300

CREATIVE COOKING

FOR EVERYONE

CREATIVE COOKING
FOR EVERYONE

Veronika Müller
and
Mechthild Piepenbrock

Photography by C.P. Fischer

HAMLYN
LONDON · NEW YORK · SYDNEY · TORONTO

English edition published by
The Hamlyn Publishing Group Limited
London . New York . Sydney . Toronto
Astronaut House, Feltham, Middlesex, England

First published under the title
Spass am Kochen — Freude Beim Essen
© Copyright BLV Verlagsgesellschaft mbH, München 1980

ISBN 0 600 32250 5

Photography by C. P. Fischer assisted by
Anneliese Kompatscher-Hoppe and Michael Henkelmann
Photograph on page 19 by Paul Kemp
Front cover photograph by Paul Williams

Phototypeset by Page Bros (Norwich) Ltd, Norwich, England in 9pt Times
Printed in Italy

Contents

Useful Facts and Figures

Notes on metrication

In this book quantities are given in metric and Imperial measures. Exact conversion from Imperial to metric measures does not usually give very convenient working quantities and so the metric measures have been rounded off into units of 25 grams. The table below shows the recommended equivalents.

Ounces	Approx g to nearest whole figure	Conversion to nearest unit of 25
1	28	25
2	57	50
3	85	75
4	113	100
5	142	150
6	170	175
7	198	200
8	227	225
9	255	250
10	283	275
11	312	300
12	340	350
13	368	375
14	396	400
15	425	425
16 (1 lb)	454	450
17	482	475
18	510	500
19	539	550
20 (1¼ lb)	567	575

Note When converting quantities over 20 oz first add the appropriate figures in the centre column, then adjust to the nearest unit of 25. As a general guide, 1 kg (1000 g) equals 2.2 lb or about 2 lb 3 oz. This method of conversion gives good results in nearly all cases, although in certain pastry and cake recipes a more accurate conversion is necessary to produce a balanced recipe.

Liquid measures The millilitre has been used in this book and the following table gives a few examples.

Imperial	Approx ml to nearest whole figure	Recommended ml
¼ pint	142	150 ml
½ pint	283	300 ml
¾ pint	425	450 ml
1 pint	567	600 ml
1½ pints	851	900 ml
1¾ pints	992	1000 ml (1 litre)

Spoon measures All spoon measures given in this book are level unless otherwise stated.

Can sizes At present, cans are marked with the exact (usually to the nearest whole number) metric equivalent of the Imperial weight of the contents, so we have followed this practice when giving cans sizes.

Oven temperatures

The table below gives recommended equivalents.

	°C	°F	Gas Mark
Very cool	110	225	¼
	120	250	½
Cool	140	275	1
	150	300	2
Moderate	160	325	3
	180	350	4
Moderately hot	190	375	5
	200	400	6
Hot	220	425	7
	230	450	8
Very hot	240	475	9

Notes for Australian users

In Australia metric measures are now used in conjunction with the standard 250-ml measuring cup. It is important to remember that the Australian tablespoon differs slightly from the British tablespoon; the table below gives a comparison. The British standard tablespoon, which has been used throughout this book, holds 17.7 ml and the Australian 20 ml. A teaspoon holds approximately 5 ml in both countries.

British	Australian
1 teaspoon	1 teaspoon
1 tablespoon	1 tablespoon
2 tablespoons	2 tablespoons
3½ tablespoons	3 tablespoons
4 tablespoons	3½ tablespoons

Note: WHEN MAKING ANY OF THE RECIPES IN THIS BOOK, ONLY FOLLOW ONE SET OF MEASURES AS THEY ARE NOT INTERCHANGEABLE.

Introduction

If you delight in gourmet food, you will enjoy cooking and preparing it, and it is for people who really enjoy good eating and find cooking fun that this book has been written. Just a glance at the beautiful photographs will show you that it is packed with imaginative recipes for every occasion and will provide countless ideas for different meals throughout the year. There are many classical dishes and original recipes created specially as well as a wide choice of wholesome family fare for every day.

To make it easy to plan a complete menu, the chapters are arranged in the classic order of a meal. There are recipes to suit every taste using a variety of fresh produce whether homely vegetables in hotpots and casseroles or luxuries such as lobster or asparagus for those really special occasions. Let yourself be inspired by the splendid photographs — every recipe is illustrated in full colour to show you how to present the food so that it looks as delicious as it tastes. What is at first a feast for the eyes is transformed in the kitchen to a feast for the palate.

We, the two authors and the photographer, have taken much time and care in putting together this unique collection of recipes and we would like to take this opportunity to thank all those who helped in the preparation of this book. We hope you will now feel fired with enthusiasm, eager to try out the recipes, and that you will enjoy everyday cooking as much as entertaining and cooking for festive occasions, or simply just cooking for fun.

Veronika Müller
Mechthild Piepenbrock
C. P. Fischer

Starters
for Special Occasions

Stuffed avocados

Serves 4

2 large, ripe avocados
2 tablespoons lemon juice
1 (400-g/14-oz) can palm hearts or
*   artichoke bottoms, drained*
4 firm, ripe tomatoes, peeled if liked
small bunch parsley, reserve a few
*   sprigs for garnish if liked*
2 hard-boiled eggs, shelled and
*   chopped*
1 small onion, peeled and finely
*   chopped*
2 tablespoons green peppercorns in
*   brine, drained and juice reserved*
*   for the dressing*

Dressing
2 tablespoons dry white wine
few drops Tabasco sauce
1 tablespoon tarragon or cider
*   vinegar*
4 tablespoons olive or walnut oil
1 clove of garlic, peeled and crushed
pinch of salt
pinch of sugar
4 sprigs of lemon balm or parsley to
*   garnish (optional)*

Halve the avocados lengthways and
carefully remove the stones.
Sprinkle with lemon juice.

Cut the palm hearts or artichoke
bottoms into 1-cm/½-in slices.
Quarter the tomatoes, remove the
seeds and stalks, and chop them.
Chop the parsley, then mix with the
chopped eggs and onion. Spoon this
mixture into the avocado halves.
Sprinkle over a few peppercorns.

To make the dressing, whisk
together the reserved peppercorn
juice, white wine, Tabasco, vinegar
and oil. Add the garlic, salt and
sugar.

Spoon a little of the dressing over
each filled avocado. Garnish with
lemon balm or parsley sprigs if
liked.

Melon and Parma ham cocktail

Serves 4

1 medium melon
3 tablespoons dry sherry
100 g/4 oz Parma ham, thinly sliced
freshly ground black pepper
1 small lettuce, washed and shaken
*   dry*

To finish
1 tablespoon lemon juice
150 ml/¼ pint double cream, stiffly
*   whipped*
few lightly crushed peppercorns

Cut the melon in half and scrape out
the seeds and threads. Using a
melon baller or teaspoon, scoop out
balls of melon flesh. Do this over a
bowl to catch the juice. Put the balls
and juice into a large bowl, pour the
sherry over, cover and chill in the
refrigerator for 2–3 hours.

Strain the melon balls, reserving
the liquid. Turn very lightly with the
slices of ham, separated from each
other, and season to taste with
pepper.

Cut the lettuce leaves into thin
strips, then put into 4 small glass
dishes or bowls. Arrange the melon
mixture on top.

Beat the reserved melon liquid
and lemon juice into the whipped
cream; spoon this over the melon
mixture. Sprinkle with a few crushed
peppercorns. Serve at once.

Bacon and olive kebabs

Serves 4

4 tablespoons olive oil
¼ teaspoon dried rosemary
¼ teaspoon dried basil
16 stuffed olives
200 g/7 oz rindless streaky bacon, thinly sliced
freshly ground black pepper

Beat the oil with the dried herbs, cover and stand for about 15 minutes to allow the flavours to develop.

Thread the olives alternately with the bacon slices, which should be loosely folded, on long metal skewers. Brush all over with the flavoured oil, then cook under a hot grill for 10–15 minutes, turning the skewers from time to time so that the bacon cooks evenly and becomes crispy. If necessary, baste from time to time with the flavoured oil.

Serve hot, with a little pepper sprinkled over, together with slices of hot French or garlic bread.

Cheesy prune kebabs

Serves 4

225 g/8 oz prunes, soaked and stones removed
6 tablespoons dry sherry
200 g/7 oz Edam or mild Cheddar cheese
3 tablespoons oil
freshly ground black pepper

Put the prunes in a bowl, pour over the sherry, cover and leave for about 4 hours.

Meanwhile, cut the cheese into pieces, 1 × 1 × 2-cm/½ × ½ × ¾-in. Stuff each prune with a piece of cheese, then thread them on to long metal skewers about six at a time. Brush over the prunes with the oil and cook under a hot grill until the cheese starts to melt. Sprinkle with a little pepper and serve hot with crusty bread if liked.

Note Very moist prunes may not soak up all the sherry. In that case pour the remainder over the skewers after cooking.

Variation
For a change, substitute stoned fresh dates, or dried ones soaked in sherry as above, for the prunes. Or use port instead of sherry.

Stuffed prunes make tasty accompaniments to grilled pork chops, liver or kidneys.

Starters

Savoury crêpes

Makes about 15

According to the filling, crêpes may be served as an entrée or dessert.

Basic plain batter
150 g/5 oz plain flour
pinch of salt
250 ml/8 fl oz milk
2 eggs
butter or lard for frying

Basic rich batter
150 g/5 oz plain flour
pinch of salt
300 ml/½ pint milk
150 ml/¼ pint of single cream
1 egg plus 2 egg yolks
butter or lard for frying

Sieve the flour and salt into a large mixing bowl. Make a well in the centre.

Whisk together the milk, cream if using, eggs and egg yolks, if using. Pour into the well in the flour and gradually whisk in the flour to form a smooth batter. Cover and leave to stand for 30 minutes.

Heat a knob of butter or lard in the crêpe pan until hot. Pour off any surplus.

Pour or spoon in about a tablespoon of batter. Swirl it round quickly, then cook for about 1 minute till golden underneath. Flip over with a flat-bladed knife or toss and cook the other side till golden.

Turn out on to a hot plate and keep warm. Repeat until all the batter is used up.

Caviar or lumpfish roe filling

Enough for 15 crêpes

1 quantity of Rich Batter (see above)
150 ml/¼ pint soured or double cream
100 g/4 oz ice-cold lumpfish roe or caviar
20 g/¾ oz flaked blanched almonds
1 tablespoon lemon juice

Make the crêpes as in basic recipe above and keep warm.

Softly whip the cream, then fold in the lumpfish roe or caviar, almonds and lemon juice.

Spread the filling over the crêpes, fold in four and arrange on a heated serving dish.

Tongue filling

Enough for 15 crêpes

1 quantity of Plain Batter (see above)
50 g/2 oz button mushrooms, wiped and coarsely chopped
1 shallot or small onion, peeled and finely chopped
15 g/½ oz butter
100 g/4 oz cooked tongue, cut in thin strips
1 tablespoon Madeira or dry sherry
½ tablespoon finely chopped parsley
salt and pepper

Make the crêpes as in the basic recipe above and keep warm.

Cook the mushrooms and onion in the butter until soft. Set aside.

Toss the tongue in the Madeira or sherry, add the parsley and season to taste. Stir into the mushroom mixture and heat through gently.

Spread each crêpe with a little of the filling, then fold in half or in four and arrange on a hot serving dish. Serve at once.

Camembert fritters

Serves 4

4 portions of Camembert, each
  weighing 40 to 50 g/1½ to 2 oz
2 tablespoons flour
1 egg, beaten
3 tablespoons fresh white
  breadcrumbs
oil for deep frying

Garnish
4 sprigs of parsley
4 tablespoons bottled cranberries or
  4 teaspoons cranberry sauce to
  finish (optional)

Scrape each Camembert portion
very lightly and carefully with a
knife, but without removing the
rind. Roll each one in flour, then in
the beaten egg, and then in the
breadcrumbs, pressing them on well
with a small knife to coat evenly.
Chill 30 minutes.

Heat the oil to 175 c/340 f. Put in
the cheese pieces, without allowing
them to touch, and cook till golden
brown (about 2–3 minutes). Lift
them out with a slotted spoon on to
absorbent kitchen paper to drain.

Meanwhile plunge the parsley into
the hot oil for a few seconds until
crisp, lift out with a slotted spoon
and drain on absorbent paper.

Serve the fritters on heated plates,
garnished with the fried parsley and
with a spoonful of cranberries or
cranberry sauce over each, if liked.

Deep-fried stuffed pears

Serves 4

4 firm but ripe pears
4 tablespoons pear liqueur or dry
  sherry
75 g/3 oz Roquefort or other blue
  cheese
3 tablespoons ground or finely
  chopped hazelnuts or walnuts
3 tablespoons flour
1 egg, beaten
75 g/3 oz fresh white breadcrumbs
oil for deep frying

Peel the pears without removing the
stalks and halve them lengthways.
Scoop out the core to leave a small
hollow in each half. At once dip the
cut surfaces into the liqueur or
sherry.

Mash the cheese with a fork, then

blend into the rest of the liqueur or
sherry. Stir in the nuts.

Fill the pear hollows with the
cheese mixture. Carefully reshape
the pears by pressing them together.
Roll the pears in the flour, then in
beaten egg, then in the
breadcrumbs, pressing them on well
with a flat-bladed knife to coat
evenly.

Heat the oil to 170 c/325 f. Dip
the frying basket in and out of the
oil, then put in the pears, without
them touching. Lower them into the
oil and fry 5–8 minutes, according
to size, until crisp and golden
brown. Lift out and drain on
absorbent paper. Serve immediately.

Note Fried stuffed pears are equally
delicious served as a dessert. Try
sprinkling over a few drops of pear
liqueur or sherry just before serving.

Starters

Onion flan

Serves 6

225 g/8 oz plain flour
pinch of salt
100 g/4 oz butter, chilled
1–2 tablespoons iced water

Filling
100 g/4 oz rindless streaky bacon,
   finely chopped
450 g/1 lb onions, peeled and finely
   chopped
40 g/1½ oz butter
salt and freshly ground black pepper
¼ to 1 teaspoon caraway seeds
2 eggs
150 ml/¼ pint soured cream
grated nutmeg

Make the pastry by sifting the flour
with the salt into a large mixing
bowl. Make a well in the middle.
Flake the butter and rub in until the
mixture resembles fine breadcrumbs.
Put the iced water into the well.
Work quickly either with your hands
or with a fork, to form a smooth
dough. Wrap the pastry in cling film
and chill for 30 minutes.
   Set the oven at 200 c, 400 f, gas 6.

Roll out the pastry on a floured
surface and use to line a 20-cm/
8-in fluted flan dish, placed on a
baking tray. Prick all over the base
of the pastry with a fork.
   Dry fry the bacon in a large pan
until the fat runs. Add the onion
and the butter and cook gently,
stirring frequently, until the onion is
soft and transparent. Remove from
the heat, cool the onion mixture a
little and season with salt, pepper
and caraway seeds to taste.
   Spread the onion mixture over the
pastry. Whisk together the eggs and
cream, season to taste with salt and
nutmeg and pour over the filling.
   Bake in the middle of the heated
oven for 30–35 minutes until golden
brown on top and set. Serve while
still hot, cut in wedges.

Variations
Cauliflower Line the pastry with
350 g/12 oz cooked cauliflower
florets mixed with 100 g/4 oz cooked
diced ham. Top with 2 eggs beaten
with 150 ml/¼ pint soured or single
cream and 100 g/4 oz grated cheese.

Leek and cheese Cover the base of
the pastry case with 100 g/4 oz
grated cheese. On this put 225 g/
8 oz crisply fried diced, rindless
bacon, then top with 2–3 lightly
cooked sliced leeks. Season with
freshly ground black pepper to taste
and top as for Onion flan.

Mushroom and ham Cover the base
of the pastry case with 225 g/8 oz
thinly sliced button mushrooms
cooked with 1 peeled and chopped
onion in 40 g/1½ oz butter, and
mixed with 75 g/3 oz cooked diced
ham and 2 tablespoons finely
chopped parsley. Season with salt
and freshly ground black pepper to
taste. Top with 2 eggs beaten with
150 ml/¼ pint single cream, and
sprinkle with 2–3 tablespoons finely
chopped chives and a generous
pinch of paprika.

Red pepper dip

Serves 4–6

5 medium red peppers
2–3 cloves of garlic, peeled and
  crushed
salt and freshly ground black pepper
1 teaspoon vinegar or lemon juice
2–3 tablespoons olive oil
1–2 tablespoons chopped chives to
  garnish

Wash and dry the peppers. Place
under a hot grill for about 8
minutes, turning them from time to
time, until the skins are well
blistered and charred. Remove them
carefully, cover with a damp cloth
and leave for a few minutes. They
will then peel easily.

Peel off the skin, and when cool,
halve the peppers, deseed and finely
chop. Put in a bowl and mix with
the garlic; season to taste with salt,
pepper, vinegar or lemon juice.
Then stir in as much olive oil as the
pepper will absorb.

Cover and chill. Sprinkle over the
chives and serve with pieces of
wholewheat bread or pumpernickel
to dip into it.

Taramasalata

Serves 4–6

225 g/8 oz cooked cod's roe or 1
  (198-g/7-oz) can pressed cod's roe
1 onion, peeled
5 slices of white bread, each 1.5-cm/
  ¾-in thick
5 tablespoons milk or water
1 clove of garlic, peeled and crushed
100 ml/4 fl oz olive oil
juice of 1 large lemon or 2 limes
salt and freshly ground black pepper
black olives to garnish

Place the roe in a large mixing bowl
and mash well. Grate the onion
finely. Remove the crusts and soak
the bread in the milk or water for a
few minutes then squeeze dry.

Add the onion, bread and garlic
to the roe. Beat together, adding the
oil alternately with the lemon or
lime juice a little at a time. Beat
until smooth and creamy.
Alternatively work all the
ingredients in a liquidiser or food
processor till smooth. Season to
taste with salt and pepper. Garnish
with olives and serve with hot
buttered toast.

Aubergine dip

Serves 6

3 medium aubergines, washed
salt
150 ml/¼ pint olive oil
2 cloves of garlic, peeled and crushed
white pepper
1 tablespoon lemon juice
2 tablespoons chopped parsley

Heat the oven to moderately hot
(180 C, 350 F, gas 4).

Prick the aubergines all over with
a fork and bake for 40–45 minutes
until the skins wrinkle. Remove
from the oven and cover with a
damp cloth until cool and the skins
can be peeled off easily.

Scoop out the flesh and squeeze in
a clean cloth to remove any excess
liquid. Mince the flesh. Whisk in the
salt, then the olive oil, drop by
drop, until completely absorbed.
Finally beat in the garlic.
Alternatively blend all the
ingredients in a liquidiser or food
processor. Season to taste with
pepper, lemon juice and a little
extra salt if necessary. Stir in the
parsley and chill.

Starters

Party vols-au-vent

Makes 6 vols-au-vent cases

*1 (215-g/7½-oz) packet frozen puff
    pastry, thawed
1 egg yolk*

Set the oven at moderately hot
(200c, 400f, gas 6).
    Roll out the pastry to a thickness
of about 5 mm/¼ in on a floured
surface. Using a 7.5-cm/3-in plain
pastry cutter, cut out 12 rounds.
Then, using a 5-cm/2-in plain
cutter, cut out the centre of six
rounds to give you six rings and six
lids.
    Brush round the edges of the
large rounds with a little cold water.
Place the rings of pastry on top,
pressing gently to seal them
together.
    Dampen a large baking tray. Place
the pastry rounds and the lids on it,
spacing them well apart. Brush the
pastry with a little beaten egg yolk.
Bake in the heated oven for about
15 minutes or till risen and golden.
Take out, cool slightly, then transfer
to a hot serving dish if serving at
once, or to a wire rack to cool.

Creamy avocado filling

Enough for 6 vols-au-vent

*50 g/2 oz fresh or frozen peas
1 large, ripe avocado
3 tablespoons lemon juice
3–4 tablespoons double cream
1–2 tablespoons finely chopped dill
    or parsley (optional)
salt and pepper*

*Garnish (optional)
50 g/2 oz lumpfish or red cod's roe
lemon wedges*

Cook the peas till tender in boiling
salted water, drain and rub through
a sieve or purée in a liquidiser.
    Halve the avocado pear
lengthways, remove the stone and
scoop out the flesh. Sieve or purée
in a liquidiser with 2 tablespoons of
the lemon juice. Then blend in the
puréed peas and cream till thick and
creamy. Stir in the herbs if using,
and season with salt and pepper and
the rest of the lemon juice.
    Spoon a little of this filling into
the vol-au-vent cases, top each with
a teaspoon of lumpfish or cod's roe.
Serve with lemon wedges, if liked.

Kidney ragoût filling

Enough for 6 vols-au-vent

*225 g/8 oz lamb's kidneys, halved
    lengthways, skinned and cored
150 ml/¼ pint milk
50 g/2 oz butter
1 small onion, peeled and finely
    chopped
15 g/½ oz flour
150 ml/¼ pint chicken stock
4 tablespoons single cream
salt and pepper
½–1 teaspoon made mustard
75 g/3 oz cooked chicken, boned and
    diced or cut in strips
2 tablespoons pistachio nuts,
    chopped*

Soak the kidneys in the milk for 30
minutes. Drain and dry on
absorbent kitchen paper, then cut
the kidneys into thin slices.
    Heat 25 g/1 oz of the butter in a
pan and fry the kidney slices, a few
at a time, for 1–2 minutes, removing
and setting aside each portion as it
cooks. Cook the onion in 15 g/½ oz
of the butter till crispy. Set aside.
    Melt the remaining butter in the
pan, add the flour and cook for 1
minute till straw-coloured. Add the
hot stock beating well till blended.
Bring to the boil, stirring all the
time, then reduce the heat and
simmer for 1 minute. Stir in the
cream. Remove from the heat and
season with salt and pepper and
mustard to taste.
    Add the chicken and kidney slices
to the sauce, and let it barely
simmer for 4–5 minutes. Add the
pistachio nuts.
    Spoon a little of the filling into
hot vols-au-vent cases, sprinkle with
the onion and put on the lids. Serve
at once on a heated dish.

Ham and mushroom filling

Enough for 6 vols-au-vent

*100 g/4 oz button mushrooms, wiped
    and thinly sliced
40 g/1½ oz butter
1 (241-g/8½-oz) can asparagus
    tips or pieces
20 g/¾ oz flour
250 ml/8 fl oz hot chicken stock
100 ml/4 fl oz dry white wine
100 ml/4 fl oz double cream
100 g/4 oz cooked lean ham, diced
    or cut in thin strips
100 g/4 oz cooked veal or chicken,
    diced
salt and white pepper
grated nutmeg
2 tomatoes, peeled, seeded and cut in
    thin strips, to garnish*

Cook the mushrooms gently in half
the butter until the liquid has
evaporated. Set aside. Heat the
asparagus in its own liquid but do
not boil; set aside.
    Heat the rest of the butter in a
saucepan, stir in the flour to make a
roux and cook for 1 minute. Whisk
in the hot stock till blended, bring to
the boil, stirring all the time, then
reduce heat and simmer for 5
minutes till thick. Stir in the wine
and cream and heat through without
boiling.
    Remove from the heat and cool
slightly. Stir in the drained
mushrooms, asparagus and ham and
veal or chicken and season with salt,
pepper and nutmeg to taste. Spoon
a little of the filling into hot vol-au-
vent cases and place on a heated
serving dish. Garnish with strips of
tomato and serve at once.

Starters

Pickled trout

Serves 4

2 trout, each weighing about 350 g/
*   12 oz, cleaned, washed and dried*
1 teaspoon white peppercorns
1 teaspoon sugar
1 teaspoon salt

Garnish
few lettuce leaves, washed and dried
chopped dill or parsley

Cut the tails and back fins off the
trout, then cut off the heads and
discard. Using kitchen scissors or a
sharp filleting knife, cut the trout
open along the belly to the tail.
Open out and place, opened side
facing downwards, on your work
surface.
   With the palm of your hand, press
down gently on the backs of the
trout to free the backbone, then
turn over each one and ease it out
with the point of a knife. Carefully
fillet them and set aside in a cool
place.
   Crush together the peppercorns,
sugar and salt; set aside.

Cover a flat dish with a piece of
greaseproof paper double its size.
Place two trout fillets on it. Place
the remaining fillets on your work
surface. Sprinkle all four equally
with the pepper mixture. Sandwich
the fillets together in pairs, place
them all on the paper, then fold it
over to enclose them completely,
tucking in well. Weight the parcel
with a small flat board or tray, with
cans stood on top, and refrigerate
for about 12 hours.
   To serve, line a flat dish with the
lettuce leaves. Open up the parcel
and lay the sandwiched fillets on a
board. With a very sharp knife, cut
off paper-thin slices with slanting
strokes. Arrange the slices on the
lettuce, garnish with dill or parsley
and serve at once. Serve with
horseradish cream or mustard sauce.

Horseradish cream

1–2 tablespoons freshly grated, or
*   2–3 tablespoons bottled*
*   horseradish*
1 teaspoon sugar
2 tablespoons lemon juice
pinch of salt
250 ml/8 fl oz whipping cream, stiffly
*   whipped*

Fold the horseradish and seasonings
into the cream. Turn into a serving
bowl and chill till needed.
Makes about 300 ml/½ pint

Mustard sauce

2 egg yolks
3 teaspoons made English mustard
300 ml/½ pint corn oil
1 teaspoon sugar
2 tablespoons vinegar
½ bunch of dill, finely chopped

Whisk the egg yolks with the mustard. Then beat in the oil, a drop at a time, until completely absorbed to give a mayonnaise-like consistency. Beat in sugar and vinegar to taste, then the dill. Pour into a sauce boat and serve.
Makes about 300 ml/½ pint

Vegetable mousses

Serves 4

275 g/10 oz frozen spinach
200 ml/7 fl oz strong chicken stock
1 (15-g/½-oz) packet gelatine
salt and pepper
pinch of grated nutmeg
150 ml/¼ pint soured cream

Simmer the spinach in the stock until tender — a few minutes after the block has thawed. Purée the mixture by pushing it through a sieve or use a liquidiser or food processor.
　Dissolve the gelatine in three tablespoons of water in a bowl over a pan of hot water. Stir into the warm vegetable purée and season to taste with salt, pepper and nutmeg. Allow to cool. When the mixture is on the point of setting fold in the soured cream. Adjust the seasoning then pour into four 150-ml/¼-pint moulds and chill until firm.
　Before serving dip the moulds into hot water for a moment and turn the mousses out on to four plates. Garnish with slices of cucumber and radish roses.

Variations
Carrot mousse Use 275 g/10 oz peeled and chopped carrots instead of the spinach and cook for 15–20 minutes until really tender before reducing to a purée. Season with salt, pepper and ginger instead of the nutmeg. Garnish with watercress.

Watercress mousse Use 2 large or 3 medium-sized bunches of watercress instead of the spinach. Wash well, trim off the roots and chop roughly before simmering for a few minutes in the stock. Season as for spinach mousse. This mousse may be garnished with slices of lemon and large prawns.

Avocado mousse Mash 3 ripe avocados with the juice of ½ lemon and purée with the stock, before adding the gelatine. Garnish the mousse with watercress and a twist of lemon.

Starters

Grilled peaches with cheese

Serves 4

about 50 g/2 oz butter, softened
4 slices of white bread
200 g/7 oz full fat cream cheese
100 g/4 oz lean cooked ham, finely
*   chopped*
40 g/1½ oz finely chopped blanched
*   almonds*
4 tablespoons brandy
salt and freshly ground black pepper
4 canned peach halves, drained and
*   thinly sliced*

Butter the bread slices on both sides
and fry until golden brown on both
sides. Drain on absorbent paper.

In a bowl blend the cheese with
the ham, almonds and brandy.
Season with salt and pepper to taste.

Spread half the cheese mixture on
one side of the slices of fried bread.
Lay the peach slices on top, then
cover with the remaining cheese
mixture. Place under a hot grill and
cook for 5–7 minutes or until
golden. Serve at once.

Prawn and avocado toasts

Serves 4

about 50 g/2 oz butter, softened
4 slices of white bread
1 ripe avocado pear, halved
*   lengthways, stoned and thinly*
*   sliced*
1 tablespoon lemon juice
200 g/7 oz peeled prawns
freshly ground black pepper
100 g/4 oz Emmental or Gruyère
*   cheese, grated*
4 tablespoons soured cream
pinch of paprika

Butter the bread on both sides then
fry the bread on one side only until
golden. Drain on absorbent kitchen
paper.

Cover the unfried side of the
bread with avocado slices and
sprinkle them with lemon juice to
stop them discoloring. Strew the
prawns over and season with
pepper.

Beat together the grated cheese,
soured cream and paprika, then
spoon over the prawns.

Cook under a hot grill for a few
minutes till browned on top.

Fried cheese sandwiches

Serves 2–4

2 eggs
4 tablespoons soured cream
salt and pepper
8 large slices of bread
350 g/12 oz mozzarella cheese, sliced
4 tablespoons olive or corn oil
20 g/¾ oz butter

Beat the eggs to a light froth with
the cream and salt and pepper to
taste. Soak the slices of bread in this
mixture.

Divide the cheese between four of
the slices of bread, cover with the
remaining slices and press to seal.

Heat the oil and butter together in
a frying pan till hot. Fry the
sandwiches, two at a time, until
golden brown on both sides. Serve
at once.

Marinated mushrooms

Serves 4

100 ml/4 fl oz white wine vinegar
100 ml/4 fl oz dry white wine
100 ml/4 fl oz sunflower or
* salad oil*
2 cloves of garlic, peeled and lightly
* crushed with a knife*
1 bay leaf
½ teaspoon salt
6 peppercorns
3 juniper berries
450 g/1 lb button mushrooms, wiped

Heat the vinegar, wine and oil in a large saucepan until simmering. Add the garlic, bay leaf, salt, peppercorns, juniper berries and mushrooms and bring rapidly to the boil. Reduce the heat and gently cook the mushrooms for 10 minutes. Remove from the heat and leave the mushrooms to cool in the liquid after removing the garlic.

When cold, turn into a non-metallic bowl or container, cover and marinate in the refrigerator for about 24 hours. To serve, drain the mushrooms and serve with hot garlic bread (see page 26).

Variations
Baby onions or green beans can be prepared in the same way; beans should be cooked for 10–15 minutes.

Marinated onions

Serves 4–6

450 g/1 lb shallots or pickling onions,
* peeled*
4 tablespoons olive oil
20 g/¾ oz butter
2 teaspoons sugar
salt
freshly ground black pepper
150 ml/¼ pint red wine

Garnish
100 ml/4 fl oz soured cream
1 tablespoon finely chopped parsley

Fry the shallots or onions in the hot oil and butter until golden brown.

Sprinkle them with the sugar and cook till they caramelise, stirring often so they don't stick to the pan. Season with salt and pepper to taste.

Add the red wine to the pan, cover and simmer the onions for 20 minutes. Turn into a serving dish and leave to get cold, then chill.

To serve, spoon a large blob of cream over the middle and sprinkle with parsley.

Variations
Other vegetables can be cooked in the same way. For leeks, trim, wash and cut across in rings; dry well, then cook as above for 10 minutes. For courgettes, wash and cut in thick slices: dry well and cook as above for about 10 minutes, adding a little finely chopped garlic for extra flavour.

Tip If the onions are very strongly flavoured, soak them in cold water for 2 hours after peeling.

Starters

Spicy prawn cocktail

Serves 4–6

350 g/12 oz peeled prawns
3 tablespoons lemon juice
225 g/8 oz button mushrooms, wiped
    and thinly sliced
2 oranges, peeled, white pith and
    pips removed and thinly sliced,
    crossways
1 egg yolk
½ teaspoon dry mustard
salt
150 ml/¼ pint olive oil
4 tablespoons orange juice
grated rind of ½ lemon
150 ml/¼ pint double cream, stiffly
    whipped
2 tablespoons green peppercorns in
    brine, mashed (optional)
4 small sprigs of mint to garnish

Sprinkle the prawns with half of the
lemon juice and marinate in the
refrigerator. If using frozen prawns,
sprinkle them with lemon juice and
leave to thaw, covered, in a cool
place.

Sprinkle the mushrooms with the
rest of the lemon juice and set aside.
Halve the orange slices and reserve.

Mix the prawns, mushrooms and
their juices with the orange pieces
and spoon into four large chilled
glasses.

Blend the egg yolk with the
mustard and a pinch of salt, then
beat in the oil, drop by drop, until
thick and creamy. Stir in the orange
juice and lemon rind and check the
seasoning. Fold in the cream
together with the peppercorns, and
chill.

Spoon the dressing over the
prawns just before serving, and
garnish each with a sprig of mint.

Fish salad

Serves 4

225 g/8 oz haddock or cod fillet,
    bones and any skin removed
4 tablespoons lemon juice
salt
100 ml/4 fl oz water
100 ml/4 fl oz dry white wine
1 bay leaf
½ onion, peeled
4 sprigs of parsley
3 peppercorns
4 anchovy fillets, drained and soaked
    in 4 tablespoons milk
225 g/8 oz tomatoes, peeled
1 bunch spring onions, trimmed,
    washed and sliced into rings
2–3 celery stalks, trimmed, washed
    and thinly sliced
1 small lettuce, washed and dried, to
    serve

Dressing
1 egg yolk
1 teaspoon dry mustard
4 tablespoons double cream
pinch of cayenne

Rinse the fish fillets and drain on
absorbent kitchen paper. Then
sprinkle with lemon juice and a little
salt and leave for 10 minutes. Cut
into bite-sized pieces.

Meanwhile bring the water and
wine to the boil with the bay leaf,
onion, parsley and peppercorns.
Season with a little salt, add the fish
with its juices, cover, reduce the
heat so the liquid is simmering
gently and cook the fish for 10
minutes. Do not let it boil.

Take out the pieces of fish with a
slotted spoon and leave to cool.
Reduce the cooking liquid to half
the quantity by fast boiling, then set
aside to cool.

Drain and halve the anchovies
lengthways. Cut the tomatoes into
eighths, discarding the seeds. Mix
together the tomatoes, spring
onions, and celery, then stir in the
fish.

To make the dressing, beat the
egg yolk with the mustard, then
gradually whisk or blend in the
strained, cooled fish stock. Add the
cream and season with cayenne to
taste, adding a little more salt if
necessary.

Pour the dressing over the fish
salad and mix carefully. Let it stand
in the refrigerator for 15 minutes.

Arrange the lettuce leaves in a
serving dish or on four individual
plates. Spoon on the fish salad and
garnish with anchovies. Serve with
warm French bread or wholemeal
bread.

Cook's Tip

This basic recipe can be varied in
many different ways. Deseeded
green and red peppers, cut into
narrow strips, go well with it, as do
apples, finely chopped and sprinkled
with lemon juice.

Oranges, lemons and grapefruit,
peeled, pips removed and cut into
segments are refreshing alternatives
as well. Thinly sliced green or black
olives also complement the flavour
of the fish.

For a really creamy sauce, beat in
a little extra double cream or natural
yogurt. If you like, substitute curly
endive or Iceberg lettuce for an
ordinary round lettuce.

Soups

Hot and Cold

Soups

Mussel soup

Serves 4

*1.15 litres/2 pints fresh mussels in the
  shell
1 onion, peeled and chopped
2 cloves of garlic, peeled and
  chopped
40 g/1½ oz butter
1 (227-g/8-oz) packet of frozen
  mixed vegetables
300 ml/½ pint dry white wine
1 bay leaf
6 peppercorns
4 juniper berries
600 ml/1 pint chicken stock
salt
freshly ground black pepper
4 celery stalks, trimmed, leaves
  reserved, and thinly sliced
2 small leeks, trimmed, well washed
  and thinly sliced
225 g/8 oz tomatoes, peeled,
  deseeded and diced
1 teaspoon Pernod*

Garnish
*1 tablespoon finely chopped parsley
1 tablespoon finely chopped dill*

Scrub each mussel under a running
cold tap. Throw away any open ones
which do not close when touched
and any which have broken shells.
Pull or scrape off with a small sharp
knife the dark 'beards' attached to
the shells.

Fry the onion and the garlic in the
butter till golden in a very large
saucepan. Add the mixed
vegetables, still frozen, and cook 2
minutes. Add the wine, bay leaf,
peppercorns and juniper berries.
Bring to the boil, add the mussels,
cover and boil until the mussels
open — about 10 minutes. Any
mussels which have not opened after
this cooking must be discarded.
Strain the mussels into a colander,
returning the liquid to a clean pan.
Shell the mussels and set aside.

Add enough stock to the reserved
mussel broth to make 1 litre/
1¾ pints. Season to taste with salt
and pepper. Add the celery, leeks
and tomatoes, cover and simmer 10
minutes. Add the mussels to the
pan, cover and reheat but do not
boil. Add the Pernod to taste and
check the seasoning.

Pour into a warm tureen and
sprinkle over the herbs. Serve with
hot garlic bread.

Note If needs be, this soup can also
be made with mussels preserved in
brine. Use about 300 g/11 oz mussel
meat packed without flavouring and,
if possible, use some fish stock, so
that it tastes of the sea!

Crème d'escargots

Serves 4

*50 g/2 oz rindless streaky bacon,
  diced
25 g/1 oz butter
1 small onion, peeled and finely
  chopped
2 cloves of garlic, peeled and crushed
24 canned snails, drained and
  roughly chopped
900 ml/1½ pints white stock
5 tablespoons dry white wine
50 g/2 oz parsley, coarsely chopped
6 dill stalks (optional)
1 egg yolk
150 ml/¼ pint double or whipping
  cream
1 tablespoon brandy
salt and freshly ground black pepper*

In a large saucepan, fry the bacon in
the butter till the fat runs. Add the
onion and the garlic and sauté till
golden brown. Add the snails and
cook for 2 minutes, stirring
constantly. Pour on the stock and
wine, cover and simmer gently for
30 minutes.

Meanwhile, set aside about 4
teaspoons of parsley and finely chop
the rest together with the dill if
using.

Whisk the egg yolk with a little of
the hot soup, then stir it back into
the pan of hot soup and reheat; do
not let it boil or the soup will
curdle.

Lightly whip the cream and fold
two-thirds of it into the soup. Add
the brandy and season well with salt
and pepper.

Set the oven at hot (230c, 450f,
gas 8).

To serve, pour into four
ovenproof bowls and top with the
rest of the cream. Heat in the hot
oven for 3 minutes, then take out
and sprinkle with the remaining
parsley. Serve at once with puff
pastry fingers or toasted French
bread.

Alternatively the cream topping
can quickly be finished under a very
hot, preheated grill, if the soup
bowls are flameproof.

Garlic bread

Set the oven at moderate (180c,
350f, gas 4).

Cut deep into, but not completely
through, a French bread stick at
intervals of about 1 cm/½ in.
Cream softened butter with crushed
garlic, salt and a little lemon juice
and spread thickly into the incisions.
Press the stick back into shape, wrap
in foil, place on a baking tray and
bake for 15–20 minutes until all the
butter has soaked in and the bread
is crisp.

Soups

Pea soup with smoked salmon

Serves 4

1 kg/2 lb fresh peas, shelled or
*   450 g/1 lb frozen peas*
600 ml/1 pint chicken or veal stock
5 tablespoons dry white wine
salt and pepper
pinch of sugar
150 ml/¼ pint single cream
2 tablespoons chopped parsley
50 g/2 oz smoked salmon, cut into
*   very thin strips (optional)*

Cook the peas in the boiling stock
for 15 minutes, lifting out about half
a cup of peas after 5 minutes. Purée
the remaining peas and stock in
liquidiser or food processor. Return
the purée to the pan, add the wine
and bring to the boil. Season to
taste, add the sugar and stir in the
cream. Add the reserved peas and
heat through gently. Serve garnished
with chopped parsley and the
salmon, if using.

Cream of cauliflower soup

Serves 4–6

1 cauliflower, broken into florets
2 large potatoes, peeled and diced
600 ml/1 pint hot chicken stock or
*   broth*
450 ml/¾ pint hot milk
150 ml/¼ pint single cream
salt
grated nutmeg
15 g/½ oz butter
2 tablespoons chopped parsley to
*   garnish*

Simmer the cauliflower and potatoes
in the boiling stock for 20–30
minutes, lifting out a few florets
after 10 minutes. Purée the mixture
in a liquidiser or food processor.
Return the purée to the pan, add
the milk, cream and reserved florets
and season lightly with salt and
nutmeg. Reheat gently but do not
boil.
   Pour the soup into a warmed
tureen and serve dotted with butter
and sprinkled with chopped parsley.

Cream of tomato soup

Serves 4

2 onions, peeled and finely chopped
1 clove of garlic, peeled and crushed
2 tablespoons oil
1 (680-g/24-oz) can peeled
*   tomatoes, puréed with their juice*
600 ml/1 pint hot chicken stock
150 ml/¼ pint red wine
salt and freshly ground black pepper
pinch each of sugar, dried thyme and
*   dried oregano*
150 ml/¼ pint soured cream
50 g/2 oz rindless streaky bacon,
*   diced*
few sprigs fresh basil (optional)

Gently fry half the onion and garlic
in the oil until transparent. Add the
puréed tomatoes, stock, wine,
seasoning to taste, sugar and dried
herbs and cook for 20 minutes.
Purée the mixture in a liquidiser or
food processor. Stir in the cream
and heat through. Fry the bacon
until the fat runs, add the reserved
onion and garlic and cook till
golden. Serve the soup sprinkled
with the bacon mixture and garnish
with basil.

Hot chicken consommé

Serves 4

1 (1.75-kg/4-lb) boiling fowl,
    cleaned
2½ litres/4½ pints cold water
salt
1 large onion, unpeeled and halved
1 bay leaf
2–3 cloves
2 carrots, peeled and sliced
2 sticks celery, washed and chopped
3–5 peppercorns
2 egg whites, beaten

Take out the giblets and rinse the
fowl inside and out. Put in the water
in a 3.5-litre/6-pint pan, cover and
bring slowly to the boil, skimming
frequently. Add the salt when the
water boils but not before. Turn
down the heat and simmer gently for
1 hour.

 Brown the cut surfaces of the
onion on a clean preheated hotplate
or in a frying pan (this helps to
colour the soup). Add it to the pan
with the bay leaf, cloves, vegetables
and peppercorns. Simmer for a
further 1 hour.

 Lift out the fowl. Strain the broth,
cool and skim.

 To clarify the broth, stir in the
beaten egg whites and bring slowly
to the boil while whisking
continuously until a thick froth starts
to form. Stop whisking at once,
reduce the heat and simmer gently,
undisturbed and uncovered, for 20
minutes. If the broth bubbles too
rapidly, the froth will break and turn
the consommé cloudy.

 Line a large fine sieve with
scalded muslin or a tea-towel. Pour
the broth through, holding back the
froth at first, then letting it fall on to
the cloth. Repeat the straining
process to clarify the broth
completely.

 Reheat, adding strips of the
chicken meat if liked, and check the
seasoning; only add salt because
anything else may turn it cloudy.

Variations

Consommé Jardinière Cook 100 g/
4 oz cauliflower florets in boiling
salted water until tender; heat 1
(280-g/10-oz) can of asparagus tips
or pieces in their own liquid. Heat 1
litre/1¾ pints chicken consommé
(made as recipe above) and add to it
the drained vegetables, together
with 1 tablespoon cooked rice and
the diced or sliced chicken breast
meat. Serve sprinkled with finely
chopped parsley. Serves 4.

Consommé Far-Eastern style Soak 2
tablespoons dried Chinese
mushrooms and 1 handful of thin
egg noodles separately in cold water
for about 30 minutes. Put 1 small
leek, trimmed and cut into rings, 1
celery stalk, trimmed and thinly
sliced, and 1 small onion, peeled
and cut into rings, or 4 small spring
onions, trimmed, into a large
saucepan with 1 litre/1¾ pints
chicken consommé (made as recipe
above). Bring slowly to the boil,
covered, and cook for 3 minutes.
Add the drained mushrooms and
noodles.

 As soon as the broth returns to
the boil, add 1 (142-g/5-oz) can of
drained bamboo shoots, cut into
narrow strips, and 75 g/3 oz washed
beansprouts. Cook for a further 2
minutes. Season to taste with soy
sauce, then stir in 2–3 tablespoons
rice wine or dry sherry. Serve
sprinkled with chopped parsley.

Soups

Cream of asparagus soup

Serves 4

50 g/2 oz butter
1 small onion, finely chopped
25 g/1 oz plain flour
150 ml/¼ pint hot milk
600 ml/1 pint hot chicken stock
1 (280-g/10-oz) can asparagus tips
  or pieces, drained and chopped
  and liquid reserved
salt and pepper
4 tablespoons single cream

Heat the butter in a large saucepan, add the onion and cook gently until soft but not browned. Stir in the flour, then add the hot milk, stock and the liquid from the can of asparagus, stirring constantly. Bring to the boil, add the asparagus, cover and simmer for 20 minutes. Rub the soup through a sieve or purée in a liquidiser or food processor.

Return the soup to the rinsed-out pan, season to taste with salt and pepper. Bring to the boil, remove from the heat and stir in the cream. Pour into a warmed tureen or individual bowls and serve at once. Garnish with fresh herbs if liked.

Cream of spinach soup

Serves 4

1 kg/2 lb fresh spinach, well washed
  and drained
1 onion, peeled and finely chopped
1–2 cloves of garlic, peeled and
  finely chopped
4 tablespoons olive oil
300 ml/½ pint hot chicken stock
salt
freshly ground black pepper
grated nutmeg
300 ml/½ pint whipping cream

Garnish
25 g/1 oz pine kernels
lemon slices (optional)

Blanch the spinach in a large pan of boiling salted water for 3 minutes. Drain, refresh under cold water, then drain again and press well to dry the leaves completely. Chop them finely, mince or purée in a blender or food processor.

Soften the onion and the garlic in 3 tablespoons of the oil till the onion is transparent but not browned. Add the spinach, let it cook for about 5 minutes, then pour on the stock. If

necessary reduce rapidly over high heat to a thick creamy consistency. Season to taste with salt, pepper and nutmeg.

Meanwhile, fry the pine kernels in the rest of the oil till golden brown. Drain on absorbent kitchen paper and set aside.

To serve, remove the pan of soup from the heat. Stir in half of the cream; stiffly whip the rest. Pour the soup into a warmed tureen or individual bowls. Spoon on top the whipped cream and sprinkle with pine kernels. Serve at once with a lemon slice placed on the edge of each bowl, if liked.

Tip If you are pressed for time use frozen instead of fresh spinach.

French onion soup

Serves 4–6

*450 g/1 lb onions, peeled and
  chopped*
50 g/2 oz butter
2 tablespoons flour
1 litre/1¾ pints clear brown stock
300 ml/½ pint dry white wine
salt and freshly ground black pepper

To finish
50 g/2 oz butter
*8 thin slices cut from a French bread
  stick*
1 tablespoon brandy
*100 g/4 oz grated Emmental or
  Cheddar cheese*

Lightly brown the onions in the
butter in a large saucepan. Sprinkle
in the flour and cook about 2
minutes till light brown.

Pour on the stock, blend, cover,
bring to the boil, then reduce the
heat and simmer gently for 20
minutes. Add the wine and season
with salt and plenty of pepper to
taste. To finish: heat the rest of the
butter in a large frying pan. Put in
the bread, in two batches if

necessary, and fry until golden
brown on both sides.

Warm the brandy a little, set fire
to it in a ladle and pour it, while still
flaming, over the bread. Let it burn
out. Set the grill at high.

Pour the soup into four
flameproof bowls, put 2 slices of
bread on top of each one and
sprinkle with grated cheese. Grill for
5 minutes or until the cheese is
bubbling and golden, then serve
immediately.

Variations

1   Use 3 instead of 2 slices of bread
per person and 150 g/5 oz grated
cheese in all. Lay the slices of fried
bread, sprinkled with the cheese,
one on top of another in the soup
bowls, and fill up with the hot soup.

2   Substitute milk for half of the
stock, and double or soured cream
for the wine. Do not use bread or
cheese in the cooking but serve toast
with the soup and, if liked, add a
little cayenne to the seasoning.

3   Thicken the soup with 2 egg
yolks beaten up with 1 tablespoon
brandy and 150 ml/¼ pint double

cream. Add this at the end of the
cooking time and do not boil after
adding, otherwise the soup will
curdle. Add fried croûtons and
sprinkle with chopped parsley.

4   Cut the onions into thin rings
instead of chopping them. Do not
add flour, but simmer with 50 g/2 oz
pearl barley for 2–2½ hours. Sprinkle
with grated Swiss or Parmesan
cheese before serving.

5   Fry the onion rings in the butter,
dust with a little flour and pour on
the hot stock. Season with salt and
pepper to taste and then add white
wine and 150 ml/¼ pint single cream.
Finally, blend 1 egg yolk with a little
hot soup, then return it to the pan
and reheat gently until the soup is
hot but not boiling. Pour into a
warmed tureen or individual bowls
and serve sprinkled with fried
croûtons and plenty of chopped
chives and parsley.

6   Soften 1–2 finely chopped or
crushed cloves of garlic with the
onions in the butter. Or, if you
prefer it less pungent, use garlic salt
to taste instead.

Soups

Mushroom and potato soup

Serves 4

*150 g/5 oz mushrooms, wiped and
  thinly sliced*
1 teaspoon lemon juice
*100 g/4 oz rindless streaky bacon,
  finely chopped*
*1 large onion, peeled and finely
  chopped*
1 clove garlic, peeled and crushed
450 g/1 lb potatoes, peeled and diced
750 ml/1¼ pints chicken stock
salt
freshly ground black pepper
2 tablespoons chopped parsley
*1 small leek, trimmed, well washed
  and thinly sliced into rings*
2 egg yolks
150 ml/¼ pint soured cream

Reserve some of the mushrooms for
the garnish. Sprinkle these with the
lemon juice or leave them to soak in
water to cover, mixed with the
lemon juice, to prevent them going
brown.

Dry fry the bacon in a large
saucepan until the fat starts to run.
Reserve 1 tablespoon of the fried
bacon for the garnish. Add the
onion and cook gently until soft but
not coloured. Add the mushrooms
and the garlic and continue to cook
over a low heat for 5 minutes.

Add the potatoes to the pan,
together with the stock. Bring to the
boil, cover and simmer gently for 20
minutes. Purée in a food processor
or liquidiser, then season to taste
with salt and pepper.

Stir half the chopped parsley into
the soup with the leek and simmer
for a further 10 minutes. Beat the
egg yolks and cream together, blend
with a little of the hot soup, then
stir back into the pan and reheat but
do not allow to boil.

Pour the soup into a warmed
tureen or individual bowls, sprinkle
with the rest of the parsley and
garnish with the reserved drained
mushrooms and fried bacon. Serve
immediately, with crusty French
bread if liked.

Note This soup is particularly tasty if
made with chanterelles or wild
mushrooms instead of field
mushrooms.

Hearty beef and potato soup

Serves 6

*450 g/1 lb veal or beef bones,
  chopped*
2 litres/3½ pints water
salt
*450 g/1 lb piece good quality lean
  beef*
675 g/1½ lb potatoes, peeled and diced
225 g/8 oz carrots, peeled and sliced
*225 g/8 oz celeriac, trimmed, peeled
  and diced*
*2 leeks, trimmed, well washed and
  cut into thin rings*
*2 celery stalks, trimmed and roughly
  chopped or cut into thin strips*
freshly ground black pepper
pinch of grated nutmeg

To finish
*100 g/4 oz rindless streaky bacon,
  finely chopped*
2 onions, peeled and chopped

Wash the bones well to remove any
splinters. Put them in a large
saucepan, cover with the cold water
and bring slowly to the boil,
skimming off any scum that forms
on the surface.

Add a pinch of salt and the beef,
cover the pan, reduce the heat and
simmer for 1 hour, skimming once
or twice. Then add all the vegetables
to the pan and simmer 30 minutes
more.

Remove all the bones. Take out
the meat, dice or slice and return to
the broth. Season to taste with extra
salt, pepper and nutmeg.

Dry fry the bacon till the fat starts
to run in a frying pan; add the
onions and fry until the bacon and
onions are golden brown and crispy.

Pour the soup into a warmed
tureen or individual bowls. Sprinkle
over the bacon and onion mixture.
Serve immediately, with Granary
bread if liked.

Cheesy potato soup

Serves 6

450 g/1 lb potatoes, peeled and diced
*1 (227-g/8-oz) packet frozen
  stewing vegetables*
2 onions, peeled and chopped
2 cloves of garlic, peeled and crushed
1 litre/1¾ pints chicken stock
300 ml/½ pint milk
150 ml/¼ pint single cream
*100 g/4 oz Emmental or mature
  Gouda cheese, finely grated*
salt and freshly ground black pepper
grated nutmeg
1 egg yolk
1 tablespoon chopped chives
1 tablespoon chopped parsley

Put all the vegetables and the garlic
in a large saucepan, add the stock
and bring to the boil. Cover and
cook for 30 minutes.

Cool the soup for a few minutes,
then rub through a sieve or purée in
a liquidiser or food processor.

Heat the milk and cream but do
not boil. Remove from the heat and
stir in the cheese until melted. Add
the cheese mixture to the potato
purée in the rinsed-out pan, and
season to taste with salt, pepper and
nutmeg. Reheat but do not boil.

Blend the egg yolk with a little of
the hot soup, then return this to the
pan and heat gently, stirring
continuously. Pour into a warmed
tureen or individual bowls and
sprinkle over the chopped herbs.
Serve at once, with Granary bread if
liked.

Soups

Gazpacho

Serves 6

200 g/7 oz stale white bread
150 ml/¼ pint water
1 kg/2 lb ripe tomatoes, peeled, cored
*   and cut into eight*
1 green pepper, deseeded and cut
*   into strips or small chunks*
1 small onion, peeled and chopped
2 cloves of garlic, peeled and crushed
2 tablespoons tomato purée
5 tablespoons olive oil
3 tablespoons red wine vinegar
300 ml/½ pt chicken stock
½ teaspoon salt

Accompaniments
4 slices of white bread, cut in small
*   dice, for croûtons*
40 g/1½ oz butter
½ cucumber, unpeeled and diced
6 shallots, peeled and finely chopped
250 g/9 oz tomatoes, peeled,
*   deseeded and finely chopped*
1 green pepper, deseeded and finely
*   chopped*
2 hard-boiled eggs, chopped
20 stuffed green olives, drained and
*   thinly sliced crossways*
ice cubes

Soak the bread in the water for 10 minutes, then squeeze it dry. Put half of the bread, tomatoes, pepper, onion, garlic and tomato purée into a liquidiser or food processor together with half of the oil, vinegar and stock. Purée until completely smooth. Tip into a tureen. Repeat this process with the remaining ingredients. Add salt to taste and chill for at least 4 hours.

Prepare the accompaniments. Fry the croûtons in the butter until golden brown. Take out, drain on absorbent kitchen paper. Put all the accompaniments, except the ice cubes, separately into dishes.

Just before serving, stir the soup well and put in some ice cubes. Arrange the dishes of accompaniments around the soup so that everyone can help themselves.

Note For a more tangy version, cook the croûtons with garlic. First fry them in the butter as above, then sprinkle finely chopped or crushed garlic over them. The quantity of garlic can vary from 1 clove to 1 teaspoon, according to taste. Continue to heat for a few seconds only or the garlic will turn bitter.

Cook's Tip

To peel tomatoes, cut a small cross in the base of each one then place in a bowl. Pour over boiling water and allow to stand for a few seconds before plunging the tomatoes into cold water. The skin can then be quickly peeled back from the cross.

Alternatively, spear each tomato firmly on a fork and hold over a naked gas flame, rotating slowly until the skin starts to blister. It will then peel easily.

Cold chicken consommé

Serves 4

1 (1.75-kg/4-lb) boiling fowl, cleaned
2½ litres/4½ pints cold water
salt
1 large onion, unpeeled and halved
1 bay leaf
2–3 cloves
2 carrots, peeled and sliced
2 sticks celery, with leaves, trimmed and chopped
3–5 peppercorns

To clarify

2 egg whites, beaten
1 egg shell, crushed
1 carrot, peeled and finely diced
1 small onion, peeled and finely diced
1 stick celery, washed and finely diced

Remove the giblets and wash the fowl inside and out. Put in a large saucepan and cover with the water. Bring to the boil, skimming from time to time. Add salt, turn down the heat and simmer gently for 1 hour.

Brown the cut surfaces of the onion on a clean hotplate or frying pan. Add it to the pan together with the bay leaf, cloves, vegetables and peppercorns. Simmer for a further 1 hour.

Lift out the fowl; strain the broth, allow to cool and skim well.

To clarify the broth, stir in the egg whites and shell and the finely diced vegetables. Bring slowly to the boil, whisking continuously until a thick froth starts to form. Stop whisking, reduce the heat and simmer very gently for about 20 minutes. It is important not to allow the consommé to bubble too rapidly as this will break up the foam and turn it cloudy.

Strain twice through a large sieve lined with scalded muslin or a clean tea towel. Pour into individual bowls and cool. Chill for about 1 hour before serving.

Variation

Consommé with pepper and peas
Warm 1 litre/1¾ pints chicken consommé (made as recipe above) until just pourable. Set aside. Blanch 1 red pepper, deseeded and diced, for 2 minutes in boiling salted water, refresh with cold water and drain. Cook 100 g/4 oz shelled fresh or frozen peas in boiling salted water for 8 minutes or till tender, then refresh and drain. Stir the diced pepper, peas and 2 tablespoons finely chopped parsley into the consommé, turn into individual bowls and chill till firm.

To add a little piquancy to this consommé, a few drops of Worcestershire sauce or lemon juice may be added with the vegetables. Other herbs such as freshly chopped tarragon, lemon balm or mint, may also be added instead of parsley, but use sparingly so that the flavouring herbs do not mask the subtle flavour of the consommé.

Soups

Cold Avocado Soup

Serves 4

3 medium ripe avocados
juice of 1 lemon
4 tablespoons dry white wine
5 tablespoons soured cream
300 ml/½ pint cold chicken stock
1–2 tablespoons olive oil
salt and pepper
dash of Worcestershire sauce
¼ teaspoon grated lemon rind
150 ml/¼ pint whipping cream, stiffly
   whipped
sprigs of lemon balm or mint to
   garnish

Halve and stone the avocados.
Scoop the flesh out of five halves
only and brush the sixth with lemon
juice immediately to prevent
discoloration; set it aside for the
garnish.

Mash the scooped-out flesh, then
rub through a sieve and beat into
the purée the remaining lemon
juice, wine and soured cream.
Alternatively purée these ingredients
in a liquidiser or food processor.

Continue to beat or blend while
adding the chicken stock and the oil,
drop by drop. When thoroughly
combined, season with salt, pepper,
Worcestershire sauce and lemon
rind, cover and chill for 30 minutes.
Then stir again, check the seasoning
and lightly fold in the whipped
cream.

Turn into individual bowls. Peel
and slice the remaining ½ avocado
and arrange 2 slices per bowl on top
of the soup, together with the sprigs
of herbs. Serve immediately.

Vichysoïsse

Serves 4–6

2 large leeks, trimmed, well washed
   and cut into thin rings
2 onions, peeled and finely chopped
50 g/2 oz butter
225 g/8 oz potatoes, peeled and cut
   into small dice
600 ml/1 pint hot chicken stock
300 ml/½ pint milk
300 ml/½ pint whipping cream
salt and pepper
dash of Tabasco sauce
1 bunch of chives, finely chopped

Gently cook the leeks and onions in
the butter in a large saucepan,
stirring frequently, until soft but not
brown — about 8 minutes. Add the
potatoes together with the stock.
Bring to the boil, cover, reduce the
heat and simmer gently for about 30
minutes.

Cool the mixture slightly, then rub
through a sieve or purée in a
liquidiser or food processor.

Gently reheat the purée in the
rinsed-out pan with the milk and
150 ml/¼ pint of the cream, whisking
it in gently. Do not allow to boil.
Remove the pan from the heat,
season to taste with salt and pepper
and Tabasco and leave to cool.
When cold, chill.

Just before serving pour the soup
into individual bowls. Stiffly whip
the rest of the cream and spoon it
over the soup, sprinkle with
chopped chives and serve, with
triangles of toasted brown bread,
spread with salted butter, or bread
sticks, or potato crisps.

Variation
If you like garlic, then cook 1–2
cloves of garlic, peeled and finely
chopped or crushed, with the onions
and leeks. Or season to taste at the
end with a little garlic salt or the
juice extracted from crushed garlic.

For a slightly sharp flavour, add a
little dry white wine or a few drops
of lemon juice, or substitute natural
yogurt for some of the cream.

You can also put very small pieces
of peeled tomato or cooked French
beans and/or chopped hard-boiled
egg yolk on each serving, to give
colour and flavour.

Fried onions or white bread
croûtons fried in garlic-flavoured oil,
also go well with this soup but
should only be sprinkled on at the
last moment.

Cook's Tip

If short of time for cooling the soup,
pour it out of the hot pan into a
glass or metal bowl and stand it in
several changes of cold water. For
extra speed, put a quantity of ice
cubes into a plastic bag, seal well
and hang it in the soup. Don't forget
to remove it before serving!

Gourmet Fish Dishes

Fish

Haddock with mussel and shrimp sauce

Serves 4

1.15 litres/2 pints mussels
300 ml/½ pint dry white wine
225 g/8 oz carrots, peeled and sliced
2 onions, peeled and coarsely
chopped
2–3 tablespoons roughly chopped
parsley
1 bay leaf
½ teaspoon white peppercorns
generous pinch of salt
1 litre/1¾ pints water
1-kg/2-lb piece haddock (preferably
middle cut)
1 egg yolk
150 ml/¼ pint soured cream
100 g/4 oz thawed frozen or canned
shrimps
salt and pepper
1 tablespoon chopped fresh dill or 2
teaspoons dried dill
springs of dill to garnish (optional)

Scrub and rinse the mussels thoroughly to remove any grit. Scrape the shells with a knife and scrape or pull away the beards. Discard any mussels which are open or damaged. Place the cleaned mussels in a large pan and pour over the wine. Bring to the boil and cover the pan. Cook over high heat, shaking the pan occasionally, for about 10 minutes until all the shells have opened — throw away any that remain closed. Drain and reserve the cooking liquid and remove the mussels from their shells.

Place the carrot, onion, parsley, bay leaf, peppercorns and salt in a fish kettle or large saucepan, pour over the water and bring to the boil. Wash and scrape the haddock to remove any scales. Add the reserved cooking liquid from the mussels to the pan, bring the liquid back to the boil and place the fish in the pan. Cover and cook gently for 15–20 minutes, then carefully remove the fish to a serving dish and keep it hot.

Strain the fish stock through a fine sieve, preferably lined with muslin or a double thickness of absorbent kitchen paper. Pour the strained stock into a pan, bring to the boil and cook rapidly, uncovered, until reduced to half its original quantity. Whisk about 4 tablespoons of this into the egg yolk, then return it to the pan together with the soured cream, shrimps and mussels and heat through, stirring continuously, without boiling. Season to taste, stir in the dill and pour a little of the sauce over the fish. Garnish the dish with a few sprigs of fresh dill, if available. Serve the remaining sauce separately.

Variations
Mussel and celery sauce Omit the shrimps. Thinly slice 1 stalk of celery, sauté it in 25 g/1 oz butter until soft and add it to the sauce just before serving.

Mussel and apple sauce Omit the shrimps. Peel, core and coarsely grate a small cooking apple, toss in a dash of lemon juice and stir it into the sauce before adding the egg yolk. The fish may then be garnished with thinly pared lemon rind cut into fine shreds and blanched in boiling water for a few minutes. A tablespoon of brandy or sherry may also be added to the sauce before the egg yolk.

Note This dish also tastes good when served cold. Prepare the sauce and fish as above, omitting the egg yolk and soured cream and allow fish and sauce to cool. Before serving stir 150 ml/¼ pint whipped double cream or yogurt into the sauce.

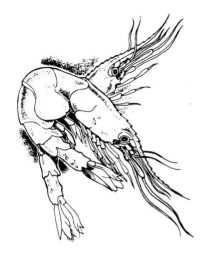

Fish

Plaice steamed in sherry

Serves 4

8 medium plaice fillets
juice of ½ lemon
pinch of salt
25 g/1 oz butter
1 small onion, peeled and thinly
    sliced
1 carrot, peeled and cut in thin strips
2 tomatoes, peeled and roughly
    chopped
1 sprig of tarragon
250 ml/8 fl oz dry sherry
tarragon or parsley sprigs to garnish

Sprinkle the fish with the lemon juice and salt, cover and leave to marinate for 30 minutes.

Melt the butter in a frying pan, add the onion and carrot and cook for a few minutes until just beginning to soften. Arrange over the base of a deep plate together with the tomatoes and tarragon. Alternatively use the steamer plate of a fish kettle or a thoroughly cleaned deep fryer basket. Lay the fish fillets neatly on top of the vegetables and sprinkle 2–3 tablespoons of the sherry over them. Pour the remaining sherry into a saucepan and bring to the boil. Cover the plate closely with cooking foil and place it over the saucepan. Reduce the heat and steam the plaice for about 10–15 minutes until cooked. Uncover the plate and carefully drain any juices into the sherry in the saucepan. Keep the fish and vegetables hot.

Bring the sherry to the boil and continue to boil rapidly until it is reduced to half its original quantity, then pour over the fish and vegetables and serve at once. The plaice may be garnished with sprigs of tarragon or parsley.

Fresh white bread or rolls are the best accompaniment to this dish and dry sherry should be served rather than dry white wine.

Note Hot butter sauce (see page 110) goes very well with this dish. Alternatively, for a richer sauce, add 150 ml/¼ pint of single cream to the reduced sherry liquid and reheat gently, without boiling.

Variation

Fillets of sole may also be cooked in sherry steam. For a stronger flavour, omit the carrots and tomatoes and replace the tarragon with 2 tablespoons chopped chives.

Sole with mushroom and prawn sauce

Serves 4

8 medium sole fillets, skinned
juice of 1 lemon
250 ml/8 fl oz dry white wine
pinch of salt
1 bay leaf
4 peppercorns
1 small onion, peeled and sliced
100 g/4 oz butter
100 g/4 oz peeled prawns
100 g/4 oz button mushrooms, wiped
    and stalks removed
1 teaspoon tomato purée
1 egg yolk
pinch of cayenne

Sprinkle the fish with a little lemon juice, roll up the fillets and secure them with a wooden cocktail stick. Heat the wine with the salt, bay leaf, peppercorns and onion, then cover and simmer for 10 minutes. Place the fish rolls in the pan and poach them gently for 10 minutes. Lift on to a warmed serving dish, standing each roll up on end, and keep hot. Remove the cocktail sticks. Strain the cooking liquid, return it to the pan and boil rapidly until reduced to half its original quantity.

Melt half the butter in a saucepan, add the prawns and sauté lightly for a few minutes. Lift the prawns out of the butter and place them on top of the fish rolls. Add the mushrooms to the butter in the pan and cook them gently for a few minutes. Add these to the fish in the serving dish and keep hot.

Add the reduced cooking liquid to the buttery pan juices and stir in the tomato purée. Heat this mixture to just below boiling point. Lightly whisk the egg yolk with any remaining lemon juice and stand it in a bowl over a saucepan of hot water. Gradually whisk in the hot cooking liquor and the remaining butter, in small pieces, until the sauce is slightly thickened and very creamy. Season lightly with a little cayenne pepper and pour the sauce over the fish. Serve immediately with hot bread rolls or freshly made toast.

Cook's Tip

Thawed frozen fish may be used successfully in both the above recipes but fresh fish, if you can get it, is even more delicious. When buying fish it is important to check that it is absolutely fresh. Look for bright eyes, firm flesh and a good sheen to the skin. Avoid fish with an unpleasant smell. Any markings such as the red spots on plaice should be clear and bright.

Fish

Fish au gratin

Serves 4

100 g/4 oz long-grain rice
salt
100 g/4 oz frozen peas, thawed
450 g/1 lb white fish fillets such as
*   cod or haddock*
100 ml/4 fl oz dry white wine
½ teaspoon peppercorns
1 shallot, peeled and chopped
1 small carrot, peeled and chopped
100 ml/4 fl oz milk
100 ml/4 fl oz single cream
100 g/4 oz Gruyère or mature
*   Cheddar cheese, grated*
2 tablespoons fresh white
*   breadcrumbs*
25 g/1 oz butter

Cook the rice in 600 ml/1 pint boiling salted water for about 20 minutes or until tender. Drain thoroughly and rinse with a little fresh boiling water, then mix with the peas.

Cut the fish into bite-sized pieces. Heat the wine with the peppercorns, shallot and carrot until it reaches boiling point. Cook for a minute then strain and pour the liquid over the fish in a saucepan. Poach gently for about 5 minutes until cooked. Add the rice and peas to the pan and continue cooking over a low heat until heated through. Spoon the mixture into a gratin or shallow ovenproof dish.

Gently heat the milk and cream together, stir in all but two tablespoons of the cheese, season to taste and pour this mixture over the fish. Top with the breadcrumbs and remaining cheese and dot with butter. Cook under a hot grill until crisp and golden.

Baked fish with vegetables

Serves 4

450 g/1 lb cod or haddock steaks
salt
juice of 1 lemon
3 tablespoons plain flour
225 g/8 oz button mushrooms, wiped
*   and thinly sliced*
1 leek, trimmed, washed and cut in
*   thin strips*
1 large carrot, peeled and cut in thin
*   strips*
¼ small celeriac root, peeled and cut
*   in thin strips (optional)*

50 g/2 oz butter
1 onion, peeled and finely chopped
1–2 cloves of garlic, finely chopped
3 ripe tomatoes, sliced
8 stuffed green olives, sliced
freshly ground black pepper
pinch of cayenne
2 tablespoons dry sherry
3 tablespoons soured cream
1 tablespoon chopped parsley to
*   garnish*

Set the oven at moderately hot (200 c, 400 f, gas 6). Cut the fish into bite-sized cubes, season it with a little salt and sprinkle over half the lemon juice. Coat lightly in the flour. Sprinkle the remaining lemon juice over the mushrooms and mix them with the leek, carrot and celeriac, if used.

Melt the butter in a large frying pan, add the onion and garlic and cook until transparent but not browned then stir in all the prepared vegetables except the tomatoes and cook gently for 5 minutes. Spoon about two-thirds of the vegetables into a lightly greased ovenproof dish and arrange the fish on top. Spoon over the remaining vegetables and top with the tomatoes and olives.

Fish

Season with a little pepper and a pinch of cayenne then pour over the sherry and cover the dish. Cook in the heated oven for 15 minutes. Uncover the dish, pour in the soured cream and cook for a further 5–10 minutes. Sprinkle the parsley over and serve immediately with boiled and buttered rice or potatoes.

Herrings with scrambled egg

Serves 4

4 medium herrings, cleaned
100 g / 4 oz butter
6 eggs
4 tablespoons single cream
salt and pepper
pinch of paprika
2 tablespoons chopped parsley

Cut the heads and tails off the herrings. Open them out and place skin side up on a board or flat surface. Press along the back of the fish with your thumb to release the backbone. Turn the fish over and remove any loose bones then fold over to re-form the shape.

Melt 50 g / 2 oz butter in a large frying pan and use to fry the herrings for about 15 minutes, turning once. Remove carefully and arrange on a warmed serving dish. Keep hot.

Whisk together the eggs and cream and season to taste with salt, pepper, and paprika. Melt the remaining butter in a saucepan and add the egg mixture. Stir over a medium heat until the eggs are just set. Arrange the scrambled egg around the herrings in the dish, sprinkle with chopped parsley and serve at once.

Marinated smoked fish

Serves 4

100 ml / 4 fl oz wine vinegar
4 tablespoons water
100 ml / 4 fl oz red wine
3 tablespoons olive oil
50 g / 2 oz castor sugar
8 black peppercorns, crushed
2 dried red chillies
pinch of salt
3 cloves of garlic, peeled and chopped
1 red pepper, deseeded and cut in strips
1 green pepper, deseeded and cut in strips
450 g / 1 lb smoked eel, cut in 5-cm / 2-in lengths
2 tablespoons capers
2 tablespoons chopped parsley
2 tomatoes, halved and cut in wedges
12 stuffed green olives, halved

Mix the vinegar, water, wine, olive oil, castor sugar, peppercorns and chillies. Season with salt and bring to the boil. Skim the mixture, allow it to cool then remove the chillies. Add the garlic, peppers and smoked eel, cover and refrigerate for 24 hours.

Add the capers, parsley, tomatoes and olives and arrange the mixture in a serving dish. Serve with fresh, warm French or rye bread. Alternatively serve with sautéed potatoes or buttered new potatoes.

Note If you cannot obtain smoked eel then try using 4 medium smoked mackerel or smoked haddock fillets — they will taste just as good. Place the fillets in a dish, prepare the marinade and proceed as above.

45

Fish

Spanish herrings

Serves 6

450 g/1 lb salted herrings, trimmed
   and filleted or rollmops
1 teaspoon sugar
250 ml/8 fl oz dry sherry
2 tablespoons wine vinegar
1 teaspoon black peppercorns,
   crushed
3 tablespoons olive oil
1 onion, peeled and sliced
2–3 cloves of garlic, peeled and
   chopped
12 stuffed green olives, halved
2 sprigs of fresh thyme
1 small dried red chilli

Soak the herrings overnight and
rinse them before use. Rinse the
rollmops, if used, and cut the fish
into thin strips. Mix the sugar with
the sherry, vinegar, peppercorns,
oil, onion and garlic. Layer the
herrings and olives in a large jar or
dish and top with the thyme and
chilli. Pour over the sherry mixture
and cover closely. Leave to marinate
in the refrigerator for 1–3 days.
   Serve with warm French bread
and a glass of dry sherry or light
white wine.

Cook's Tip

Oily fish such as herrings or
mackerel are delicious when pickled
in a vinegar or brine solution which
stabilises the protein in the flesh in
the same way that cooking does.
Salted herrings are usually sold
whole and need to be soaked
overnight before being trimmed and
filleted.

Herrings in yogurt

Serves 6

450 g/1 lb salted herrings, trimmed
   and filleted or rollmops
2 onions, peeled and chopped
1 large cooking apple, peeled, cored
   and chopped
2 gherkins, chopped
2 pickled beetroot, sliced
1 teaspoon capers
150 ml/¼ pint double cream
3 tablespoons natural yogurt
1 teaspoon creamed horseradish
pinch of sugar
pinch of freshly ground white pepper
1 tablespoon tarragon vinegar
1 tablespoon red wine vinegar
2 tablespoons chopped mixed fresh
   herbs
1 tablespoon chopped chives

Salted herrings should be soaked
overnight and rinsed before use.
Rinse the rollmops, if used, and cut
the fish into bite-sized pieces. Mix
the onion, apple, gherkin and
beetroot together with the fish and
capers. Stir in the cream and yogurt
together with the horseradish, sugar,
pepper and vinegars. Add the mixed
herbs and stir well. Cover and leave
to marinate in the refrigerator for
1–2 days. Serve sprinkled with
chives.
   Fresh bread or jacket potatoes go
well with this dish.

Herrings in red wine

Serves 6

450 g/1 lb salted herrings, trimmed
   and filleted or rollmops
1 leek, sliced and thoroughly washed
1 onion, peeled and sliced
2 tablespoons green peppercorns
pinch of sugar
2 cloves
2 juniper berries
1 bay leaf
1 carrot, peeled and sliced
1 small red pepper, deseeded and
   finely chopped
grated rind of 1 orange
250 ml/8 fl oz red wine
4 tablespoons red wine vinegar
2 tablespoons olive oil (optional)

Soak the salted herrings in water
overnight. Rinse the rollmops, if
used, and cut the fish into strips.
Place all the ingredients except the
wine, vinegar and oil in an
earthenware terrine or covered dish
and stir lightly. Mix together the
wine, vinegar and oil, if using, and
pour over the mixture in the terrine.
Cover well and leave to marinate in
the refrigerator for 24 hours. Serve
with baked potatoes.

Swedish style herrings

Serves 6

6 fresh herrings, cleaned and filleted
300 ml/½ pint white wine vinegar
300 ml/½ pint water
175 g/6 oz sugar
1 tablespoon whole allspice
1 tablespoon black peppercorns
1 teaspoon mustard seed
2–3 small bay leaves
2 shallots, peeled and sliced
1 carrot, peeled and chopped
3-cm/1½-in piece horseradish root,
   scraped and finely sliced (optional)
1-cm/½-in piece fresh root ginger,
   peeled and finely sliced
sprig of dill or parsley to garnish

Cut the fish into strips. Put the wine
vinegar and water with the sugar,
spices and bay leaves in a saucepan,
bring to the boil and simmer for 5
minutes. Add the fish, bring back to
the boil and remove from the heat.
Allow to cool.
   Layer the fish with the vegetables,
horseradish, if using, and ginger in a
large jar or covered dish and pour
over the cooled marinade. Cover
and marinate in the refrigerator for
2 days. Garnish with a sprig of dill
or parsley before serving with plenty
of fresh bread and butter.

Fish

Mackerel with avocado stuffing

Serves 4

4 medium mackerel, cleaned
juice of 2 lemons
salt and freshly ground black pepper
1 ripe avocado
100 g/4 oz lean, rindless bacon
2 tablespoons flour
100 g/4 oz butter
1 small leek, trimmed, washed and
   thinly sliced
2 carrots, peeled and cut in julienne
   strips
100 ml/4 fl oz dry white wine
3 tablespoons dry vermouth
150 ml/¼ pint soured cream

Garnish
1 lemon, cut in wedges
sprigs of dill or parsley

Heat the oven to moderate (180 c,
350 f, gas 4). Dry the fish on
absorbent kitchen paper and trim off
the fins. Sprinkle the inside of the
fish with about half the lemon juice
and seasoning. Halve the avocado,
remove the stone and peel and
sprinkle the flesh with lemon juice.
Mash the avocado with the
remaining lemon juice. Chop the
bacon finely and stir it into the
avocado then season the stuffing
generously.
   Divide the mixture between the
mackerel and sew up the opening.
Alternatively use wooden cocktail
sticks to secure the opening. Dust
the fish with the flour and melt half
the butter in a frying pan. Brown
the fish quickly in the butter, turning
carefully, then remove to an
ovenproof dish. Toss the leek and
carrots quickly in the pan and
arrange them around the fish. Pour
over the wine and dot the top of the
fish with a little of the remaining
butter. Cook in the heated oven for
30 minutes.
   Arrange the fish on a warmed
serving dish on four individual
dishes together with the vegetables.
Pour the cooking liquid into a pan,
stir in the vermouth and boil rapidly
until reduced by half. Stir in the
cream and heat gently without
boiling. Finally beat in the
remaining butter in small pieces.
Pour the sauce over the fish and
garnish with lemon wedges and
sprigs of dill and parsley. Serve with
boiled rice and a green salad.

Mushroom-stuffed fish steaks

Serves 4

4 large monkfish or cod steaks
4 tablespoons oil
4 tablespoons lemon juice
100 ml/4 fl oz dry white wine
salt and freshly ground black pepper
225 g/8 oz button mushrooms, wiped
   and thinly sliced
1 teaspoon chopped parsley
1 small onion, peeled and finely
   chopped
50 g/2 oz butter
2 egg yolks
1 teaspoon wine or tarragon vinegar

Heat the oven to moderate (180 c,
350 f, gas 4). Rinse the fish steaks
and dry them on absorbent kitchen
paper. Remove the central bone
then arrange them in a shallow dish.
Mix the oil, lemon juice and wine
together and season generously.
pour this marinade over the fish and
leave to stand for 15–30 minutes.
   Mix the mushrooms with the
herbs and onion and season lightly.
Arrange the fish in an ovenproof
dish, spoon the stuffing into the
middle of the steaks and arrange any
remaining mixture over the top. Dot
the top with the butter and pour
over the marinade. Cover the dish
and bake in the heated oven for 20–
30 minutes. Carefully lift the fish on
to a warmed serving dish and keep
hot.
   Place the egg yolks and vinegar in
a basin over a pan of hot water or in
a double boiler and whisk until
foamy. Gradually whisk in the
cooking liquor from the fish until
pale and creamy. Season lightly.
Pour a little of the sauce over the
fish and serve the remainder
separately. Boiled and buttered new
potatoes and a fresh green salad are
the ideal accompaniments for this
dish. Alternatively use a melon
scoop to cut out pieces of raw
potato and simmer them gently in
lightly salted water to about 10
minutes or until cooked. Toss in
butter before serving with the fish.

Note Monkfish is not always easily
obtainable so any other firm white
fish steaks may be substituted.

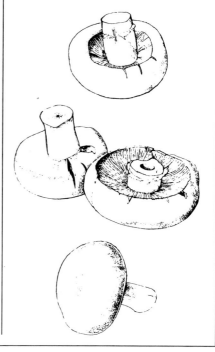

Gravad lax

Serves 6–8 as a starter

1 kg/2 lb middle cut fresh salmon
small bunch of dill, tarragon or
* parsley*
1 tablespoon white peppercorns,
* crushed*
4 tablespoons coarse salt
3 tablespoons sugar
sprigs of dill to garnish (optional)

Rinse the salmon and dry it on
absorbent kitchen paper. Using a
sharp knife, make a horizontal cut
along the back of the fish. Continue
cutting lengthways along either side
of the backbone, keeping the knife
as close to the bones as possible
until the uppermost fillet is free. Slip
the tip of the knife under the
backbone and, keeping the knife
horizontal, cut the bone free from
the remaining fillet. Remove any
small bones from the fillets with a
small knife or tweezers.
  Rinse and dry the herbs. Mix the
peppercorns with the salt and sugar.
Place one piece of fish, skin side
down, in a deep dish and spread half
the salt mixture evenly over it.
Arrange the herbs on top, reserving
a few sprigs for garnish, and sprinkle
over the remaining salt mixture. Lay
the second piece of salmon, skin
side uppermost, on top and press
down well. Cover with a double
thickness of greaseproof paper and a
plate or small chopping board, then
weight down well and leave in the
refrigerator for 2 days. Turn the
salmon over twice during this time.
  Pat the prepared salmon dry on
absorbent kitchen paper and, using a
sharp knife, cut it diagonally across
the grain into very thin slices.
Arrange these on a platter and serve
with a little mustard sauce poured
over. Garnish with sprigs of dill, if
available. Thinly sliced bread and
butter or boiled new potatoes should
be served as accompaniments.

Mustard sauce

2 egg yolks
4 teaspoons made English mustard
6 tablespoons oil
caster sugar to taste
3 tablespoons chopped dill, tarragon
* or parsley*
4 tablespoons juices from the Gravad
* lax or 2 tablespoons lemon juice*
salt and pepper

Whisk the egg yolks with the
mustard then gradually add the oil
drop by drop, whisking continuously
to produce a mayonnaise. Stir in a
little caster sugar, the chopped dill,
tarragon or parsley and the juices
from the Gravad lax or lemon juice.
Taste the sauce and adjust the
sweetness and seasoning if
necessary.

Poached salmon in watercress sauce

Serves 4

4 (225-g/8-oz) salmon steaks
salt and freshly ground white pepper
juice of ½ lemon
50 g/2 oz butter
1 small onion, peeled and finely
* chopped*
1 bunch of watercress, washed,
* trimmed and chopped*
100 ml/4 fl oz fish stock or water
100 ml/4 fl oz dry white wine
100 ml/4 fl oz single cream

Season the salmon steaks lightly
with a little salt and pepper.
Sprinkle over half the lemon juice
and leave to marinate for 10
minutes. Melt the butter, add the
onion and cook, stirring
occasionally, until softened but not
browned. Stir in remaining lemon
juice and half the watercress, season
lightly then add the stock and wine.
Heat gently to simmering point, add
the salmon steaks and simmer for
about 5–7 minutes until just cooked.
  Remove the fish to a warmed
serving dish and keep hot. Stir the
remaining watercress and cream into
the sauce and heat through gently
without boiling. Pour over the
salmon and serve immediately with
boiled potatoes and a cucumber
salad or buttered asparagas.

Variations

Sorrel sauce Fresh sorrel is delicious
with salmon. Substitute 225 g/8 oz
sorrel for the watercress, wash, dry
and chop it finely then cook as
above.

Tarragon or chive sauce Both of
these well-flavoured herbs may be
substituted for the watercress in the
above recipe. They should be used
sparingly, about 1–2 tablespoons is
enough, and should be added to the
sauce with the cream.

Lemon sauce Thinly pare the rind
from 1 lemon and cut it into needle-
fine shreds. Cook it with the salmon
steaks, omitting the watercress from
the recipe, and serve as above.

Grilled salmon Alternatively the
sauce can be prepared as above and
the salmon cooked separately under
a hot grill. Dot the fish steaks with
butter and grill them for about 3
minutes on each side. Pour the
sauce over them before serving.

Cook's Tip

Gravad lax is a traditional Swedish
delicacy and, as it can be made
some time in advance, is excellent as
a starter for a dinner party or as
part of a cold buffet meal. Maintain
the Scandinavian mood by serving it
on a wooden board garnished with
lemon wedges and dill and
accompanied by thinly sliced rye
bread or crispbread.

Fish

Trout au bleu

Serves 4

4 freshly caught trout, cleaned
100 ml/4 fl oz vinegar
1 small onion, peeled and sliced
1 carrot, peeled and sliced
1 bay leaf
few sprigs of parsley
generous pinch of salt
2.25 litres/4 pints water
1 lemon, cut in wedges to garnish

Handle the trout with care so as not to remove the natural coating on the skin. Mix the vinegar, onion, carrot, bay leaf, half the parsley, salt and water in a large saucepan or fish kettle and bring it to the boil. Add the fish, curving them slightly in the pan and bring back to a gentle simmer. Cook for 7–10 minutes then carefully lift the trout out of the pan and arrange them on warmed serving dishes. Garnish with lemon wedges and the remaining parsley.

Serve with plenty of melted butter, boiled potatoes and a fresh green salad. Creamed horesradish goes well with fresh trout.

Tip If you cannot obtain freshly caught trout bring the vinegar to the boil separately from the other ingredients and pour this over the fish before cooking it.

Variation
Trout au bleu may also be served cold. Allow the fish to cool in the cooking liquid then carefully remove the skin, leaving the head and tail in place. Arrange them on a large serving platter, lightly coat with aspic and garnish with boiled or steamed mixed vegetables, lemon wedges and sprigs of parsley or dill.

Trout meunière

Serves 4

4 medium trout, cleaned
salt and freshly ground white pepper
juice of 2 lemons
4–6 tablespoons seasoned flour
75 g/3 oz butter
1 tablespoon oil
2 tablespoons chopped parsley

Rinse the trout under running water and dry on absorbent kitchen paper. Season the cavities lightly and sprinkle with half the lemon juice. Coat with seasoned flour.

Melt about half the butter and the oil in a large frying pan and cook the trout over medium heat for about 8–10 minutes, turning once. Remove to a warmed serving dish.

Add the remaining butter to the pan juices and cook for a few minutes then stir in the remaining lemon juice and parsley. Heat through for a few seconds before pouring over the fish. Serve immediately with boiled new potatoes and a fresh green salad.

Tip When cooking trout, take care not to overcook the outside before the middle is cooked. Medium heat is necessary for this and to avoid breaking up the flesh.

Variation
A few sprigs of fresh parsley, dill or lemon balm may be placed in the body cavity of the fish before cooking or try cooking orange or lemon wedges in the pan with the fish to provide extra juices and a lovely flavour. A little ground aniseed may also be added to the flour before coating the fish — unorthodox, but delicious!

Fish

Trout en papillote

Serves 4

4 medium trout, cleaned
juice of ½ lemon
salt and pepper
50 g/2 oz butter
small bunch of parsley, washed and dried
4 sprigs of tarragon, washed and dried (optional)
4 sprigs of dill, washed and dried (optional)
3 large tomatoes, peeled, deseeded and chopped
2 onions, peeled and finely chopped
2 tablespoons chopped parsley
sprigs of parsley to garnish

Set the oven at moderate (180 C, 350 F, gas 4). Rinse the trout well, both inside and out, and pat dry on absorbent kitchen paper. Sprinkle the inside of each with a little lemon juice and season generously. Divide the butter into four and place in the cavity of each fish, along with the herbs, if using. Soak eight pieces of greaseproof paper in cold water and use to wrap each trout up in a double thickness. Lay the fish in a

roasting tin, making sure that the ends of the parcels are tucked in well and bake in the heated oven for 10 minutes. Carefully turn the fish over, again ensuring that the parcels are secure, and cook for a further 10 minutes.

Carefully open the paper, removing the skin of the fish with it and lift the uppermost fillet on to a warmed serving dish. Remove and discard the bone and cooked herbs and carefully lift the lower fillet off the skin, arranging it on the serving dish with the first piece of fish.

Mix the tomatoes with the onions and parsley. Season to taste and serve this mixture with the fish. Garnish with sprigs of parsley. A green salad with a tangy lemon dressing would be the ideal accompaniment to this dish.

Note Mackerel or herrings can also be prepared very successfully in this way. Alternatively the fish can be wrapped in cooking foil and cooked over a barbecue.

Tip A few dried dill or fennel seeds may be sprinkled in the fish during cooking to add extra flavour.

Cook's Tip

Cooking trout in paper is a traditional method of cooking fish which has very practical reasons behind it. Whilst the paper keeps in all the natural flavour and juices it also adheres to the skin of the fish making it easy to remove. For successful results make sure that the paper is moistened and that the 'parcels' are neat and well folded.

Moules marinière

Serves 4

2.25 litres/4 pints mussels
50 g/2 oz butter or 6 tablespoons
* olive oil*
3 spring onions, chopped
1 large carrot, peeled and finely diced
freshly ground black pepper
450 ml/¾ pint dry white wine

Scrub and wash the mussels
thoroughly. Scrape the shells to
ensure that they are clean and
scrape or pull away the beards.
Discard any mussels that remain
open as they are inedible. Melt the
butter or heat the oil in a large
saucepan with a close fitting lid.
Add the prepared vegetables and
cook until soft but not browned —
about 15 minutes. Season generously
with black pepper and pour over the
wine. Bring to the boil, add the
mussels and cover the pan. Cook
over fairly high heat, shaking the
pan frequently, for about 10 minutes
until all the mussels have opened.

Discard any mussels which have
not opened and arrange the rest in
four serving bowls. Pour the cooking
liquor over the mussels taking care
not to transfer any grit which may
have settled in the bottom of the
pan. Alternatively the liquid may be
strained through a sieve lined with
muslin or a double thickness of
absorbent kitchen paper.

Serve with home-baked
wholemeal bread, French bread or
pumpernickel.

Tip The mussels can be flavoured
with a chopped clove of garlic,
added to the vegetables, a peeled,
deseeded and diced tomato or a bay
leaf, sprig of rosemary or chopped
parsley which may be added to the
cooking liquid. The sauce may be
enriched by the addition of 2–4
tablespoons of double cream which
should be gently heated in the sauce
just before serving.

Note Mussels should not be cooked
for longer than is required to open
the shells as continued cooking
toughens and wrinkles the mussel
meat, destroying its delicate flavour.

Variation
Grilled mussels Place the cooked
mussels in a large flat ovenproof
dish. Top with a mixture of 50 g/
2 oz fresh breadcrumbs, 1 finely
chopped clove of garlic, 1
tablespoon chopped parsley, mint or
grated lemon rind and 2 tablespoons
finely grated cheese. Sprinkle
generously with olive oil and cook
under a hot grill until lightly
browned and crisp. Serve with warm
French bread.

Fish

Boiled lobster

Serves 2

*1 live lobster, about 675 g/1½ lb in
    weight*
1 tablespoon salt
1.75 litres/3 pints water
1 lemon or lime
50 g/2 oz butter, melted
sprigs of dill or parsley to garnish

Rinse the lobster under cold running
water leaving any rubber bands
which secure the claws. Place the
salt in a large deep saucepan with a
lid. Add the water and bring it to
the boil then plunge in the lobster,
head downwards. Place the lid on
the pan and, holding it down firmly,
bring the water back to the boil.
Reduce the heat and simmer for 15
minutes. The lobster turns the
characteristic red colour during
cooking.

Lift out the lobster with tongs or a
large fish slice and fork and split it
down the back. Using a large sharp
knife and starting at the point where
the head and tail meet, cut firmly
down through the tail then up
through the head. Use a small
hammer or steak mallet to tap the
knife through the shell if necessary.
Remove the white gills which are
found in both halves of the head and
the black intestine which runs down
the length of the body. Remove and
reserve any roe and the bright red
roe or coral that is found in a female
lobster. Place the lobster on a
warmed serving dish and serve with
wedges of lemon or lime and a little
melted butter. The lobster may be
garnished with sprigs of dill or
parsley.

Note When buying live lobsters it is
important to ensure that they are
really fresh. Hold the lobster by the
back and lift it up — if it is strong
and fresh it should strike out with its
tail. Lobsters with only sluggish
movements should be avoided as
these are not at the peak of
freshness.

Lobster thermidor

Serves 4

2 (675-g/1½-lb) lobsters, cooked
75 g/3 oz butter
2 shallots, peeled and chopped
salt and pepper
pinch of dry mustard
2 tablespoons flour
150 ml/¾ pint dry white wine
150 ml/¼ pint milk
*2 tablespoons grated Parmesan or
    Gruyère cheese*
1 egg yolk
2 tablespoons single cream
50 g/2 oz fresh white breadcrumbs
sprigs of dill or parsley to garnish

Remove the claws and legs from the
lobster, crack the claws with lobster
crackers or nutcrackers and remove
all the meat making sure that bits of
shell do not get into it. Remove all
the meat from the shell and flake
slightly.

Melt 25 g/1 oz of the butter in a
small saucepan, add the shallots and
cook until soft but not browned. Stir
in a little seasonong and the
mustard, then add the flour and stir
in the wine. Bring to the boil,
stirring continuously, then gradually
stir in the milk and heat through
thoroughly. Remove the sauce from
the heat and stir in the cheese until
well blended. Mix the egg yolk with
the cream and beat this into the
sauce. Reheat without boiling to
prevent the egg curdling.

Stir the lobster meat into the
sauce and replace it in the halved
shells. Sprinkle the breadcrumbs
over the top then dot with the
remaining butter and brown under a
hot grill. Garnish with sprigs of dill
or parsley before serving.

Tip When finishing the lobster under
the grill take care not to cook for
too long as this will cause the
delicate lobster meat to dry up and
become stringy. Some gourmets
insist that lobster should be served
lukewarm to bring out the
characteristic delicate flavour but
this is entirely a matter of personal
preference.

Fish

Scallops in mushroom sauce

Serves 4

450 g/1 lb scallops, cleaned
300 ml/½ pint water
100 ml/4 fl oz dry white wine
2 shallots, peeled and sliced
sprig of thyme
· 1 bay leaf
6 peppercorns
1 clove
salt and freshly ground black pepper
100 g/4 oz butter
100 g/4 oz button mushrooms, wiped
  and sliced
2 teaspoons flour
2 tablespoons soured cream
1 egg yolk
1 tablespoon chopped parsley

Cut the red coral away from the scallops and halve the white flesh. Place the water, wine, shallots, herbs and spices in a saucepan and boil rapidly for 10–15 minutes until reduced to about half its original volume. Add the white scallop flesh, season lightly and cook gently for 5 minutes. Add the corals and cook for a further 3–4 minutes. Lift the

flesh out of the stock and slice if the scallops are large.

Strain the stock and reserve. Melt 25 g/1 oz of the butter in a saucepan and use to cook the mushrooms until all the liquid is evaporated. Melt another 25 g/1 oz of butter in another pan and stir in the flour. Cook until golden then gradually whisk in the reserved cooking liquor. Add the soured cream and simmer gently for 2 minutes, stirring all the time. Whisk the egg yolk with a little of the sauce and blend this mixture back into the rest. Heat through without boiling.

Whisk in the remaining 50 g/2 oz butter, a piece at a time, then add the scallops and mushrooms. Season to taste. Serve in clean scallop shells or individual dishes, sprinkled with parsley.

Serve with thinly sliced bread and butter and a finely shredded green salad or with plain boiled rice.

Variations
Scallops au gratin Top the scallops with 25 g/1 oz breadcrumbs mixed with 1 tablespoon grated Parmesan cheese and grill until golden and bubbling.

Saffron scallops Prepare the scallops as above, adding ¼ teaspoon saffron strands to the cooking liquid. Stir a teaspoon each of brandy and vermouth into the sauce and add 2 peeled, deseeded and chopped tomatoes before serving.

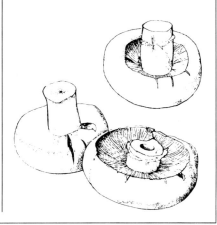

Japanese seafood fritters

Serves 4

Most fish and seafood with firm flesh can be cooked in batter and deep fried. The batter protects the fish from the hot oil and should be crisp, light and tasty.

450 g/1 lb bite-sized pieces of prepared fish and seafood (see below)

Batter
3 egg whites
3 tablespoons sherry
20 g/¾ oz rice flour
20 g/¾ oz plain flour
oil for deep frying

Garnish
1 lemon, cut in wedges
few sprigs of parsley

Prepare the fish and seafood following the instructions below.

Whisk the egg whites until stiff then lightly stir in the sherry, rice flour and plain flour. Heat the oil to 180c/350f. Dip bite-sized pieces of the prepared seafoods in the batter and fry them in the hot oil for the suggested length of time. Drain on absorbent kitchen paper and serve immediately garnished with wedges of lemon and parsley. The fritters go well with a crunchy mixed salad and freshly cut bread and butter.

Note Do not make the batter in advance. It only forms a thin delicate crust if used at once.

Cod, plaice and whiting
Skin the fillets and remove any bones. Season lightly and sprinkle with lemon juice. Cut into bite-sized pieces, coat in the batter as above and deep fry for 7–10 minutes.

Smoked halibut and haddock
Skin the fish fillets and remove any bones. Cut the flesh into strips, coat in the batter and cook for about 5 minutes.

Prawns and scallops
Peeled large and small prawns should be coated in batter and fried for 5 minutes. Scallops should be cleaned, rinsed and cut in half then coated in batter and cooked for 7–10 minutes.

Squid
Remove the heads, tentacles and intestines from the squid, carefully pulling out the transparent cartilage. Pull off the skin and rinse and dry the flesh. Cut it into rings and coat in the prepared batter. Cook the pieces of squid for 10 minutes.

Scampi
Cooked and peeled scampi can be dipped in batter and deep fried for 7–10 minutes.

Roasts
and Grills

Roasts and Grills

Roast beef in a salt crust

Serves 6

*1 (1.25-kg/2½-lb) piece fillet of beef
   or topside*
4 egg whites
450 g/1 lb coarse sea salt

Set the oven at hot (230c, 450F, gas 8). Dry the meat with absorbent kitchen paper. Carefully score any fat several times, without cutting into the meat. Lightly whisk the egg whites and salt together to a dry paste.

Line a roasting tin with a double thickness of foil. Spread over it a layer of the salt paste as long and as wide as the meat. Lay the meat, fat side up, on the salt paste and cover it completely with the rest of the paste. Wrap the foil carefully over the top to enclose the meat completely and cook in the heated oven for 55 minutes to 1 hour for rare meat; cook 10 minutes longer for medium done meat. Place the foil-wrapped meat on a large dish; fold down or tear off the foil.

To serve, carefully break open the salt crust with a hammer or meat mallet. Lift the meat off its bed of salt on to a warmed serving dish, brushing off any salt adhering to it, then let it rest for a few minutes before carving.

Serve with Cumberland or Cranberry sauce (see recipes, page 115) handed round separately, together with croquette potatoes, runner beans or fried mushrooms.

Note This roast appears to do the impossible. In general salt attracts moisture and draws it out of food, thereby drying out anything it comes into contact with — on this occasion a joint of beef. But here the beef remains very juicy and succulent because there is a trick to it. The salt is mixed with a liquid (the egg whites) which it soaks up like a sponge. The salt paste then bakes into a hard shell which, while it imparts a flavour to the meat, ensures it doesn't dry out or overcook.

To make the salt and egg white bind more easily, add about 40 g/1½ oz flour with the salt: it has no noticeable effect on the taste. For the best results choose unrefined sea salt (iodised salt) which imparts a delicious aroma to the meat. Moreover, the crust does not have to be thrown away once opened: pounded in a mortar or worked in a liquidiser or food processor it can be used as a seasoning for other meats as it will have taken on the unmistakeable flavour of a roast. For a stronger flavour, push a few slivers of garlic in between the fat and the meat, or mix some dried herbs with the salt.

Saddle of lamb provençale

Serves 6

*2.25-kg/5-lb saddle of lamb, dressed
   or 1.75-kg/4-lb leg of lamb*
3 cloves of garlic, peeled
2 teaspoons salt
4 juniper berries
6 peppercorns
3 allspice berries
*1 teaspoon fresh rosemary leaves or
   ⅓ teaspoon dried rosemary*
4 tablespoons olive oil
*450 g/1 lb tomatoes, peeled, deseeded
   and finely chopped*
100 ml/4 fl oz stock
100 ml/4 fl oz red wine

Wipe the lamb with a damp cloth and cut off excess fat. Crush the garlic with the salt, juniper berries, peppercorns, allspice berries and rosemary in a mortar. A little of the olive oil may be added to make it smooth. Rub this mixture over the lamb.

Set the oven to hot (220c, 425F, gas 7). Heat the oil in a roasting tin, together with the fat trimmings from the lamb. Put in the lamb and cook for 10 minutes. Reduce the heat to moderately hot (190c, 375F, gas 5), put the tomatoes round the meat, mix the stock with the wine and pour half over the lamb. Put the lamb back in the oven and cook for 1¼–1½ hours, basting from time to time with the juices in the tin. Top

up the stock and wine from time to time.

At the end of the cooking time turn the oven off and let the lamb rest for 5 minutes.

Strain the roasting juices, skim off the fat and serve as gravy, together with ratatouille and French bread, or noodles and garden peas or mangetouts.

Tip Sauce lovers may add more wine to the gravy if liked, then boil to reduce it a little and thicken with a little kneaded butter or cornflour.

Cook's Tip

Saddle is a prime joint consisting of both loins of lamb (these are more usually cut into chops) but the butcher will probably require some notice to dress it for you. A saddle varies in weight from 2.25–3.5 kg/5–8 lb and is therefore an excellent cut for a party or celebration meal. For a family meal a leg of lamb makes a good alternative.

Roasts and Grills

Roast chicken with cream cheese and herb stuffing

Serves 4–6

*1.25-kg/2¾-lb oven-ready chicken,
  thawed if frozen
2 cloves of garlic, peeled and crushed
salt and freshly ground black pepper
50 g/2 oz butter*

Stuffing
*225 g/8 oz cream cheese
2 tablespoons soured cream
1 egg yolk
50 g/2 oz fresh breadcrumbs
1 shallot or small onion, peeled and
  finely chopped
3 tablespoons chopped parsley
½–1 tablespoon chopped chives or
  rosemary
salt and pepper*

To finish
*100 ml/4 fl oz soured cream
2 tablespoons tomato purée
1 teaspoon lemon juice
1 tablespoon brandy*

First make the stuffing: beat the cream cheese, soured cream and egg yolk into the breadcrumbs. Stir in the shallot or onion and the herbs. Season to taste with salt and pepper and set aside.

Set the oven at moderately hot (200 C, 400 F, gas 6).

Using a sharp knife, cut into the skin of the chicken along the backbone. Carefully cut the meat from the bones without detaching it from the skin. Put in the stuffing through this opening, and push it down under the breast meat. Pull the skin together and sew it up. Alternatively use the mixture to stuff the body cavity of the chicken. Mix the garlic to a paste with salt and pepper, then spread over the chicken.

Grease a large piece of foil with some of the butter, put the chicken on it, breast side up, then dot with the rest of the butter, cut into flakes. Draw the foil up and over the chicken loosely and pinch the edges together to seal. Place in a roasting dish and roast for about 1 hour in the heated oven, then open up the foil for 5–10 minutes more to let the chicken brown.

Remove from the oven and place the chicken on a warmed serving dish. Pour off some of the fat from the roasting tin and transfer the juices to a saucepan. Whisk in the cream and reduce the mixture by about one-third over gentle heat. Flavour to taste with tomato purée, lemon juice and brandy. Carve the bird and serve the gravy separately.

Variation
This stuffing is also excellent with chicken legs. Either remove the leg bones from the chicken yourself or get the butcher to do it for you. Fill the cavities with the stuffing and cook in foil as above, reducing the overall cooking time to 30 minutes.

Roast stuffed turkey

Serves 6–8

A whole turkey should in principle be cooked with a stuffing, whether or not both are to be eaten at the same time. The stuffing imparts a special flavour to the meat, and helps to keep it moist during long cooking.

1 (4-kg/9-lb) oven-ready turkey,
  thawed if frozen
½ lemon
salt and pepper
100 g/4 oz streaky bacon
50 g/2 oz butter, melted

Stuffing
100 g/4 oz sultanas
150 ml/¼ pint port or sherry
450 g/1 lb pork sausagemeat
butter for frying
turkey liver from giblets, finely
  chopped
1 egg
salt and pepper
dried thyme

First make the stuffing. Steep the sultanas in the port or sherry for 1 hour, then drain, reserving any juices for the gravy. Fry the sausagemeat in a little butter, then stir in the sultanas and liver, and cook 1–2 minutes longer. Remove from the heat, cool and stir in the beaten egg. Season to taste with salt, pepper and thyme. Set aside in a cool place.

Set the oven at moderate (190 C, 375 F, gas 5).

Rub the lemon around the body cavity of the turkey, then season inside and out with salt and pepper. Fill the body cavity with the stuffing.

Wrap the bacon rashers over the breast and legs, then truss the bird. Place in a large roasting tin. Pour over the melted butter and roast in the heated oven for about 3½ hours, basting from time to time with the juices in the tin and occasionally sprinkling with a little water.

Ten minutes before the end of cooking time, remove the bacon, spoon over some of the juices from the tin and leave to brown off the breast. Test with a skewer — the bird is done if the thigh juices run out clear. Remove from the oven

and pour off the cooking juices. Cover the turkey with foil and if possible stand in a warm place for 10 minutes before carving, to allow the meat and juices to settle.

Strain the pan juices into a saucepan and skim off any fat. Add strained giblet stock (see note below) and if you like, thicken the gravy by whisking in a little kneaded butter and add 1–2 tablespoons of red wine or sherry or the port left over from making the stuffing. Bring to the boil, check the seasoning and pour into a gravy boat to serve.

Note To make giblet stock: wash the gizzard and heart and simmer in about 900 ml/1½ pints water seasoned with salt, pepper and bouquet garni for 1 hour. Strain well before using.

Roasts and Grills

Roast stuffed goose

Serves 8

1 (4-kg/9-lb) oven-ready goose,
*   thawed if frozen*
salt and pepper
25 g/1 oz butter
300 ml/½ pint boiling water

Stuffing
450 g/1 lb cooking apples, peeled,
*   cored and diced*
1 onion, peeled and finely chopped
100 g/4 oz fresh breadcrumbs
100 g/4 oz sultanas

Rub inside the goose with salt and pepper. Set the oven at hot (200c, 400f, gas 6).

For the stuffing, mix together the apples, onion, breadcrumbs and sultanas. Stuff the breast of the goose with this mixture and sew up with fine string or secure with skewers. Rub all over the bird with salt and pepper and prick it with a fork in several places so that the fat can run out during roasting. Remember to prick under the breast and under the legs. Spread the butter over the breast.

Pour the boiling water into the roasting tin. Put in the goose on a rack, breast side uppermost. Cook in the heated oven for about 2½ hours, basting from time to time with the cooking juices. Then turn the bird over and brown the back for about 20 minutes. Turn it over again, brush well with salted water and let it brown until crisp, about 10 minutes. Take out, cover with foil and let it stand for 10 minutes in a warm place before carving.

Serve with croquette potatoes, glazed chestnuts, Brussels sprouts and chopped, fried mushrooms. The goose itself may be garnished with fried apple rings and parsley sprigs.

Sage gravy

Pour 300 ml/½ pint boiling water into the roasting tin to dissolve the meat juices. Skim off as much fat as possible. Pour the liquid into a saucepan and add 2 tablespoons chopped fresh or 2 teaspoons dried sage. Reduce over high heat for a few minutes. Strain, and season to taste with salt and pepper. Stir in a little cream if liked, and serve separately in a gravy boat.

Brussels sprouts

Serves 8

1 kg/2 lb Brussels sprouts
25 g/1 oz butter
grated nutmeg
freshly ground black pepper

Clean the sprouts and make shallow cuts crosswise in the stalk ends. Plunge them into the boiling salted water, cover and cook for about 10 minutes until just tender. Drain well. Melt the butter in the same saucepan, put in the sprouts, season with nutmeg and pepper to taste and toss them well. Serve hot.

Glazed chestnuts

Serves 6–8

675 g/1½ lb fresh chestnuts or 350 g/
*   12 oz dried chestnuts, soaked in*
*   cold water*
6 tablespoons stock
50 g/2 oz butter
1 tablespoon sugar

Slit open the chestnut skins (crosswise), if using fresh ones, cook in boiling water to cover for 5 minutes or until the skins curl outwards. Drain and peel them, removing the furry inside skin as well. Or drain the dried chestnuts.

In another pan, bring the stock to the boil, put in the chestnuts, butter and sugar, cover and cook for 15–20 minutes. Remove the lid and cook for a further 5 minutes until the chestnuts are soft and lightly caramelised. Serve hot.

Variations
Potato stuffing Cook 450 g/1 lb peeled potatoes in boiling salted water for 10 minutes. Drain and dice them. Mix with 1 chopped onion and 2 tablespoons chopped parsley, then season to taste with dried marjoram and sage. Use to stuff the goose as above.

Orange stuffing Peel 4 large oranges and divide into segments. Mix with 2 large cooking apples, peeled, cored and diced, 100 g/4 oz fresh breadcrumbs and 1 egg to bind. Use to stuff the goose as above. 50 g/2 oz each sultanas and chopped, blanched almonds may also be added, if liked.

Alternative accompaniments Try red cabbage braised with apples, and flavoured with cinnamon and ginger. Or canned sauerkraut, drained and heated with a little dry white wine and mixed with pineapple chunks or slices of orange.

Note The same stuffings and accompaniments can be used for roast duck.

Cook's Tip

Goose is a delicious meat, traditionally eaten at Christmas, but is avoided by some because it has a reputation for being somewhat fatty. However if cooked using the method above the fat will run out of the bird and collect in the roasting tin. The skimmed fat can be used for making well-flavoured roast or sautéed potatoes and in many cooked dishes.

Roasts and Grills

Roast pheasant with mushroom cream

Serves 2

100 g/4 oz button mushrooms, wiped
or 20 g/¾ oz dried morels, soaked
in lukewarm water
1 oven-ready hen pheasant (about
675 g/1½ lb), thawed if frozen
salt and pepper
2 large slices streaky bacon
100 g/4 oz butter
2 shallots, peeled and finely chopped
1 tablespoon brandy
150 ml/¼ pint double cream
½ teaspoon lemon juice
1 tablespoon chopped parsley

Set the oven at hot (220 c, 425 f,
gas 7).
  If using fresh mushrooms, halve
or quarter them if large. If using
morels, drain and rinse well under a
running cold water to wash out any
grit trapped inside their crinkly caps;
halve, quarter or coarsely chop if
large.
  Rub inside the pheasant with salt
and pepper. Wrap the bacon around
the breast meat. Tie with fine string
and season all over the outside. Lay
the pheasant on its side on a rack in
a roasting tin and pour over 75 g/
3 oz of the butter, melted.
  Place the roasting tin with the bird
in the heated oven and roast for
35–50 minutes, according to size,
basting frequently with cooking
juices, and turning the bird halfway
through so it cooks evenly. About 5
minutes from the end of the cooking
time, remove the bacon so the
breast can brown lightly, and baste
again.
  Lift out the pheasant, wrap it in
foil and stand in the turned-off oven
or with the door ajar for 10 minutes
so the meat juices can settle.
  Put the roasting tin back on the
stove and reheat the cooking juices.
Add the shallots and cook till
softened, then add the mushrooms
or morels, cook briefly and add the
brandy. Skim off any fat, stir in the
cream and cook gently for 6–8
minutes. Add the lemon juice and
parsley to the sauce, remove the pan
from the heat and stir in the rest of
the butter in small pieces.
  Cut the legs off the pheasant, then
the wings, and lastly carve the
breast. Put all the pieces on a warm
serving dish and pour the mushroom
cream around them. Serve with
game chips or croquette potatoes.

Note Leeks, cut into 7.5-cm/3-in
pieces, then blanched, softened in
butter and seasoned with salt and
pepper, go extremely well with this
dish as do baby sprouts. White
cabbage cut into wide strips and
cooked in the same way as the
leeks, but seasoned with grated
nutmeg as well, is also very good
with the pheasant.

Tip A hen pheasant generally serves
2 people whereas a cock pheasant
which is much larger will serve 3 or
sometimes 4 people.

Fillet of beef in bacon

Serves 6

1-kg/2¼-lb fillet of beef
1 clove of garlic, peeled and crushed
1 teaspoon salt
1 teaspoon freshly ground black
  pepper or roughly crushed black
  peppercorns
1 teaspoon paprika
100 g/4 oz barding fat or streaky
  bacon, cut into paper-thin rashers

Carefully skin the fillet with a sharp, pointed knife and wipe it with absorbent kitchen paper. Mix the garlic to a thick paste with the salt, pepper and paprika. Rub this paste all over the beef, working it in well. Set the oven at hot (230 c, 450 f, gas 8)

Wrap the barding fat or bacon round the beef and tie with thin string. Put the beef on a rack in the roasting tin and roast in the heated oven for 30–35 minutes, depending on the thickness of the cut: the beef should still be pink inside. For well done meat, cook 5–10 minutes longer.

When cooked, let the meat stand for 5 minutes in a warm place before removing the string. Carve and arrange on a warm serving dish. Serve with croquette potatoes and gooseberry chutney.

Gooseberry chutney

450 g/1 lb green gooseberries, topped
  and tailed
450 g/1 lb ripe apples, peeled, cored
  and thinly sliced
3 onions, peeled and finely chopped
100 ml/4 fl oz white wine vinegar
225 g/8 oz sugar
½ teaspoon powdered cinnamon
½ teaspoon powdered ginger
pinch of ground coriander
grated rind of ½ lemon
3 tablespoons white rum

Thoroughly wash and drain the gooseberries. Mix with the apples, onions, wine vinegar, sugar and spices and put in a large saucepan. Cover and leave to stand for 2 hours. Slowly bring to the boil, stirring continuously, until the fruits are quite soft but the gooseberries are still whole.

Remove the pan of chutney from the heat and stir in the lemon rind and rum. Pour into hot, clean jars or bottles, seal, label and keep in a cool, dry place or the fridge for at least 14 days. Once opened, keep for about a week only and store in the refrigerator.

Serve with the fillet of beef, or with individual steaks or chops.

Variations
Apple chutney Replace the gooseberries and apples with 1 kg/ 2 lb apples and add 100 g/4 oz chopped raisins.

Peach chutney Use 1 kg/2 lb peaches, peeled and chopped, instead of the apples and gooseberries. Omit the cinnamon and replace the grated lemon rind with the grated rind of 1 orange.

Roasts and Grills

Roast leg of pork

Serves 6

1.5-kg/3-lb leg of pork, well scored
salt and freshly ground black pepper
25 g/1 oz lard
300 ml/½ pint boiling water
1 onion, peeled and quartered
1 bay leaf
2 cloves
4 juniper berries
6 tablespoons sweet brown ale
stock
1 tablespoon cornflour, blended with
a little cold water

Set the oven at hot (200 C, 400 F, gas 6).

Rub the pork very thoroughly with salt and pepper. Heat the lard in a roasting tin and fry the pork in it for 15 minutes or until browned all over. Pour on half of the boiling water. Add the onion, bay leaf and spices and roast in the heated oven for 2 hours, basting it at intervals with a little of the brown ale. Transfer to a warm serving dish and keep warm.

Dissolve the meat juices in the roasting tin with the rest of the water and beer, bring to the boil and then strain. Skim off any fat. Make the liquid up to 450 ml/¾ pint with stock, and stir in the cornflour mixture. Bring back to the boil, taste for seasoning and pour into a gravy boat.

Serve the roast pork with roast potatoes and braised cabbage with caraway seeds.

Variation
Roast pork with apple The sharp taste of apple complements the flavour of pork well. Add two cooking apples, peeled, cored and halved, to the onion when roasting the meat and use dry cider instead of brown ale.

Baked pork

Serves 4–6

1 large carrot, peeled and chopped
2 sticks celery, washed and chopped
1 onion, peeled and stuck with
4 cloves
1 bay leaf
5 juniper berries
10 peppercorns
2 tablespoons vinegar
1-kg/2-lb piece boneless roasting
pork
75 g/3 oz butter, melted
100 ml/4 fl oz dry white wine
1 teaspoon cornflour, blended with a
little cold water
1 tablespoon tomato purée
2 tablespoons single cream
salt and freshly ground white pepper
1 teaspoon sugar

Put the vegetables, bay leaf, spices and vinegar in a large pan with the meat. Cover with water and bring to the boil. Cook over moderate heat for 20 minutes. Then lift out the meat, drain it well and cool for a few minutes. Strain and reserve the stock. Meanwhile, set the oven at hot (200 C, 400 F, gas 6).

Heat half the butter in a roasting tin, put in the joint and brush with a little of the melted butter. Roast in the heated oven for 60–70 minutes, basting it frequently.

When done, remove from the oven, cover with foil and stand in a warm place for 10 minutes. Place on a warmed serving dish and pour the remaining butter over it.

Dissolve the juices in the roasting tin with 300 ml/½ pint of the reserved, stock then pour into a saucepan, add the wine and boil rapidly until reduced by about one-third. Stir in the cornflour mixture, bring back to the boil, stirring, then add the tomato purée and cream and season to taste with salt, pepper and sugar. Simmer for 5 minutes, then pour into a gravy boat.

Serve with green vegetables or salad if you prefer, together with mashed potatoes or ribbon noodles. Try also a light potato salad, with plenty of herbs, mixed with thinly sliced cucumber and chopped dill.

German style roast pork

Serves 4

1-kg/2¼-lb leg of pork, with the
rind scored in a diamond pattern
salt and freshly ground black pepper
6 cloves (optional)
2 onions, peeled and halved
1 clove of garlic, peeled
2 carrots, peeled and chopped
1 turnip, peeled and chopped
4 tablespoons beer or cider
2 teaspoons cornflour mixed with a
little cold water

Set the oven at hot (200 C, 400 F, gas 6).

Rub the meat with salt and pepper, push the cloves, if using, into the pork rind where the incisions cross.

Bring a little water to the boil in a roasting tin, put in the joint, rindside downwards and roast in the heated oven for 30 minutes. Remove from the oven. Place the joint on a rack with the rind uppermost, put back in the roasting tin and continue cooking for 30 minutes longer. Then add to the roasting tin the onions, garlic, carrot and turnip and cook 30 minutes more. If necessary add more water from time to time. Ten minutes before the end of the cooking time, brush the rind with the beer or cider to help it crisp. Remove the joint from the oven to a warmed serving dish, cover with foil and stand in a warm place for at least 10 minutes.

To make the gravy, dissolve the juices in the roasting tin with 450 ml/¾ pint boiling water or stock, then strain into a saucepan. Bring to the boil and stir in the cornflour mixture. Bring back to the boil, stirring, and pour into a gravy boat.

Serve the pork with croquette potatoes and braised red cabbage with apple.

Roasts and Grills

Veal Olives

Serves 4

*4 thin slices of veal escalope (each
  about 175 g/6 oz)*
1 teaspoon anchovy paste
*4 very thin rindless rashers of back
  bacon*
4 hard-boiled eggs, shelled
25 g/1 oz butter or dripping
1 onion, peeled and finely chopped
300 ml/½ pint stock
150 ml/¼ pint dry white wine
2 tablespoons tomato purée
4 tablespoons soured cream
salt and pepper
parsley sprigs to garnish

Beat out the escalopes as for Beef
olives. Spread each one thinly with
the anchovy paste, then cover with a
bacon rasher. Place a whole egg on
each one, then roll up the escalopes
to enclose the eggs completely and
fasten with wooden cocktail sticks or
fine string.

Heat the fat in a large heavy pan.
Put in the 'olives' and brown them
all over for 5 minutes, then add the
chopped onion and cook for a
further 5 minutes. Pour on the stock

and wine, cover and simmer for 20
minutes. Lift the 'olives' out of the
pan, remove the cocktail sticks or
string and place on a warmed
serving dish. Keep warm.

Reduce the sauce by about one-
third over high heat, stir in the
tomato purée and cream and season
to taste.

Halve the 'olives' widthways, pour
some of the sauce round them and
serve the rest separately. Garnish
with parsley.

Beef olives

Serves 4

*4 thin slices of topside or rump
  steak (each about 175 g/6 oz)*
1 teaspoon made English mustard
salt and freshly ground black pepper
*75 g/3 oz rindless streaky bacon, cut
  into thin strips*
2 gherkins, finely chopped
1 onion, peeled and finely chopped
25 g/1 oz lard or 2 tablespoons oil
450 ml/¾ pint stock
1 bay leaf
3 juniper berries
100 ml/4 fl oz soured cream

Lay the slices of meat between two
sheets of dampened greaseproof
paper and beat each one with a
meat mallet or rolling pin as thinly
as possible. Remove from the paper,
then spread each one thinly with
mustard and sprinkle with salt and
pepper.

Mix together the bacon, gherkins
and onion, then cover about two-
thirds of each slice of meat with the
mixture. Roll up the meat and
secure with wooden cocktail sticks
or tie with fine string.

Heat the fat in a large heavy pan.
Put in the 'olives' and brown them
well on all sides for 10 minutes.
Pour on the stock, add the bay leaf
and juniper berries, cover and
simmer gently for 1¼ hours. Take
out the meat, put on a heated
serving dish, remove the cocktail
sticks or string and keep the meat
warm. Reduce the liquid in the pan
over high heat by about half, strain,
then stir in the soured cream and
reheat slowly; do not let it boil.
Season to taste with salt and pepper
and pour into a sauce boat.

Serve the 'olives' with macaroni or
noodles and a green salad, or boiled
potatoes and a green vegetable.

Steak tartare

Serves 1

*100 g/4 oz fillet or rump steak, very
finely minced*
salt and freshly ground black pepper
1 tablespoon vodka
1 egg yolk
*6 anchovy fillets, soaked, drained
and finely chopped*
1 tablespoon chopped parsley
1 tablespoon chopped black olives
*1 tablespoon chopped pickled dill
cucumbers*
*1 tablespoon chopped cooked
beetroot*
1 tablespoon chopped onion
1 tablespoon chopped red pepper

Season the steak well and mix with
the vodka. Shape into a round in the
centre of a large serving plate and
place the egg yolk in the centre as
for Steak tartare with herbs (see
below). Arrange the chopped
ingredients in little mounds around
the meat. Serve with Granary bread
or pumpernickel and mix the meat
with any of the accompaniments to
taste.

Steak tartare with herbs

Serves 1

*100 g/4 oz fillet or rump steak, very
finely minced.*
salt and freshly ground black pepper
pinch of paprika pepper
1 tablespoon grated onion
1 teaspoon chopped capers
1 teaspoon chopped mixed herbs
1 teaspoon oil
dash of Worcestershire sauce
1 egg yolk

Season the steak well with salt,
pepper and paprika. Add the onion,
capers, herbs, oil and
Worcestershire sauce and mix well.
Shape into a round on a serving
plate. Make a shallow depression in
the centre of the round with a whole
egg or the back of a spoon and
carefully slip the egg yolk into this.
    Serve with thinly sliced, buttered
rye or wholemeal bread.

Chicken liver tartare

Serves 3–4

50 g/2 oz butter
*225 g/8 oz chicken livers, finely
minced or chopped*
2 teaspoons grated onion
*1 dessert apple, peeled, cored and
finely diced*
1 tablespoon Calvados or brandy
salt
pinch of dried thyme
pinch of dried marjoram

Melt the butter in a frying pan. Add
the chopped liver and the onion and
fry gently for about 2 minutes,
stirring constantly until just cooked.
Allow to cool.
    Blend the apple into the liver
mixture, together with the Calvados
or brandy. Season to taste with salt
and the herbs.
    Spoon into individual dishes and
chill; serve with hot toast.

Note For a milder onion flavour,
cook it in the butter by itself for a
while before adding the liver to the
pan.

Roasts and Grills

Chateaubriand steak

Serves 2

12 oz–1 lb /350 g–450 g piece middle
*   cut fillet of beef*
2 tablespoons oil
freshly ground black pepper
25 g/1 oz butter or butter and
*   dripping mixed*

Rub the beef well with the oil.
Cover and let it stand for 1 hour at
room temperature. Then rub over it
with pepper. Brown it quickly to
seal the meat in a pan for 5 seconds,
without adding any fat. Remove and
set the meat aside.

Heat the butter or butter and
dripping in the pan, and put back
the meat and fry for 4–5 minutes on
each side. The outside should be
brown and crisp, the inside
remaining bright pink and tender.
Do not season the meat after frying
it but let it stand in a warm place for
5 minutes before serving. Slice
diagonally and arrange on a warmed
serving dish.

The classic accompaniment is
Béarnaise sauce (page 122).

Steak bordelaise

Serves 2

25 g/1 oz butter
2 shallots, peeled and chopped
½ clove of garlic, peeled and crushed
5 peppercorns, crushed
½ bay leaf, crumbled
½ teaspoon dried thyme
300 ml/½ pint red wine
salt
50 g/2 oz fresh beef marrow, wiped
*   (optional)*
12 oz–1 lb/350 g–450 g middle cut
*   fillet of beef*
freshly ground black pepper
4 tablespoons oil

Heat the butter in a frying pan, add
the shallots and garlic and fry till
golden brown. Add the peppercorns,
bay leaf, thyme and wine, and bring
to the boil. Cook rapidly until
reduced by a good two-thirds.
Season to taste with salt.

Meanwhile cut the beef marrow, if
using, into six slices and blanch
them in boiling water. Drain well,
then finely chop two of the slices.

Strain the sauce from the pan and
mix in the sliced marrow. Set aside

in a warm place.

Gently press out the steak with
the ball of your hand; score the fat
with a knife and rub well with
pepper. Sear it in a hot heavy pan,
without adding any fat, for 3
seconds on each side, then remove
from the pan.

Heat the oil in the same pan and
use to fry the meat quickly for 2
minutes on each side to brown and
crisp the outside but still leaving the
inside a rosy pink. Season with salt,
leave for 3 minutes, then slice
diagonally and arrange on a warmed
serving dish. Heat the marrow slices
in the sauce and arrange them on
top of the meat; serve the rest of the
sauce separately.

Stuffed tournedos

Serves 4

8 (75-g/3-oz) tournedos of beef
50 g/2 oz smooth liver sausage
1 tablespoon brandy
1 tablespoon green peppercorns,
    drained and chopped
2 fresh sage leaves, finely chopped or
    pinch of dried sage
4 thin rashers of streaky bacon
3 tablespoons oil
25 g/1 oz butter
salt and freshly ground black pepper

Press out the tournedos with the ball
of your hand. Cream the liver
sausage with the brandy and stir in
the peppercorns and sage. Spread
this mixture over four of the
tournedos, lay each of the remaining
four on top and press gently
together. Wrap a bacon rasher
around each tournedos "sandwich"
then tie with fine string.

Heat the oil and butter in a pan,
put in the tournedos and brown for
1 minute on each side over high
heat. Lower the heat and cook them
for 2–3 minutes on each side,
according to how well done you like
your meat. Season with salt and
pepper and serve at once.

Suitable accompaniments are corn
salad (lamb's lettuce) tossed in
vinaigrette, or green beans or
broccoli plus little potato pancakes
or croquette potatoes.

Tournedos with tomatoes and shallot sauce

Serves 4

4 (100- to 165-g/4- to 6-oz)
    tournedos of beef
3 shallots, peeled and finely chopped
50 g/2 oz butter
1 tablespoon red wine vinegar
100 ml/4 fl oz dry white wine
4 tablespoons soured cream
salt and pepper
2 cloves of garlic, peeled and finely
    chopped or crushed
8 ripe tomatoes, peeled, deseeded
    and finely chopped
1 tablespoon chopped fresh or
    1 teaspoon dried basil
3 tablespoons oil
freshly ground black pepper
sprigs of fresh basil to garnish
    (optional)

Wipe the tournedos and press into
shape with the ball of the hand.
Cook the shallots till transparent but
not browned in half the butter. Add
the vinegar and wine, stir in the
cream and reduce the sauce over
high heat to a creamy consistency.
Season to taste with salt and pepper.

Cook the garlic and tomatoes in
15 g/½ oz of the remaining butter for
2–3 minutes, then add the basil and
salt and pepper to taste and keep
warm.

In another pan heat the oil with
the rest of the butter. Put in the
tournedos and brown them 2–3
minutes on either side. Season them
with salt and black pepper and serve
with the tomatoes and the shallot
sauce. Garnish with sprigs of fresh
basil, if available.

Variation
Instead of the tomatoes and shallot
sauce serve the tournedos with a
white wine sauce and garnish with a
slice of truffle.

Roasts and Grills

Grilled steaks

Grilled steaks should be served as soon as they are cooked so prepare any sauces or accompaniments ahead so that they are ready at the same time as the meat. Season the meat with a little salt just before serving.

Marinating steaks before they are cooked helps to tenderise them and give them a special flavour. The marinade liquid can then be turned into a sauce to serve with the steak, or reserved for adding to gravy, soups or stews. As long as the basis of a marinade comprises oil with vinegar, lemon juice or wine you can experiment to produce endless combinations of delicious flavours.

Types of steak

Rump steak This is boneless and cut from the top of the rump. It should have a good 5 mm/¼ inch of fat on the outside edge.

Entrecôte steak Cut from the tender centre of a boned sirloin, it is usually about 2.5–3.5 cm/1–1½ in thick.

Sirloin steak This is cut from the large joint of the same name, including the fillet, and is boneless.

T-bone steak Taken from between the chump end and wing rib, it comes with a bone, shaped like a 'T', hence its name, and includes a piece of fillet. It may be cut to serve 2 or as a large individual steak.

Porterhouse steak This steak is cut from the thick end of the sirloin, giving a large succulent piece that can weigh about 900 g/1¾ lb. When cooked on the bone it is called a T-bone steak.

Tournedos steaks A small steak cut from the centre of the fillet. Also known as filet or steak mignon.

Fillet steak This prime cut is taken from the sirloin joint and usually weighs about 1 kg/2 lb. It is boneless and can be cooked whole, or cut into individual steaks.

Chateaubriand steak This is cut from the centre of the fillet, and is usually about 2.5–3.5 cm/1–1½ inches thick. It is usually large enough to serve 2.

Tips for cooking steaks

Steaks taste better if left to stand for a few minutes in a warm place before serving as this allows the juices to permeate the meat. Grilling times are always calculated in minutes. The grill must be heated long enough to have reached its maximum heat when the meat is put on. The thinner the steak, the nearer it should be to the heat source. Meat grilled on a charcoal fire tastes the best, and the wood from fruit trees or vines gives the best aroma. But this type of grilling is not available for most of us, so ordinary charcoal or briquettes have to suffice. An equally irresistible aroma can be achieved by sprinkling sprigs of herbs like rosemary, bay or juniper over the fire, or even spoonfuls of mixed dried herbs.

Grilling times for steaks

The length of cooking time is dependent on the thickness of the steak, rather than the type, and the degree to which you like your meat cooked: rare, medium rare or well done, are the usual terms, although even these are somewhat arbitrary. The table below will give a rough guide. All the times are given in minutes.

Thickness	Rare	Medium Rare	Well Done
2 cm/¾ in	5	9–10	12–15
2.5 cm/1 in	7	12	15–18
3.5 cm/1½ in	10	15	18–20

The times given are total cooking times. It is best to grill the meat at high on either side for 1–2 minutes according to thickness and to finish at a lower temperature. It must be stressed that the times can only be approximate because the quality and thickness of the meat, personal taste and the strength of the grill all play a part. It is best therefore to begin testing the meat a couple of minutes before the end of the estimated cooking time.

Accompaniments for grilled steaks

Béarnaise sauce (page 122) or a pat of Maître d'hôtel (parsley) butter put on top are traditional accompaniments. Other delicious accompaniments are matchstick or chipped potatoes, grilled tomatoes and mushrooms, or green or mixed salad.

Marinades for steaks

Basic marinade Mix equal parts of wine or vermouth and olive oil and flavour as required with lemon juice and crushed garlic. Put the meat in the marinade, cover and place in the refrigerator for 6–24 hours, turning the meat from time to time. Drain the meat well, and dry with absorbent kitchen paper before grilling. Use for all small steaks.

Wine marinade Mix 600 ml/1 pint red wine with 6 tablespoons lemon juice or vinegar, 6 tablespoons olive oil, 2 peeled, chopped onions, 2 peeled, diced carrots, a few peppercorns, 1 crumbled bay leaf, 2 tablespoons chopped parsley and a sprig of thyme. Particularly good for large steaks. Marinate and drain as above.

Spicy marinade Mix together 6 tablespoons tomato juice, 6 tablespoons red wine and 6 tablespoons olive oil. Add 3 peeled, chopped cloves of garlic, 2 deseeded, chopped fresh chillies, 1 teaspoon sugar and 2 tablespoons soy sauce. Thin steaks need 30–60 minutes only in this marinade; large ones should be left for up to 6 hours in the refrigerator. Drain as above.

Roasts and Grills

Austrian boiled beef

Serves 4

1.5 litres/2¾ pints salted water
800-g/1¾-lb piece salt beef (brisket
* or silverside)*
1 onion, peeled and halved
1 bay leaf
1 teaspoon white peppercorns
1 large carrot, peeled and chopped
2 sticks celery, washed and chopped

Bring the water to the boil in a deep
pan. Put in the beef and let it come
back to the boil before putting in
the onion, bay leaf and peppercorns.
Cover and simmer for 30 minutes;
add the carrots and celery and cook
1½ hours or until the meat is tender.
    Remove the meat and let it stand
for a few minutes in a warm place
before carving and arranging on a
hot serving dish. Serve with boiled
potatoes, tossed in parsley, as well
as Apple and horseradish sauce and
Chive sauce (recipes below).

Note Extra vegetables can be added
to the pan towards the end of
cooking and served with the meat.
Diced potatoes may also be cooked
in the meat broth.

Chive sauce

Serves 4

3 slices of bread, crusts removed
100 ml/4 fl oz hot milk
2 hard-boiled eggs, shelled
2 teaspoons made English mustard
6 tablespoons oil
salt
sugar
about 2 tablespoons lemon juice or
* vinegar*
3 tablespoons finely chopped chives

Soak the bread in the hot milk for
10 minutes. Squeeze it dry then
sieve, blend or process with the
hard-boiled eggs. Stir in the
mustard, then beat in the oil, drop
by drop, to make a thick
mayonnaise-like sauce. Season with
salt, sugar and lemon juice or
vinegar to taste, then stir in the
chives.

Apple and horseradish sauce

Serves 4

3 tablespoons horseradish sauce
2 tablespoons beef stock, reserved
* from cooking liquid*
3 tablespoons corn oil
1 teaspoon sugar
salt
1 small cooking apple, cored and
* grated*

Add the horseradish to the hot stock
and reheat but do not let it boil.
Remove from the heat and cool,
then whisk in the oil, drop by drop,
to make a thick sauce. Season to
taste with the sugar and salt. Add
the freshly grated apple just before
serving. Hand separately with the
boiled beef. If a smooth sauce is
preferred, purée in a liquidiser or
food processor before serving.

Vitello tonnato

Serves 4

1-kg/2-lb leg or loin of veal, boned
* and rolled*
450 ml/¾ pint dry white wine
450 ml/¾ pint water
1 onion, peeled and chopped
1 carrot, peeled and chopped
1 stalk celery, with leaves, chopped
1 bay leaf
sprig of tarragon (optional)
5 peppercorns
2 cloves
salt

Sauce
1 (198-g/7-oz) can tuna in oil,
* drained*
4 anchovies, drained
4 tablespoons olive oil
1 egg yolk
1 tablespoon lemon juice
1 tablespoon capers, drained
salt and pepper

Put the veal into a deep pan with
the wine and water. The meat must
be completely covered by the liquid,
so add more wine and water in
equal quantities if necessary. Bring
slowly to the boil, skim and then
add the vegetables, herbs and spices.
Season with salt, cover, reduce the
heat and simmer for about 1½ hours
or until the meat is tender.
    Make the tuna sauce. Mash the
tuna and anchovies together with 1
tablespoon oil. Beat in the egg yolk,
then rub through a sieve. Stir in 1
teaspoon of the lemon juice, then
add the rest of the oil, drop by
drop, beating well after each
addition. Alternatively put the fish,
egg yolk, and 1 tablespoon of oil in
a blender or food processor and
work until smooth, then add the
lemon juice and oil as above. When
thick, like mayonnaise, stir in about
2 tablespoons of the cooled veal
broth to give a pouring consistency.
Add the capers, seasoning and
lemon juice to taste.
    Drain the meat, allow to cool and
carve into slices. Arrange on a
serving dish. Pour over the sauce,
cover with foil and chill at least 30
minutes before serving with a green
salad.

Roasts and Grills

Chicken liver kebabs

Serves 4–6

450 g/1 lb chicken livers
100 g/4 oz thin rindless rashers
*   streaky bacon*
16 button mushrooms, wiped
8 shallots, peeled and halved
freshly ground black pepper
50 g/2 oz butter
3 teaspoons flour
150 ml/¼ pint hot water or stock
3 tablespoons sherry
100 ml/4 fl oz double cream
2 tablespoons tomato purée
dash of Worcestershire sauce
salt

Rinse the livers under cold running water, then dry them with absorbent kitchen paper. Cut them into bite-sized pieces, if necessary, and wrap them in the bacon. Thread these parcels and the mushrooms and shallots alternately on to small skewers or kebab sticks and season well with pepper. Melt the butter in a large frying pan and fry the kebabs all over for 8 minutes, then take them out of the pan and keep warm.

Add the flour to the juices in the pan and stir well. Add the hot water or stock, sherry and cream and bring to the boil, stirring constantly. Add the tomato purée and Worcestershire sauce and season to taste. Pour into a sauceboat and serve immediately.

Plain boiled rice or ribbon noodles and a green salad go well with these kebabs.

Beef olive kebabs

Serves 4

4 thin slices of rump or fillet steak
2 teaspoons strong made mustard
8 rindless thin rashers of bacon
12 small onions, peeled and halved
3 green or red peppers, deseeded and
*   cut in large chunks*
2 tablespoons oil
1 teaspoon celery salt
1 teaspoon paprika
pinch cayenne

Lay the slices of beef on your work surface. Spread them with mustard and then cover each one with two rashers of bacon. Roll up the slices, then cut each one into six equal pieces. Heat the grill

Thread 8 small skewers or kebab sticks with three pieces of beef roll each, alternating the meat with the onions and peppers. Mix the oil, celery salt, paprika and cayenne together, lay the skewers across the grill rack and brush them all over with the oil mixture. Place the rack with the kebabs in the grill pan and cook for about 15 minutes or until browned all over.

As soon as they are cooked, serve with noodles in tomato sauce and a mixed salad, or a sauce made by dissolving the meat juices in the pan over the heat in equal quantities of stock and wine, then thickening it with a little cream.

Tip Soak wooden kebab sticks for at least 45 minutes in cold water before use to stop charring.

Liver Berlin-style

Serves 4

100 g/4 oz butter
2 sharp apples, peeled, cored and cut
*   into 5-mm/¼-in thick rounds*
4 medium-sized onions, peeled and
*   cut into rings*
450 g/1 lb lamb's liver, thinly sliced
2 tablespoons flour
salt and freshly ground black pepper

Heat 25 g/1 oz of the butter in a
frying pan, put in the sliced apples
and cook until golden brown on
both sides — about 2–3 minutes.
Remove them from the pan and
keep warm.

Add another 25 g/1 oz butter to
the pan, put in the onions and cook
till a crisp brown, turning them
frequently, then take out and keep
warm.

Meanwhile lightly dust the liver
with the flour. Heat the rest of the
butter in another pan. Quickly fry
the liver on both sides (about 2–4
minutes each side). It should still be
light pink inside. Season with salt
and pepper to taste and serve at
once, topped with the hot apple and
onion rings. Pour over any pan
juices and serve with mashed
potatoes and a green salad with a
herby dressing.

Turkey breast with fruity curry sauce

Serves 4

4 (175-g/6-oz) slices of turkey
*   breast, thawed if frozen*
75 g/3 oz butter
salt and white pepper
1 (396-g/14-oz) can fruit cocktail,
*   drained and syrup reserved*
juice of ½ lemon
1 teaspoon honey
1–2 tablespoons curry powder
sprigs of parsley to garnish

Dry the turkey slices thoroughly
with absorbent kitchen paper. Heat
the fat in a frying pan, put in the
turkey slices and cook for about
2 minutes on each side until just
cooked through. Remove them from
the pan, season with salt and pepper
to taste and keep warm.

Add the fruit cocktail to the juices
in the frying pan and cook them
quickly over high heat for about a
minute to warm through. Stir in the
lemon juice, honey and curry
powder, moisten with some of the
reserved syrup, then simmer for
2 minutes.

Check the seasoning, then pour
over the turkey slices and garnish
with parsley. Serve with boiled rice
and a salad.

Tip A few drops of wine vinegar and
a liberal amount of finely chopped
dill added at the end impart a
subtle, sweet-sour flavour to the
sauce.

Roasts and Grills

Chops with cheese sauce

Serves 4

4 pork or veal chops
salt and pepper
1 tablespoon paprika
2 tablespoons olive oil
25 g/1 oz butter
100 ml/4 fl oz dry white wine
1 tablespoon brandy
100 g/4 oz cream cheese with herbs,
  cut into pieces
150 ml/¼ pint soured cream
2 tablespoons chopped fresh mixed
  herbs

Season the chops with salt and
pepper then dust lightly with
paprika; rub this in well.

Heat the oil and butter together in
a pan till hot, put in the chops, two
at a time if necessary, and cook
gently for about 8 minutes on each
side until cooked through. Remove
from the pan to a hot plate and
keep warm.

Dissolve the juices in the pan over
a moderate heat in the wine and boil
rapidly until reduced by half. Add
the brandy, cheese and cream and
stir until the cheese has melted; do

not let it boil. Pour over the chops,
then sprinkle with the herbs.

Serve with tender young
vegetables or with a vegetable purée
for a change.

Cheesy stuffed meatballs

Serves 4

450 g/1 lb minced beef
1 onion, peeled and finely chopped
1 clove of garlic, peeled and finely
  chopped
1 teaspoon chopped dill
2 tablespoons chopped parsley
2 tablespoons chopped mint
200 g/7 oz fresh breadcrumbs
1 egg plus 1 egg yolk
salt and freshly ground black pepper
pinch of cayenne
150 g/5 oz cream cheese, cut into
  2-cm/¾-in cubes
oil for deep frying

In a large bowl or a food processor,
combine the beef, onion, garlic,
herbs, half the breadcrumbs, the egg
and yolk till smooth. Season to taste
with salt, pepper and cayenne.

Shape the meat mixture into
5-cm/2-in balls. Press into the

centre of each one a cube of cheese,
making sure it is completely
enclosed. Roll the balls in the
remaining breadcrumbs, pressing
them on lightly with a palette knife.

Heat the oil till hot (190c/375 f)
and fry the meatballs, a few at a
time, for 5 minutes till crisp and
brown. Lift out and drain on
absorbent kitchen paper. Serve them
hot or cold, with a mixed or potato
salad.

Cook's Tip

When making meatballs or burgers
wet your hands under the tap before
handling the meat. This will prevent
the meat sticking to your hands and
make it easier to shape.

Crispy stuffed pork

Serves 6

1.25-kg/2½-lb belly of pork, boned
salt and freshly ground black pepper
2 tablespoons oil
1 tablespoon paprika
1 teaspoon dried rosemary
pinch of garlic salt

Stuffing
2 onions, peeled and finely chopped
1 clove of garlic, peeled and finely
  chopped
1 green pepper, deseeded and finely
  chopped
150 g/5 oz ham, fat removed and
  finely diced
2 tablespoons chopped parsley
1 bay leaf, crushed

Trim any surplus fat from the meat.
Flatten it out a little with a rolling
pin or meat mallet. Rub over with
salt and pepper. Heat the grill.
  Mix all the stuffing ingredients
together. Spread this evenly over the
meat, leaving a 5-cm/2-inch border
at the end nearest you. Roll up the
roast starting at the far end and
secure with wooden cocktail sticks

or skewers, then tie with fine string.
  Mix together the oil, remaining
flavourings and a little salt to a thick
paste and rub this into the outside of
the meat roll. Thread it on to a
rotary spit and place under the
heated grill. Cook for 1 hour 20
minutes till a crisp brown all over
and cooked through, brushing it
from time to time with the juices in
the pan underneath. Alternatively
cook in a moderately hot oven
(220 C, 400 F, gas 6) for 1 hour then
reduce the temperature to moderate
(180 C, 350 F, gas 4) and cook for a
further hour. Baste as above.
Remove the meat from the spit or
the oven, let it stand in a warm
place for a few minutes, then slice it
thickly. Serve with potato salad
made with plenty of fresh herbs, and
radishes.

Variations
Use any of the following to replace
the ham and pepper stuffing:

Plenty of freshly chopped herbs
mixed with crushed green
peppercorns, grated apple and
sieved or finely chopped hard-boiled
egg yolk.

Small cubes of white bread, soaked
in seasoned beaten egg, with
chopped cooked ham and plenty of
chopped parsley.

Blue cheese creamed with freshly
chopped herbs.

Finely chopped garlic mixed with
chopped sage and finely chopped
spring onions.

Tip Other suitable prime cuts for
cooking by the rotisserie method are
pork fillet, veal escalopes (cooking
time about 35 minutes), rack of
lamb (30 minutes), or sirloin of beef
(this is best when rubbed with oil
and left to marinate for about 5
hours before cooking with a very
moist stuffing). Any of the above
stuffings may be used with the meat
of your choice.

Roasts and Grills

Grilled veal or pork chops

Serves 4

4 veal or pork chops
40 g/1½ oz butter, melted
paprika
salt and freshly ground black pepper
extra butter or oil for greasing
4 sprigs of rosemary
4 sprigs of thyme

Heat the grill. Flatten the chops a little with a rolling pin or meat mallet. Brush the melted butter thinly over the chops, then sprinkle them with the seasonings.

Grease the grill rack with a little butter or oil and arrange the herbs on it. Lay the chops on top and cook under a moderate grill, brushing frequently with melted butter. After about 6 minutes, turn the chops over and brush again with more melted butter. Cook for a further 5 minutes or until cooked through.

Tip If you want to barbecue the chops, remember that the barbecue grill temperature cannot be controlled as precisely as a conventional grill. Brush over the bars of the grill as well as the meat with oil as this doesn't burn as readily as butter. The chops can also be basted with butter during the last few minutes cooking to give them a special buttery flavour. Before you start cooking on the barbecue, make sure it has reached the right heat: there should be no red flames and the coals should be covered with a layer of white ash.

Spicy lamb cutlets

Serves 4

12 small lamb cutlets, trimmed
2 tablespoons olive oil
3 tablespoons tomato purée
1 teaspoon dried marjoram
pinch of powdered cinnamon
pinch of ground cloves
salt

Marinade
250 ml/8 fl oz red wine
4 tablespoons olive oil
4 cloves of garlic, peeled and finely crushed
8 peppercorns, crushed
1 bay leaf, crumbled
1 teaspoon dried rosemary

Put all the marinade ingredients in a large non-metallic bowl and mix together. Put in the cutlets, cover and marinate in the refrigerator overnight. If the cutlets are not covered completely by the liquid, turn them occasionally.

Heat the grill. Drain the cutlets and dry them carefully on absorbent kitchen paper. Mix the remaining oil with the tomato purée, marjoram, spices and salt and brush over the cutlets on both sides. Lay them on an oiled grill rack and cook under the heated grill for 4–5 minutes on each side. Season with salt just before serving with hot garlic bread, and a tomato, cucumber and pepper salad in a yogurt or lemon dressing.

Note These cutlets can also be barbecued. If you like the flavour and smell of rosemary, marjoram or sage, then sprinkle more of these herbs into the barbecue fire: the rising smoke gives off a wonderful aroma that pervades the cutlets.

Spit-roast garlic chicken

Serves 4

150 ml/¼ pint olive oil
4 tablespoons lemon juice
1 teaspoon salt
10 cloves of garlic, peeled and crushed
50 g/2 oz parsley
2 oven-ready poussins, thawed if frozen
75 g/3 oz butter, well chilled

Mix together the oil, lemon juice, salt and garlic; finely chop 25 g/1 oz of the parsley and add to the garlic mixture.

Put each poussin on a piece of foil large enough to enclose it, then rub with the garlic oil. Wrap them up in the foil and leave to marinate for 10 minutes.

Heat the grill. Open up the parcels, and carefully wipe off the oil with absorbent kitchen paper. Push half of the butter, cut up in little pieces, under the skin of each chicken breast without breaking the skin; divide up the rest of the parsley and put a little inside each chicken.

Thread the birds on to a spit, fastening the wings and legs with wooden cocktail sticks or skewers and the fold of the skin at the neck. Cook for 40–45 minutes under the heated grill, turning and basting them from time to time with the juices in the pan underneath.

When cooked, remove the birds from the spit, cut in half and remove the parsley. Serve with boiled rice, mixed with chopped dill or parsley, plus sautéed onions and a salad.

Tip Blisters sometimes form on the poultry skin during grilling, especially if the grill is too hot. Don't make the mistake of pricking these blisters as this will cause the juices to run out; instead brush them with a little melted fat.

Heartwarming Casseroles

Casseroles

Pork and orange stew

Serves 6

25 g/1 oz butter
1 kg/2 lb loin of pork, boned,
*   trimmed and cut into bite-sized*
*   pieces*
150 g/5 oz shallots or pickling
*   onions, peeled and finely chopped*
grated rind of 1 orange
150 ml/¼ pint fresh orange juice
4 tablespoons dry sherry
salt and pepper
small pinch of sugar
1 bay leaf
1 teaspoon cornflour, blended with a
*   little cold water (optional)*
150 ml/¼ pint single cream
1 orange, peeled, white pith removed
*   and cut into segments*

Set the oven at moderate (180c, 350f, gas 4).

Heat the butter in a flameproof casserole, put in the meat, a third at a time, brown quickly and remove. Add the shallots or onions to the casserole and brown them all over, then put back the meat and stir in the orange rind and juice and sherry. Season with plenty of salt, pepper and the sugar. Add the bay leaf, cover and cook in the heated oven for 1½ hours or till tender. Remove the bay leaf. If necessary, thicken the liquid with the cornflour and adjust the seasoning. Stir in the cream.

Put the orange segments into the stew and heat through. Serve immediately, with noodles lightly fried in butter, or boiled rice mixed with cooked peas.

Tip Blood oranges, although not available all year round, do give a very special flavour and appearance to the sauce. If you like a strongly flavoured stew, add some green peppercorns.

Yugoslavian meat medley

Serves 4

225 g/8 oz lean beef
225 g/8 oz lean pork
225 g/8 oz lean lamb
6 tablespoons olive oil
350 g/12 oz onions, peeled and
*   chopped*
2 cloves of garlic, peeled and crushed
1 small red pepper, deseeded and
*   diced*
1 small green pepper, deseeded and
*   diced*
1 small aubergine, diced
575 g/1¼ lb ripe tomatoes, peeled and
*   chopped*
salt and pepper
paprika
100 g/4 oz green beans, trimmed and
*   cut into 5-cm/2-inch pieces*
100 g/4 oz shelled peas, fresh or
*   frozen*
175 g/6 oz courgettes, trimmed and
*   diced*

Set the oven at moderately hot (180c, 350f, gas 4)

Cut the meats into bite-sized pieces. Grease inside a large casserole with half the oil and put in the meats, onions, garlic, peppers, aubergine and tomatoes. Season with plenty of salt, pepper and paprika and pour over the rest of the oil. Cover, place in the heated oven and cook for 1½ hours or till the meat is tender, if necessary adding a little water to prevent the meat sticking. Add the green beans, peas and courgettes for the last 20 minutes of the cooking time. Serve immediately with crusty bread.

Variations
To the above ingredients, add 100 g/ 4 oz long-grain rice together with 6 tablespoons each stock and wine or equal quantities of wine and tomato juice. Or make with lamb or mutton only and include 225 g/8 oz okra.

Try making it with veal only, with tomatoes and peas but omitting the aubergine and courgette, and adding instead 225 g/8 oz white seedless grapes.

Cook's Tip

Casseroles and stews may be cooked on top of the stove as well as in the oven. It is important to use a thick-based flameproof casserole or saucepan with a heavy close-fitting lid. Enamelled cast iron is ideal as it ensures even distribution of the heat and can be used to seal the meat before the liquid is added. When casseroling on top of the stove make sure that the heat is turned to the lowest setting so that the liquid is only just bubbling, otherwise the meat may become toughened by too rapid cooking.

Casseroles

Ratatouille

Serves 4

225 g/8 oz aubergines, trimmed and
sliced into thin rounds
salt
150 ml/¼ pint olive oil
225 g/8 oz onions, peeled and sliced
into rings
225 g/8 oz green peppers, deseeded
and cut into strips
225 g/8 oz courgettes, cut in rounds
1 (227-g/8-oz) can tomatoes, or
225 g/8 oz fresh tomatoes, coarsely
chopped
3 large cloves of garlic, peeled and
crushed
2 tablespoons mixed dried herbs

Place the aubergine slices in a
colander, sprinkle with salt, place a
plate on top and leave for 10
minutes. Rinse and pat dry with
absorbent kitchen paper.

Heat 2 tablespoons of the oil in a
large saucepan and add the
vegetables in layers so there are two
layers of each type. Season as you
go with salt, garlic and herbs,
sprinkling a little oil over each layer.
Finish with a layer of aubergines and

season only with salt; spoon over the
rest of the oil. Bring to the boil,
cover, reduce the heat and simmer
for 45–60 minutes.

Ratatouille can be eaten by itself
with crusty bread or served as an
accompaniment to roast or grilled
meats, fish or sausages.

Sausage goulash

Serves 4–6

225 g/8 oz beef or smoked pork
sausages
225 g/8 oz pork and herb sausages
4 tablespoons dry sherry
1 tablespoon Worcestershire sauce
1 tablespoon pickled green
peppercorns, drained (optional)
100 g/4 oz rindless rashers streaky
bacon, diced
225 g/8 oz onions, peeled and
chopped
1 clove of garlic, peeled and crushed
2 tablespoons paprika
1 (425-g/15-oz) can tomatoes
1 tablespoon tomato purée
salt
freshly ground black pepper
2 tablespoons chopped parsley
150 ml/¼ pint soured cream (optional)

Cut each sausage in half. Put them
in a bowl with the sherry,
Worcestershire sauce and
peppercorns, cover and marinate for
1 hour in the refrigerator.

Dry-fry the bacon in a pan till the
fat runs. Add the onion and garlic
and fry rapidly till golden brown.

Drain the sausages and dry on
absorbent kitchen paper. Add them
to the onion in the pan with the
paprika and cook for 1 minute. Stir
in the tomatoes with their juice,
tomato purée and seasoning to taste,
cover and simmer for 15 minutes.
Taste for seasoning, sprinkle with
the parsley and serve with the cream
spooned into the middle, if you like.
Serve at once.

Variation
Curried sausages A few apple pieces
can be added to the onion, and the
goulash then flavoured to taste with
curry powder instead of the paprika,
lemon juice, mango chutney and
honey. For this version, substitute
single cream for the soured cream.

Oxtail ragoût

Serves 4

100 g/4 oz rindless rashers streaky
    bacon, diced
25 g/1 oz butter
1.25 kg/2½ lb oxtail, jointed
2 large onions, peeled and chopped
2–3 cloves of garlic, peeled and
    crushed
100 g/4 oz mushrooms, wiped and
    thinly sliced
4 stalks of celery, trimmed and
    chopped
2 carrots, peeled and chopped
4 large tomatoes, peeled, deseeded
    and chopped
few sprigs of parsley, thyme or
    marjoram
salt and black pepper
1 teaspoon paprika
pinch of sugar
1 tablespoon brandy
150 ml/¼ pint dry white wine
450 ml/¾ pint hot stock
150 ml/¼ pint single cream

Dry fry the bacon in a large flameproof casserole. Add the butter to
the casserole, put in the oxtail pieces
and the onion and brown. Then add
the garlic, mushrooms, celery and
carrots and let them brown. Add the
tomatoes and the parsley, thyme and
marjoram, tied together. Season to
taste, add the paprika, sugar,
brandy, wine and stock. Cover and
simmer for about 2 hours till the
meat is just falling off the bones.

    Remove the herbs. Reduce the
liquid by boiling over high heat till
thick and syrupy, stir in the cream
and serve immediately.

Heart ragoût

Serves 6

50 g/2 oz butter
800 g/1¾ lb lamb's hearts, ducts and
    fat removed, and cut into bite-
    sized pieces
3 large onions, peeled and sliced into
    rings
1–2 cloves of garlic, peeled and
    crushed
1 small leek, trimmed, washed and
    cut into rings
2 carrots, peeled and cut into julienne
    strips
1–2 tablespoons flour
450 ml/¾ pint hot stock
100 ml/4 fl oz red wine
1 tablespoon tomato purée
225 g/8 oz ripe tomatoes, skinned
    and chopped
salt and freshly ground black pepper
pinch of sugar
½ teaspoon dried thyme
½ teaspoon dried rosemary
2 gherkins, finely chopped
2 teaspoons capers, drained
150 ml/¼ pint single cream
1 tablespoon chopped chives to
    garnish

Heat the butter in a flameproof
casserole. Put in the pieces of heart
and sauté them quickly, then
remove and keep warm.

    Add all the vegetables, except the
tomatoes, and let them brown.
Return the meat to the pan, stir in
the flour and cook for about 1
minute till brown. Pour in the stock
and wine, stir in the tomato purée
and tomatoes, season to taste and
add the sugar and the herbs.

    Cover and simmer for about 50
minutes or until the heart is tender.
Stir in the gherkins, capers and
cream. Sprinkle with chives just
before serving accompanied by plain
boiled rice.

Casseroles

Cassoulet

Serves 6

350 g/12 oz dried haricot beans,
* soaked overnight in cold water to*
* cover*
1 tablespoon dried mixed herbs
4 cloves of garlic, peeled and
* chopped*
2 smoked bacon rinds
50 g/2 oz dripping or lard
225 g/8 oz smoked streaky bacon, cut
* into bite-sized pieces*
450 g/1 lb shoulder of pork, boned,
* or pork spare rib, cut into bite-*
* sized pieces*
2 onions, peeled and chopped
4 carrots, peeled and sliced
450 g/1 lb tomatoes, peeled and
* chopped*
4 tablespoons chopped parsley
225 g/8 oz pork boiling sausage with
* garlic, sliced*
150 ml/¼ pint red wine
salt and pepper

Drain the beans, then put in a pan
with fresh water to cover, add the
herbs, 2 chopped cloves of garlic
and the bacon rinds. Cover and

simmer for 1 hour. Discard the
bacon rinds.

Heat the dripping or lard in a
large flameproof pan. Put in the
meats and brown them all over, then
add the onion and carrots with the
remaining garlic and fry for 5
minutes till browned. Stir in the
tomatoes and half the parsley and
cook gently for 30 minutes. Add the
sausage to the pan, together with
the wine and the bean mixture,
cover and simmer for 30 minutes.
Taste for seasoning.

Chop the rest of the parsley and
sprinkle it over just before serving.

Chilli con carne

Serves 4

350 g/12 oz dried red kidney or black
* beans, soaked overnight in cold*
* water to cover*
4 tablespoons olive oil
450 g/1 lb minced beef
1 tablespoon paprika
½–1 teaspoon chilli powder
4 onions, peeled and finely chopped
2 cloves garlic, peeled and chopped

2 red or green chillies, deseeded and
* finely chopped, optional*
2 carrots, peeled and diced
2 leeks, washed, trimmed and sliced
675 g/1½ lb tomatoes, peeled and
* chopped or 1 (396-g/14-oz) can*
* tomatoes*
1 beef stock cube
1 teaspoon dried thyme
3 bay leaves
salt

Drain the beans, cover with fresh
cold water, bring to the boil and
cook for at least 30 minutes. Set
aside.

Meanwhile, heat the oil in a deep
pan, put in the beef and cook till
lightly browned; sprinkle over the
paprika, with chilli powder to taste.
Add the onion, garlic and chillies if
using and fry till golden brown.

Stir in the carrots, leeks, tomatoes
and beans with their cooking liquid;
crumble in the stock cube, add the
herbs, cover and simmer gently for
35 minutes. Remove the bay leaves
and season to taste with salt.

Serve immediately with crusty
French bread.

Casseroles

Country pork stew

Serves 4

350 g/12 oz dried split peas, soaked overnight in cold water to cover
2–3 bacon or ham rinds plus a rinsed ham bone, if available
350-g/12-oz piece belly of pork
2 cloves of garlic, peeled and crushed
1 onion, peeled and chopped
250 ml/8 fl oz red wine
1 large carrot, peeled and chopped
2 leeks, washed and finely sliced
salt and freshly ground black pepper

Drain the peas, cover with fresh cold water and bring to the boil; cook for 20 minutes then add the rinds and ham bone, if using. Cook for 20 minutes more.

Add the belly pork, garlic, onion and wine, cover and cook gently for 20 minutes, then add the carrot and leeks and cook for a further 20 minutes. Remove the bacon rinds and ham bone.

Take out the pork and slice, return the slices to the pot and season with salt and pepper to taste. Pour into a warmed casserole dish and serve immediately.

Thick pea and bacon hotpot

Serves 4

450 g/1 lb dried peas, soaked in cold water overnight
3 onions, peeled
4 cloves
1 bay leaf
25 g/1 oz lard
450-g/1-lb piece of unsmoked bacon
2 carrots, peeled and diced
½ root of celeriac, peeled and diced
1 leek, trimmed, washed and sliced
salt
pinch of dried thyme
pinch of dried marjoram
2 tablespoons chopped parsley

Drain the peas, cover with fresh cold water in a pan and bring to the boil, together with 1 onion, stuck with the cloves, and the bay leaf. Cover, reduce the heat and simmer for 30 minutes. Remove the onion and bay leaf.

Meanwhile, heat the lard in a large flameproof pan, put in the bacon and brown all over. Chop the remaining onions, add to the pan and fry till golden.

Add the peas with their cooking liquid to the pan and cook for 15 minutes. Add the carrots and celeriac and cook for 15 minutes, then add the leek. Season to taste with salt and the dried herbs and cook for 15 minutes.

To serve: take out the bacon and carve into 4 slices. Sprinkle the parsley over the pea and vegetable mixture, put the bacon slices on top and serve immediately, with boiled potatoes.

Casseroles

Veal and pepper stew

Serves 4

50 g / 2 oz lard
675 g / 1½ lb lean stewing veal, cut into
bite-sized pieces
3 large onions, peeled and sliced
1–2 cloves of garlic, peeled and
crushed
2 red or yellow peppers, deseeded
and cut into thick strips
450 g / 1 lb ripe tomatoes, peeled and
coarsely chopped
3 tablespoons paprika
1 tablespoon tomato purée
150 ml / ¼ pint red wine
300 ml / ½ pint stock
salt and freshly ground black pepper
pinch each of caraway seeds and
sugar
225 g / 8 oz potatoes, peeled and diced
150 ml / ¼ pint soured cream to finish

Heat the lard in a flameproof
casserole, put in the meat and
brown all over. Remove and keep
warm. Add the onion, garlic and
peppers to the pan and fry till
browned. Put back the meat
together with the tomatoes, paprika
and tomato purée, and cook

together for a few seconds. Pour on
the wine and stock, season to taste,
add the caraway seeds and sugar and
bring to the boil.

Add the potatoes, cover, reduce
the heat to simmering point and
cook for 40–60 minutes till the meat
is tender. Spoon the soured cream
over the middle just before serving.

Chicken curry

Serves 4–6

50 g / 2 oz seedless raisins
2 tablespoons sherry
1.5-kg / 3-lb oven-ready chicken
salt and freshly ground white pepper
1 teaspoon paprika
50 g / 2 oz butter
1 tablespoon oil
1 onion, peeled and chopped
1 apple, peeled, cored and diced
1–2 teaspoons honey
1–2 teaspoons curry powder to taste
450 ml / ¾ pint chicken stock
100 ml / 4 fl oz dry white wine
1 large banana, peeled and mashed
with 2 tablespoons lemon juice
4 tablespoons single cream
40 g / 1½ oz flaked blanched almonds,
toasted to garnish

Soak the raisins in the sherry for
about 30 minutes. Divide the
chicken into 4 or 6 portions; sprinkle
all over with salt, pepper and
paprika.

Heat two-thirds of the butter with
the oil in a frying pan and sauté the
chicken till golden brown.

Heat the remaining butter in the
pan, add the onion and the apple
and cook gently till the onion is soft.
Stir in the honey and curry powder
to taste, then pour in the stock and
wine and the raisins in the sherry.
Add the chicken, cover and cook
gently for about 40 minutes till the
chicken is tender.

Remove the chicken portions.
Reduce the liquid in the pan by
boiling hard for 10 minutes. Stir in
the banana mixture and cream.
Replace the chicken portions and
heat through gently. Serve with
boiled rice with a sprinkling of
almonds over the chicken.

Chicken fricassée

Serves 4

75 g/3 oz butter
25 g/1 oz flour
750 ml/1¼ pints chicken stock
150 ml/¼ pint double cream
1 carrot, peeled and chopped
100 g/4 oz parsnips, peeled and
  sliced
100 g/4 oz shallots, peeled
100 g/4 oz mushrooms, wiped
1 (1.5-kg/3-lb) chicken, cooked and
  boned
salt and pepper
grated rind of ½ lemon

Heat 25 g/1 oz of the butter in a
saucepan, stir in the flour to make a
roux. Gradually blend in the stock,
stirring continuously, then add the
cream. Cook for 1 minute till thick.
Reduce over high heat for 2
minutes.

Cook the carrot, parsnips and
shallots in boiling salted water for
12 minutes, then drain and sauté
them gently in half the remaining
butter for 10 minutes.

In another pan, fry the
mushrooms in the rest of the butter

for 1–2 minutes.

Add the chicken meat and
vegetables to the sauce. Season to
taste and stir in the lemon rind.
Serve immediately with boiled
potatoes.

Veal fricassée

Serves 4

25 g/1 oz butter
1 kg/2 lb shoulder of veal, boned
  and cut in bite-sized pieces
20 g/¾ oz flour
150 ml/¼ pint dry white wine
450 ml/¾ pint white stock
1 onion, peeled and stuck with 2
  cloves
1 large carrot, peeled and chopped
1 stick celery, wiped and sliced
1 bay leaf
1 sprig parsley
4 peppercorns

Dumplings
2 raw chicken breasts, finely minced
2 tablespoons chopped parsley
1 egg yolk
2–3 tablespoons fresh breadcrumbs
salt and pepper
grated nutmeg

To finish
4 tablespoons single cream
1 egg yolk
225 g/8 oz cooked peas
100 g/4 oz cooked tongue, cut in
  strips

In a flameproof casserole heat the
butter and sauté the veal until light
golden. Sprinkle on the flour and
stir, then stir in the wine and stock.

Add the onion, carrot, celery, bay
leaf, parsley and peppercorns. Cover
and cook for 50 minutes over a
gentle heat.

For the dumplings, mix the
minced chicken with the parsley, egg
yolk, breadcrumbs and seasonings.
Roll into walnut-sized pieces and
simmer gently in salted water for 10
minutes. Drain well and set aside.

Remove the veal. Strain the sauce
and reduce it by boiling hard. Mix
together the cream and egg yolk, stir
into the sauce and reheat until
thickened, but do not boil. Season
to taste. Return the meat, add the
peas, tongue and dumplings and
heat through. Serve with boiled rice.

Casseroles

Sliced bean hotpot

Serves 4–6

225 g/8 oz ham bone or pork rinds
2 litres/3½ pints water
450 g/1 lb potatoes, peeled and
*   roughly chopped*
450 g/1 lb runner or French beans,
*   trimmed and sliced diagonally*
salt
3 sprigs of savory or thyme
100 g/4 oz rindless rashers streaky
*   bacon, diced*
1 large onion, peeled and chopped
freshly ground black pepper
½ teaspoon vinegar

Wash the ham bone or rinds, put them in a large pan with the water and bring to the boil. Reduce the heat, cover and simmer for 2 hours. Remove the bone or rinds.

Cook the potatoes in the broth till just soft. Cook the beans in boiling salted water for 5 minutes, then drain, rinse under cold running water and drain again.

Mash the cooked potatoes into the broth, then add the beans and the savory or thyme. Simmer for 15 minutes.

Meanwhile, dry-fry the bacon till the fat runs, put in the onion and cook till golden brown. Season with salt and pepper to taste, and add the vinegar. Pour the potato and bean hotpot into a hot tureen, sprinkle over the bacon and onion mixture and serve at once.

Note A little single or soured cream may be stirred in just before serving.

Layered meat casserole

Serves 6

225 g/8 oz stewing beef
225 g/8 oz shoulder of pork, boned
225 g/8 oz shoulder of lamb, boned
225 g/8 oz shoulder of veal, boned
225 g/8 oz celeriac, peeled and diced
225 g/8 oz onions, peeled and sliced
225 g/8 oz carrots, peeled and sliced
225 g/8 oz potatoes, peeled and diced
350 g/12 oz white cabbage, shredded
salt and pepper
grated nutmeg
dried marjoram
450 ml/¾ pint stock
3 tablespoons chopped parsley to
*   garnish*

Cut all the meats into bite-sized pieces and layer with vegetables in a large flameproof pan or casserole, seasoning each layer with salt, pepper, nutmeg and marjoram to taste.

Pour in the stock, cover and bring to the boil. Reduce the heat and simmer for about 1½ hours, or cook in a heated moderate oven (180 C, 350 F, gas 4) for about 2 hours.

Serve from the pan, sprinkled with chopped parsley.

Note If you like, flavour the hotpot additionally with caraway seeds, bay leaf and/or lovage.

Spanish hotpot

Serves 6

100 g / 4 oz dried chickpeas or yellow
  peas, soaked overnight in cold
  water to cover
4 tablespoons olive oil
1 ham bone or beef marrowbone
3 cloves of garlic, peeled
1 small pig's trotter (optional)
350-g/12-oz piece beef skirt
225 g/8 oz shoulder of lamb, boned
1½ litres/2¾ pints water
2 carrots, peeled and cut into strips
2 leeks, trimmed, washed and cut
  into strips
1 onion, peeled and chopped
1 small celeriac root, peeled and cut
  into strips
350 g/12 oz potatoes, peeled and
  diced
6 small tomatoes, peeled and
  chopped
salt and pepper
1 bay leaf
100 g/4 oz chorizo or boiling garlic
  sausage

To finish
2 tablespoons chopped parsley
1 small lettuce, shredded

Drain the peas, rinse well, and drain
again. Heat the oil in a large
flameproof pan, add the ham bone
or marrowbone and garlic and
brown. Put in the pig's trotter, if
using with the meats and water and
bring to the boil slowly; cover, then
cook gently for 1 hour, skimming
from time to time.

Add the peas to the pan and cook
for 30 minutes. Then add the
remaining vegetables and the
tomatoes, season with salt and
pepper to taste, add the bay leaf and
the sausage. Cook 25–30 minutes.

Take out all the meat, slice and
arrange on a warmed platter. Throw
away the bone and trotter. Boil up
the broth again, add the parsley and
lettuce and cook for 1 minute.
Check the seasoning. Serve the
broth separately in a hot tureen with
platter of meats.

Cook's Tip

If you do not have time to soak the
chickpeas try substituting canned
chickpeas. These should be drained
and added to the hotpot towards the
end of the cooking time. Other
types of canned pulses, such as
cannellini beans, could be used
instead.

Casseroles

Casseroled duck with cabbage

Serves 4

2 tablespoons oil
4 duck portions, thawed if frozen
salt and black pepper
½ small white cabbage (about 350 g/
*   12 oz), finely sliced*
1 small bulb of fennel, trimmed and
*   finely sliced*
2 onions, peeled and finely sliced
2–3 cloves of garlic, peeled and
*   crushed*
pinch of dried marjoram
pinch of dried thyme
4 tablespoons white wine vinegar
50 g/2 oz rindless rashers back
*   bacon, finely chopped to garnish*

Heat the oil in a frying pan, put in
the duck portions and brown them
all over. Take them out and drain
well on absorbent kitchen paper.
Sprinkle with salt and pepper.

Set the oven at moderate (180 c,
350 f, gas 4).

Layer the vegetables and garlic in
a large casserole. Sprinkle with the
herbs then arrange the duck portions
on top. Pour the vinegar over the

duck, cover and cook in the heated
oven for 50–60 minutes.

Dry fry the bacon until crisp and
sprinkle over the casserole just
before serving.

Osso buco

Serves 4

2–3 cloves of garlic, peeled
salt
25 g/1 oz butter
2 onions, peeled and finely chopped
2 carrots, peeled and finely chopped
5 stalks of celery, trimmed and diced
freshly ground black pepper
8 equal-sized pieces of shin of veal,
*   tied with string (about 1 kg/2 lb*
*   altogether)*
2 tablespoons flour
3 tablespoons oil
150 ml/¼ pint dry white wine
150 ml/¼ strong stock
¼ teaspoon dried basil
¼ teaspoon dried thyme
1 bay leaf
4 tablespoons chopped parsley
1 (227-g/8-oz) can tomatoes,
*   drained and roughly chopped*
grated rind of 1 lemon

Crush the garlic with a little salt and
set aside. Heat the butter in a large
flameproof casserole. Put in the
vegetables and brown lightly for
about 10 minutes, then remove from
the pan.

Season the veal pieces with salt
and pepper and dip them in the
flour. Add the oil to the casserole,
put in the veal, a few pieces at a
time, and brown all over, adding a
little more oil if necessary. Remove
the veal and set aside.

Dissolve the juices in the pan with
the wine, over high heat, then boil
hard to reduce the liquid by half.
Put back the veal, together with the
vegetables, stock, herbs, half of the
parsley and the tomatoes. Cover and
simmer for 1 hour till the veal is
tender.

Mix the remaining parsley with
the lemon rind and sprinkle on top.
Serve immediately with risotto (page
163).

Veal or pork stroganoff

Serves 4–6

50 g/2 oz butter
2 tablespoons oil
575 g/1¼ lb veal escalopes or pork
*   fillet, cut into thin strips, about*
*   4-cm/1½-in long*
2 shallots, peeled and finely chopped
150 ml/1¼ pint dry white wine
150 ml/¼ pint single or soured cream
salt and pepper
1 tablespoon chopped parsley

Heat half the butter with 1
tablespoon oil in a large sauté pan.
Put in half of the meat and cook
rapidly, turning all the time, for 2
minutes. Remove the meat and put
in a colander over a bowl to catch
the juices. Sauté the rest of the
meat, using the remaining butter
and oil, then drain as above.

Add the shallots to the pan and
cook gently till soft but not
browned. Pour in the wine. Over
high heat, stir in the cream, with the
meat juices, and continue stirring
while reducing the liquid over a
moderate heat to about half its
original quantity.

Put the meat back in the pan and
cook gently for about 3 minutes to
warm through. Season to taste with
salt and pepper and sprinkle with
parsley. Serve at once with noodles
or boiled rice.

Beef with wine and pepper sauce

Serves 4–6

50 g/2 oz butter
2 onions peeled and sliced into rings
1 clove of garlic, peeled and crushed
1 red pepper, deseeded and cut into
*   strips*
1 green pepper, deseeded and cut
*   into strips*
2 large, ripe tomatoes, peeled,
*   deseeded and sliced*
salt and freshly ground black pepper
2 tablespoons oil
450 g/1 lb frying steak, cut into
*   1-cm/½-inch strips*
150 ml/¼ pint red wine
3 tablespoons soured cream
2 sprigs of basil to garnish (optional)

Heat half the butter in a heavy stew
pan or flameproof casserole. Put in
the onion, garlic and peppers and
cook till the onion is soft and
transparent but not browned. Add
the tomatoes. Season with salt and
pepper, cover and cook gently for 10
minutes.

In another pan, heat the oil with
the rest of the butter, put in the
steak in two batches, and sauté to
seal for 1–2 minutes. Remove the
meat and place in a colander over a
bowl to catch any juices.

When all the meat has been
sautéed, dissolve the juices in the
pan with the wine, then reduce the
liquid by boiling hard for 1 minute.
Pour this over the vegetables in the
stew pan or casserole, adding the
juices from the meat.

Bring the mixture to the boil, add
the meat and reheat gently but do
not boil. Remove from the heat,
check the seasoning, then stir in the
cream. Garnish with basil, if
available, and serve at once with
noodles or boiled rice.

Casseroles

Rabbit stew

Serves 4

3 tablespoons oil
2 cloves of garlic, peeled
25 g/1 oz butter
4 large portions of rabbit
100 g/4 oz shallots or pickling
* onions, peeled*
225 g/8 oz mushrooms, wiped
450 g/1 lb ripe tomatoes, peeled and
* chopped*
150 ml/¼ pint dry white wine
1 chicken stock cube
1 teaspoon dried basil
1 tablespoon chopped parsley
salt
paprika

Heat the oil in a frying pan and fry the garlic until golden, then remove and discard it.

Heat the butter in the oil, add the rabbit pieces and brown on all sides. Remove them and set aside.

Add the shallots or onions and mushrooms to the pan and cook for 2–3 minutes, then add the tomatoes, wine, crumbled stock cube and basil. Cook for 1–2 minutes.

Put the rabbit pieces into a large flameproof casserole, add the onion and mushroom mixture, cover and simmer for 25 minutes; add the parsley and cook for a further 15 minutes.

Remove the lid and reduce the liquid by boiling over high heat for about 5 minutes till it becomes syrupy. Season to taste with salt and paprika.

Serve immediately with paprika or saffron rice (page 150), or green noodles tossed with fried breadcrumbs and a salad in season with a soured cream or yogurt dressing.

Note The sauce can also have cream stirred into it to give it a creamy, glossy finish. Or a little soured cream can be spooned over the casserole just before serving.

Variations
Use 25 g/1 oz dried mushrooms, soaked overnight, instead of fresh mushrooms to enrich the flavour. If the sauce needs thickening, stir in a little beurre manié at the end. The white wine can be replaced by a full-bodied red wine to darken the stew and give it a more robust flavour.

Other additions to try Add thin rings of red or green pepper with the tomatoes, or stir in finely chopped gherkins and capers at the end. Or add frozen peas — put them in still frozen about 10 minutes before the end of the cooking time. Canned sweet corn is also tasty: just heat through in the stew for the last few minutes.

Jugged hare or rabbit

Serves 4

1 hare or rabbit, cleaned, skinned
* and jointed*
1 onion, peeled and sliced
2 cloves of garlic, peeled and crushed
1 carrot, scraped and diced
8 peppercorns
1 bay leaf
150 ml/¼ pint red wine vinegar
450 ml/¾ pint red wine
100 g/4 oz rindless rashers streaky
* bacon diced*
16 shallots or pickling onions, peeled
300 ml/½ pint hot stock
salt and freshly ground black pepper
2 sprigs of thyme
pinch of powdered cinnamon

Rinse the hare or rabbit pieces and place them in a large, non-metallic bowl. Cover them with the sliced onions, garlic, carrot, peppercorns and bay leaf. Mix together the vinegar and half the wine and pour this over the meat and vegetables. Cover and marinate for 12 hours in the refrigerator, turning the meat from time to time.

Dry fry the bacon in a flameproof casserole till the fat runs, then take it out and reserve. Drain the hare or rabbit portions and pat dry with absorbent kitchen paper. Put them in the pan and brown all over in the bacon fat. Then take out and add the shallots or pickling onions and brown them.

Return the meat to the pan, add the strained marinade, the stock and the rest of the wine, season with salt and pepper and add the thyme. Cover and simmer gently for 1 hour or till the meat is tender.

Remove the lid and reduce the liquid by about half by boiling hard. Return the bacon to the casserole and check the seasoning, then add the cinnamon. Serve at once with boiled potatoes.

Casseroles

Italian pork and cabbage casserole

Serves 6

6 large loin of pork chops
2 tablespoons olive oil
100 ml/4 fl oz dry white wine
300 ml/½ pint hot stock
450 g/1 lb carrots, scraped and sliced
3 sticks of celery, chopped
3 leeks, trimmed, washed and sliced
2 cloves of garlic, peeled and crushed
salt and freshly ground black pepper
450 g/1 lb garlic sausage
1 small white cabbage, shredded

Heat the oven to moderate (180c, 350f, gas 4).

Trim any excess fat from the chops then rinse and pat dry with absorbent kitchen paper. Heat the oil in a large frying pan and fry the chops until browned on both sides. Do this in two batches, adding more oil if necessary.

Transfer the chops to a large ovenproof casserole and pour over the wine and stock. Add the carrots, celery, leeks and garlic and season to taste with a little salt and pepper. Cover the casserole with a tight fitting lid and cook in the moderate oven for 30–40 minutes.

Remove any skin from the garlic sausage and slice thickly. Add the garlic sausage with the shredded cabbage to the casserole and return it to the oven for a further 20 minutes or until the cabbage is tender but not unpleasantly soft. Alternatively put the whole garlic sausage in with the cabbage and remove and slice it just before serving.

Serve piping hot with crispy French bread or oven-baked potatoes.

Variations
A bay leaf and some chopped mixed herbs such as sage or thyme go very well with this casserole. Or for a more unusual subtle flavour add the grated rind of half an orange with the stock and wine.

Cook's Tip

When frying meat that is to be casseroled it is important to have the fat hot so that the outside of the meat browns quickly, sealing in the juices. This will help to keep the meat tender and moist and also give the gravy a good flavour and colour. Pork chops can additionally be browned along the edge by holding each chop in turn on its side until the fat colours.

Irish stew

Serves 6

1 kg/2 lb potatoes, peeled and sliced
800 g/1¾ lb onions, peeled and sliced
12 middle neck lamb chops, trimmed
  of fat
salt and freshly ground black pepper
dried thyme
chopped parsley

Put alternate layers of potato, onion and chops in a deep saucepan, seasoning as you go with salt, pepper and thyme, and finishing with a layer of onions and potato.

Pour in enough water just to cover the top layer of potatoes, cover and simmer gently for 1½–2 hours. Add a few tablespoons of boiling water from time to time to prevent the stew from burning. Sprinkle with chopped parsley just before serving.

Polish hunter's hotpot

Serves 6

100 g/4 oz streaky bacon, chopped
675 g/1½ lb pork spare rib, boned and
  cut into bite-sized pieces
4 onions, peeled and finely chopped
450 g/1 lb white cabbage, shredded
1 (454-g/1-lb) can sauerkraut,
  drained and pulled apart with 2
  forks
225 g/8 oz ripe tomatoes, peeled and
  chopped
2 cloves of garlic, peeled and crushed
  with a little salt
20 g/¾ oz dried mushrooms, soaked
  in water for 2 hours, then drained
salt
1 tablespoon paprika
1 teaspoon caraway seeds
1 teaspoon dried marjoram
4 bay leaves
300 ml/½ pint stock
225 g/8 oz smoked or boiling
  sausage, sliced

Set the oven at moderate (180c, 350f, gas 4).

Dry fry the bacon in a large flameproof casserole till the fat runs. Add the pork with the onions and brown all over.

Add the cabbage, sauerkraut, tomatoes, garlic and drained mushrooms, stir well and season with salt, paprika, caraway seeds and herbs. Pour on the stock and lay slices of sausage on top.

Cover and cook for 1½ hours in the heated oven, or till the meat is tender. Remove the bay leaves before serving.

Note This casserole makes a good party dish. The dried mushrooms can be replaced by 100 g/4 oz fresh mushrooms if liked. Serve with a crisp salad to start with, and a light sweet to follow.

Casseroles

Boeuf à la mode

Serves 8

1.5 - kg/3 - lb piece of beef topside,
  silverside or brisket, rolled and
  tied with string
100 g/4 oz rindless rashers streaky
  bacon
450 g/1 lb shallots or pickling onions,
  peeled
salt and freshly ground black pepper
2 tablespoons brandy, warmed
  (optional)
1 bouquet garni
450 g/1 lb carrots, scraped and sliced

Marinade
600 ml/1 pint red wine
2 onions, peeled and chopped
2 carrots, peeled and sliced
2 cloves of garlic, peeled and crushed
2 bay leaves, crumbled
1 teaspoon dried thyme
4 tablespoons chopped parsley

Put the meat in a deep non-metallic bowl, pour over the wine, then add the rest of the marinade ingredients. Cover and marinate for 12 hours in the refrigerator, turning the meat occasionally.

Set aside 2–3 bacon rashers and dice the rest. Dry fry the diced bacon in a large heavy pan or flameproof casserole until the fat runs. Remove it and reserve (see *Tip*). Put in the shallots or pickling onions and brown them all over. Remove and put them to one side.

Drain the meat, reserving the marinade, and dry the meat thoroughly with absorbent kitchen paper. Rub over it with a little salt and pepper then brown it in the remaining bacon fat for about 15 minutes. Take it out, pour off any fat remaining, then line the botton of the pot with the rest of the bacon rashers.

Put in the beef and heat till the bacon slowly begins to cook. Flame the brandy, if using, pour it over the meat and let it burn itself out.

Add the strained marinade and add enough water so that the liquid three-quarters covers the beef. Add the bouquet garni, cover with a lid and simmer very gently for 2 hours.

Add the carrots and the browned onions to the pan, cover, and simmer gently for another hour. Remove the pan or casserole from the heat, take out the meat and let it stand in a warm place for about 5 minutes. Then carve and arrange the slices on a warm serving dish, surrounded by the vegetables.

Strain the sauce, skimming off any fat, bring to the boil and taste for seasoning. Pour a little over the meat and serve the rest separately.

Serve at once with boiled new potatoes.

Tip Make this dish even more tasty by warming up the reserved cooked diced bacon at the end, browning it with a little chopped garlic, then scattering over the meat with 2 tablespoons chopped parsley.

Hungarian goulash

Serves 6

25 g/1 oz lard
225 g/8 oz onions, peeled and finely
  chopped
1 kg/2 lb stewing beef, trimmed and
  cut into 2 - cm/¾-inch cubes
1 clove of garlic, peeled
1 teaspoon caraway seeds
salt
2 tablespoons paprika
600 ml/1 pint hot water
225 g/8 oz tomatoes, peeled and
  chopped
2 green peppers, deseeded and cut
  into strips
350 g/12 oz potatoes, peeled and
  diced

Heat the lard in a frying pan, put in the onion and cook till soft but not coloured. Put in the meat and brown for 10 minutes, stirring all the time.

In a pestle and mortar or with a rolling pin, pound the garlic with the caraway seeds and a little salt. Mix with the paprika and stir into the meat mixture over medium heat until well blended. Add the hot water, bring to the boil and simmer very gently for 1 hour.

Add the tomatoes, the strips of pepper and the diced potato. Cook for a further hour, then check the seasoning.

Serve very hot with small fancy pasta shapes.

German mixed-meat hotpot

Serves 6

225 g/8 oz lean stewing beef
225 g/8 oz lean stewing veal
225 g/8 oz lean shoulder of pork,
  boned
2 onions, peeled and chopped
25 g/1 oz lard or dripping
225 g/8 oz tomatoes, peeled and
  chopped
1 green pepper, deseeded and diced
1 tablespoon paprika
salt
8 peppercorns, crushed
2 bay leaves
1 teaspoon caraway seeds
300 ml/½ pint hot stock
1 (454-g/1-lb) can sauerkraut,
  drained
150 ml/¼ pint soured cream to finish

Cut the meat into 3- × 1-cm (1½- × ½-in) strips. Fry the onions in the lard or dripping till golden. Add the tomatoes and pepper, cover and cook gently for 15 minutes.

Add the meat and paprika, and increase the heat a little; stir until the paprika has been absorbed. Then season with salt, the crushed peppercorns, bay leaves and caraway seeds. Pour on the hot stock, cover and simmer for 30 minutes. Stir in the sauerkraut and cook gently for 40 minutes. Remove the bay leaves.

Serve immediately, with the soured cream stirred in, together with boiled potatoes or dumplings or crispy French bread.

Sauces

the Finishing Touch

Sauces

Béchamel sauce

1 large onion, peeled
50 g/2 oz ham or lean rindless bacon
25 g/1 oz butter
25 g/1 oz flour
300 ml/½ pint boiling milk
300 ml/½ pint hot white stock
salt and pepper
grated nutmeg

Chop the onion finely with the ham or bacon. Heat the butter in a saucepan and gently cook the bacon or ham and onion till the onion is soft and transparent. Sprinkle in the flour and stir over low heat until it makes a soft paste. Whisk in the boiling milk, a little at a time, making sure each addition is blended in before adding the next lot. When all the milk is incorporated, add the stock then simmer gently over very low heat for 15 minutes.

Season to taste with salt, pepper and nutmeg, strain through a fine sieve and serve at once.
Makes about 600 ml/1 pint

Tip If serving with vegetables such as cabbage or potatoes, there's no need to strain the béchamel sauce.

Variations
Prepared according to this basic recipe, béchamel sauce can be served with a variety of dishes. It can also be used as a basis for many other sauces.

Mornay (cheese) sauce Blend the finished sauce with 75–100 g/3–4 oz grated cheese, then thicken with an egg yolk mixed with 1–2 tablespoons double cream.

Herb sauce Stir chopped herbs such as parsley or chives into the finished sauce.

Brown sauce Cook the flour and butter mixture until it is well browned, stirring constantly. Replace the milk with a mixture of red wine, tomato purée and gravy or brown stock

Mushroom sauce

50 g/2 oz rindless fat streaky bacon, diced
25 g/1 oz butter
2 onions, peeled and diced
1 clove of garlic, peeled and finely chopped or crushed
350 g/12 oz mushrooms, wiped and chopped
20 g/¾ oz flour
350 ml/12 fl oz hot stock
6 tablespoons red wine
salt and freshly ground black pepper
pinch of dried thyme
pinch of sugar
pinch of paprika
4 tablespoons soured cream
1 tablespoon chopped parsley

Dry fry the bacon in a saucepan (non-stick if possible) until the fat runs. Remove the bacon and reserve for use in another dish or for adding to the sauce at the end.

Melt the butter in the bacon fat remaining in the pan. Add the onions, garlic and mushrooms and cook, stirring constantly, until the onions are lightly coloured. Sprinkle in the flour and continue cooking over a moderate heat until it turns golden brown. Add the stock and wine, a little at a time, beating constantly. When all is incorporated smoothly, bring to the boil, then simmer gently over a low heat for 20 minutes.

Season with salt and pepper, thyme, sugar and paprika to taste and stir in the cream just before serving. Strain, if preferred, into a sauce boat, sprinkle with chopped parsley and serve.

Mushroom sauce is good served with most meats. The meat juices left in the pan after cooking can be stirred into the sauce. Serve also with boiled or steamed cauliflower, pasta or rice.
Makes about 600 ml/1 pint

Note For a more extravagant mushroom sauce, use dried mushrooms but soak and drain them first. Adding finely chopped or sieved cooked chestnuts also gives the sauce an unusual delicate flavour.

Mock béchamel with wine and herbs

100 g/4 oz rindless smoked streaky bacon, diced
2 onions, peeled and finely chopped
1 clove of garlic, peeled and finely chopped or crushed
100 ml/4 fl oz dry white wine
100 ml/4 fl oz single cream
salt and pepper
pinch of sugar
pinch of grated nutmeg
150 ml/¼ pint soured cream
1 tablespoon chopped chives
1 tablespoon chopped parsley

Dry fry the bacon in a saucepan, preferably non-stick, until the fat runs. Add the onions and garlic and cook until golden brown. Stir in the wine and cream and season with salt, plenty of pepper, sugar and nutmeg. Heat through over a gentle heat, stir in the soured cream and, if necessary, allow the sauce to reduce to a thick creamy consistency over a low heat.

Add the herbs and cook without boiling for a few minutes, then serve at once with hot potato salad, or vegetables like cauliflower, kohlrabi, or salsify.
Makes about 300 ml/½ pint

Tip For a stronger vegetable flavour, stir in some very thin slices of cooked leek or some cooked puréed celery and heat thoroughly in the sauce.

Sauces

Hollandaise sauce

2 egg yolks
1 teaspoon cold water
1 teaspoon lemon juice
225 g/8 oz chilled butter, cut into
  small cubes
salt and pepper
cayenne (optional)

Whisk the egg yolks in a small pan or heatproof bowl with the water and lemon juice. Stand the pan or bowl in a roasting pan half-filled with hot water and continue beating till the yolks are pale and frothy. Whisk in the pieces of butter, one at a time, making sure each one is completely blended in before adding the next.

When all the butter is incorporated, season to taste with salt, pepper and cayenne if liked and add a little more lemon juice if necessary.

Serve with boiled, poached or steamed fish, or with delicate vegetables such as asparagas, broccoli, globe artichokes, or with quick-fried meat dishes.
Makes about 300 ml/½ pint

Variation
Mousseline sauce Make the basic Hollandaise sauce as above. Allow to cool a little, then fold in 100 ml/ 4 fl oz stiffly whipped cream.
Makes about 450 ml/¾ pint.

Tip Should a butter sauce get too hot and start to separate, it can usually be saved by removing the pan or bowl from the heat immediately and whisking in a little cold water or an ice cube. If this fails, whisk in an extra beaten egg yolk.

Hot butter sauce

3 tablespoons dry white wine
3 tablespoons wine vinegar
2 shallots, peeled and finely chopped
salt and pepper
225 g/8 oz chilled butter, cut into
  small pieces

Place the wine and vinegar in a small pan with the shallots and a pinch of salt. Cook, uncovered, over a medium heat until reduced to about 1½ tablespoons. Season with pepper to taste and, with the pan

over a low heat, beat in the butter a piece at a time. When all is incorporated, serve at once.

This sauce is excellent served with boiled, poached or steamed fish. It is also good with shell fish and delicate vegetables.
Makes about 300 ml/½ pint

Noisette butter-sauce

The French word noisette literally means hazelnut, and describes the colour of the finished sauce; no nuts of any kind are added to it.

Allowing 20–25 g/¾–1 oz butter per person, carefully heat a quantity of butter in a frying pan or saucepan until it just turns a golden brown. Serve at once poured over baked, poached or grilled fish.

Horseradish sauce

3 stale rolls
300 ml/½ pint clear stock
salt and pepper
grated nutmeg
good pinch of sugar
juice of ½–1 lemon
15 g/½ oz butter
100 g/4 oz freshly grated horseradish
   or 3 tablespoons bottled
   horseradish sauce
2 tablespoons double cream
1 egg yolk

Grate the rolls to remove the crusts. Slice them thinly and soak in the stock for about 5 minutes, then work through a sieve into a small pan. Heat till hot but not boiling, then season to taste with salt, pepper and nutmeg, sugar and lemon juice.

   Stir in the butter in small pieces, then add the horseradish. Mix 2–3 tablespoons of the sauce with the cream and egg yolk, whisk together then blend back into the hot sauce. Reheat without boiling or it will curdle. Serve immediately with boiled or roast beef.
Makes about 600 ml/1 pint

Note Several variations of this sauce are possible. It can be mixed with grated apple and/or chopped blanched or ground almonds, with crushed garlic, finely chopped herbs, made mustard or green peppercorns.

Mustard sauce

25 g/1 oz butter or margarine
1 small onion, peeled and grated
25 g/1 oz flour
3–4 tablespoons made mild mustard
   to taste
450 ml/¾ pint hot stock
salt and pepper
good pinch of sugar
juice of ½ lemon
100 ml/4 fl oz double cream

Melt the fat in a saucepan. Stir in the onion and flour and cook gently, stirring, until all the fat is absorbed and the mixture becomes foamy. Stir in the mustard and continue cooking for 2 minutes.

   Pour on the hot stock, a little at a time, blending till smooth after each addition. Bring to the boil, then reduce the heat and cook gently for 5 minutes till thickened, stirring from time to time. Season well with salt, pepper, sugar and lemon juice, adding a little more mustard if necessary. Stir in the cream and heat without boiling until thick and smooth. Turn into a sauce boat and serve at once, with baked or grilled fish such as herrings or mackerel.
Makes about 600 ml/1 pint

Variation
To make a stronger flavoured sauce, add green peppercorns and snipped chives to taste. Make it even stronger by substituting mustard powder mixed with vinegar and/or dry white wine for some of the made mustard.

Sauces

Mayonnaise

3 large egg yolks
good pinch of salt
1 tablespoon vinegar or lemon juice
1–2 teaspoons made English mustard
450 ml/¾ pint corn or sunflower oil
white pepper or cayenne (optional)

To make mayonnaise successfully, it is essential to have all the ingredients at room temperature to reduce the risks of the eggs curdling while the oil is being added.

Beat the yolks with the salt, a few drops of vinegar or lemon juice and the mustard to a creamy foam (use either a rotary whisk or an electric beater as it is important to beat steadily and continuously).

Beat in the oil, drop by drop at first then in a steady stream, until thick and completely incorporated. Flavour with the remaining vinegar or lemon juice, and season to taste with a little pepper or cayenne and salt.
Makes about 600 ml/1 pint

Note Mayonnaise can also be made with olive, almond, walnut or hazelnut oil mixed with corn or sunflower oil. Each different oil gives the mayonnaise a subtly different flavour.

Cook's Tip

If mayonnaise should curdle while you are making it remove the curdled mixture to another bowl and beat up a further egg yolk with a little vinegar and seasoning. Add the curdled mixture a little at a time as for the oil to produce a smooth mayonnaise again.

Variations

Mayonnaise is used as the basis for many other sauces.

Tartare sauce Stir into the basic mayonnaise finely chopped gherkins, capers and herbs to taste. Very finely grated onion or chopped pickled onions can also be added.

Cream mayonnaise Make the basic mayonnaise with lemon juice instead of vinegar. Fold in 4 tablespoons stiffly whipped cream and adjust the seasoning, using cayenne, salt and lemon juice. Soured cream may also be used instead of ordinary cream.

Russian mayonnaise Make a cream mayonnaise (see above) using tarragon vinegar instead of lemon juice and soured cream; season to taste with freshly grated horseradish.

Ham mayonnaise Mix into the basic mayonnaise very finely chopped ham and a few peppercorns to taste.

Fruit mayonnaise For every 150 ml/¼ pint basic mayonnaise, fold in a purée made with 1 cooking apple, peeled and cored and cooked in 1 tablespoon water and 1 ripe peach, skinned and stoned. Season with curry powder and lemon juice to taste, and a pinch of sugar.

Olive mayonnaise Mix 150 ml/¼ pint basic mayonnaise with 3 tablespoons soured cream, 10 chopped green olives, 25 g/1 oz chopped blanched almonds and freshly ground black pepper to taste. Season to taste with freshly ground black pepper, vinegar and a little sugar.

Fish roe mayonnaise Make the basic mayonnaise with lemon juice only. Stir in one-third as much soured cream as the quantity of mayonnaise. Just before serving, fold in red or black lumpfish roe to taste.

Shrimp mayonnaise For every 150 ml/¼ pint basic mayonnaise, fold in 50 g/2 oz very finely chopped cooked shrimps and 1 tablespoon red lumpfish roe. Season to taste with lemon juice, a little Worcestershire sauce and a pinch of sugar.

Swedish-style mayonnaise Beat grated apple, freshly grated horseradish to taste and a little white wine into the basic mayonnaise. Season to taste with salt and sugar.

Gribiche sauce

4 eggs
2 teaspoons strong made mustard
1 tablespoon white vinegar
salt
250 ml/8 fl oz olive oil
1 teaspoon chopped chervil
1 teaspoon chopped tarragon
1 tablespoon chopped parsley
1 tablespoon snipped chives
1 teaspoon capers, drained
1 small pickled gherkin, drained and
*   finely chopped*
½ carton cress, washed and drained

Boil the eggs for 4 minutes only. Cool under running water, remove the shells and sieve. Beat them to a smooth paste with the mustard, vinegar and salt to taste. Then beat in the oil, a drop at a time. Mix in the chopped herbs, the capers and the gherkin. Just before serving add the cress.
Makes about 300 ml/½ pint

Serving suggestions for mayonnaise based sauces All mayonnaise based sauces go excellently with cold meats, steamed or poached fish, with hard-boiled eggs or with cold pickled or smoked fish. Gribiche sauce is especially good as a dip for all kinds of fresh vegetables or for serving with boiled potatoes.

Sauces

Aïoli

20 g/¾ oz white bread, crusts removed
2 tablespoons milk
4–5 cloves of garlic, peeled and
finely chopped
salt
2 egg yolks
250-350 ml/8-12 fl oz olive oil
1 tablespoon lemon juice
freshly ground white pepper

Soak the bread in the milk for about
2 minutes, then squeeze dry. Pound
the garlic with the bread and a little
salt in a mortar to a smooth paste.
Transfer to a small basin, beat in the
egg yolks and 2 tablespoons of the
oil until well blended together. Then
stir in the lemon juice, a drop at a
time, followed by the rest of the oil,
beating it in a drop at a time at first,
then in a thin steady stream till
thoroughly combined. Season to
taste with salt and pepper.

Aïoli is especially good with
poached fish, grilled meat or baked
jacket potatoes. It is also excellent
as a dip for pieces of fresh
vegetables, or as a fondue sauce for
meat.
Makes about 450 ml/¾ pint

Note In the making of aïoli, as with
all other mayonnaise-based sauces,
all the ingredients must be at the
same temperature — ideally room
temperature — to help prevent the
sauce curdling.

Tip Aïoli needs first-class
ingredients. Use only the best olive
oil and the freshest possible garlic. If
you buy garlic towards the end of
the season, the green shoot in the
centre of each clove should be
removed as it will taste bitter.

The bread is soaked in milk to
stabilise this rather oily sauce and
help keep it from separating. You
can also mix a few tablespoons of
fresh breadcrumbs with the chopped
garlic and work this into a smooth
paste in a mortar and then make the
sauce as above.

Rémoulade sauce

2 egg yolks
1 tablespoon made English mustard
1 tablespoon lemon juice
salt and pepper
300 ml/½ pint corn oil
3 small gherkins, drained and finely
chopped
1 tablespoon capers, drained and
chopped
2 sprigs of tarragon, finely chopped
1 tablespoon chopped parsley
¼ teaspoon anchovy paste

Beat or blend the egg yolks with the
mustard, lemon juice, salt and
pepper to taste. Beat in the oil, a
drop at a time, with a rotary whisk
or electric beater or work in a
blender or food processor to a
creamy mayonnaise.

Mix in the rest of the ingredients
seasoning it to taste with anchovy
paste. Chill until ready to serve.
Makes about 300 ml/½ pint

Cranberry sauce

225 g/8 oz bottled cranberries
pinch of ground ginger
½ teaspoon mustard powder
½ teaspoon turmeric
2 tablespoons orange juice
1 tablespoon lemon juice
1 tablespoon sweet sherry
1 tablespoon brandy

Blend the cranberries with the spices, fruit juices, sherry and brandy. Cover and chill till needed, and adjust the seasoning before serving.

Serve with hot or cold roast poultry, especially turkey, roast beef, tongue or ham.
Makes about 300 ml/½ pint

Tip Cooked unsweetened cranberry purée, made from fresh or frozen cranberries can be used instead of bottled cranberries.

Cumberland sauce

thinly pared rind and juice of
½ lemon
thinly pared rind and juice of
½ orange
1 shallot, peeled and finely chopped
3 tablespoons red wine
8 tablespoons redcurrant jelly
1 teaspoon mustard powder
pinch of ground ginger
1 tablespoon port
cayenne

Cut the lemon and orange rinds into very narrow shreds. Put them in a pan with the shallot and the red wine, bring to the boil, cover, reduce the heat and simmer over a low heat for 5 minutes. Add the lemon and orange juice with the redcurrant jelly, mustard powder and ginger and stir over a gentle heat until thoroughly blended. Leave to cool before seasoning to taste with the port and cayenne.

Serve with roast game, roast beef, or cold meats.
Makes about 300 ml/½ pint

Gooseberry sauce

450 g/1 lb gooseberries, trimmed
50 g/2 oz sugar
100 ml/4 fl oz dry white wine
50 g/2 oz butter
2 small onions, peeled and chopped
grated rind of ½ lemon
2 tablespoons orange marmalade
1 tablespoon Kirsch
salt
cayenne

Sprinkle the gooseberries with the sugar in a large bowl and leave to stand for 30 minutes.

Bring the wine to the boil in a large pan, add the gooseberries and cook over a low heat for 15 minutes till they are very soft.

Meanwhile heat the butter, add the onions and cook gently till soft. Add to the gooseberries, together with the lemon rind, marmalade, Kirsch, salt and cayenne to taste.

Serve with rich meats like roast pork, liver or boiled or baked fish.
Makes about 450 ml/¾ pint

Sauces

Hot Mango chutney

*3 ripe but firm mangoes, peeled and
    stoned
100 g/4 oz seedless raisins
2 red chillies, seeded and finely
    chopped
4 large cloves of garlic, peeled and
    finely chopped
1 piece of fresh root ginger, about
    5 cm/2 in long, peeled and finely
    chopped
150 g/5 oz dark soft brown sugar
250 ml/8 fl oz wine vinegar
1 teaspoon salt
1 teaspoon turmeric*

Weigh out 450 g/1 lb of mango flesh
and cut it into 1-cm/½-in cubes. Put
the raisins in a large bowl together
with the pieces of mango, chillies,
garlic, ginger and sugar, cover and
stand overnight.

Next day, turn into a large
preserving pan or saucepan, add the
vinegar and bring slowly to the boil,
stirring all the time. Reduce the heat
and simmer gently for 15 minutes.
Add the salt and simmer for 10
minutes more. Add the turmeric and
simmer for a further 5 minutes.

Pour into hot sterilised jars, seal
and label. Store in a cool, dry place
for up to 1 year.

Serve with curries or with cold
meat, baked fish, grilled poultry or
pilaffs.
Makes about 500 g/1¼ lb

Variations
Peach chutney Substitute 4 large ripe
peaches, peeled and stoned, for the
mangoes and add 3 tablespoons very
finely chopped parsley.

Apricot chutney Use 800 g/1¾ lb
apricots, peeled and stoned; add
100 g/4 oz pistachio nut kernels and
substitute mustard for the turmeric.

Tomato chutney Peel, seed and
finely chop 1 kg/2¼ lb ripe tomatoes.
Make the chutney as above, adding
the tomatoes and a little ground
allspice instead of the turmeric.

Tomato ketchup

*2 kg/4½ lb ripe tomatoes, peeled,
    halved and stems removed
450 g/1 lb onions, peeled and roughly
    chopped
6–8 cloves of garlic, peeled
4 tablespoons roughly chopped
    parsley
3 tablespoons finely chopped dill
    (optional)
1 tablespoon dried basil or
    2 tablespoons chopped basil
1 tablespoon dried oregano or
    2 tablespoons chopped marjoram
2 celery stalks, chopped
4 chillies, seeded and finely chopped
200 g/7 oz soft light brown sugar
450 ml/¾ pint wine vinegar
6 tablespoons olive oil*

Put the tomatoes, onions and garlic
in a blender or food processor and
work to a coarse pulp or chop by
hand. Put the pulp in a large
aluminium or enamel preserving pan
or saucepan, add the herbs, celery
and chillies and bring slowly to the
boil, gradually stirring in the sugar
and vinegar.

Cook, uncovered, over a high
heat, stirring all the time, until
reduced and thick. Stir in the oil and
bring to the boil. Remove the pan
from the heat.

Pour into hot sterilised bottles,
seal and label. Store in a cool, dry
place for up to 1 year.

Serve with sausages, cold meats,
fried or scrambled eggs, grilled
steaks etc.
Makes about 2 litres/3¼ pints

Variation
To make a red pepper ketchup, grill
2 kg/4 lb red peppers until the skins
become charred and blistered. Rub
or peel them off, remove the seeds
and proceed as for the tomato
ketchup, above. Makes about
1¼ litres/2½ pints.

Tomato and onion
chilli relish

*5-cm/2-in long piece of fresh
    horseradish, peeled and grated or
    2 tablespoons horseradish sauce
salt
750 g/1¾ lb green tomatoes, finely
    chopped
4 red peppers, deseeded and chopped
750 g/1¾ lb onions, peeled and finely
    chopped
6 cloves of garlic, peeled and crushed
300 ml/½ pint red wine vinegar
225 g/8 oz soft dark brown sugar
¼ teaspoon ground coriander
¼ teaspoon aniseed
3 green or red chillies, deseeded and
    finely chopped*

If using fresh horseradish, pound or
blend with a little salt. Then mix the
fresh or bottled horseradish with the
tomatoes, peppers, onions and
garlic. Stir in the vinegar, sugar and
2 teaspoons salt, cover and leave to
marinate overnight.

Next day, heat the mixture in a
large pan and bring to the boil
stirring all the time. Then turn down
the heat to low, add all the spices
and cook gently for 30–40 minutes
until the mixture is very thick.
Adjust the seasoning. Pour into
warm, sterilised jars, seal and label.
Store in a cool, dry place for up to 1
year.

Serve this relish with all sorts of
cold meats, sausages, grilled steaks,
fried chicken or baked fish.
Makes about 1.5 kg/3 lb

Variations
Onion relish Substitute equal
quantities of extra onions and red
peppers for the green tomatoes.
Add a few tablespoons of chopped
parsley and 2 crumbled bay leaves.
When bottling, spoon a little
vegetable oil on top.

Vegetable relish Use 450 g/1 lb each
of firm, red tomatoes, celery, green
peppers and onions with 175 g/6 oz
sugar only. Season additionally with
some yellow mustard seeds and
roughly crushed black peppercorns.
A little finely sliced leek, peeled and
chopped celeriac or diced apple may
also be added.

Sauces

Herb sauce

6 hard-boiled egg yolks, sieved
2 teaspoons made mustard
2 tablespoons white wine vinegar
salt and pepper
up to 250 ml/8 fl oz olive oil
4 tablespoons chopped fresh mixed
  herbs (for example dill, chives,
  parsley, chervil, borage, burnet,
  tarragon, lovage, lemon balm)

Blend the egg yolks with the
mustard, vinegar and salt to taste.
Whisk in the oil, a drop at a time,
until a mayonnaise-like sauce is
obtained. Season with salt and
pepper to taste, then add the herbs.
Makes about 300 ml/½ pint

Cheese sauce with basil

4 cloves of garlic, peeled and roughly
  chopped
1 tablespoon chopped basil or
  ¼ teaspoon dried basil
salt
4 tablespoons pine kernels
50 g/2 oz mild goat's cheese,
  crumbled
50 g/2 oz Parmesan cheese, grated
8 tablespoons olive oil

Work all the ingredients together in
a blender or food processor to a
smooth, thick sauce. If making by
hand, pound the garlic and the basil
leaves with salt in a mortar, then
gradually add the pine kernels,
cheese and oil, pounding all the
time.
Makes about 150 ml/¼ pt

Vinaigrette sauce

½ teaspoon made mustard
2 tablespoons herb vinegar
175 ml/6 fl oz vegetable oil
4 tablespoons chopped mixed fresh
  herbs (for example parsley,
  chervil, chives, dill, tarragon)
2 teaspoons capers, drained and
  chopped
salt and white pepper

Blend the mustard with the vinegar.
Beat in the oil, drop by drop. Stir in
the herbs and capers and season well
with salt and pepper.
Makes about 250 ml/⅓ pint

Note Substitute a little walnut or
hazelnut oil for the vegetable oil to
give your vinaigrette sauce extra
flavour.

Cucumber cream dip

½ cucumber, unpeeled and finely
   diced
salt
225 g/8 oz quark or other cream
   cheese
2 egg yolks
300 ml/½ pint soured cream
2 tablespoons lemon juice
1 tablespoon chopped watercress
1 tablespoon finely chopped mint
1 tablespoon chopped parsley
2 cloves of garlic, peeled and crushed
freshly ground black pepper

Put the cucumber in a colander and
sprinkle with 1 teaspoon salt to draw
out the juices; leave for 10 minutes,
then rinse and pat dry with
absorbent kitchen paper.

   Beat the cheese, egg yolks, cream
and lemon juice until smooth, add
the watercress, mint, parsley, garlic
and cucumber, and season to taste
with salt and pepper. Chill before
serving.
Makes about 600 ml/1 pint

Parsley cream sauce

1 onion, peeled and finely chopped
1 clove of garlic, peeled and finely
   chopped
40 g/1½ oz butter
3 tablespoons chopped parsley
300 ml/½ pint soured cream
2 egg yolks
pinch of salt
2 teaspoons lemon juice
white pepper
1 tablespoon snipped chives

Gently cook the onion and garlic in
the butter till soft and transparent.
Add 2 tablespoons of the chopped
parsley and cook gently for 2
minutes, stirring all the time. Stir in
the soured cream and heat until
almost boiling. Remove from the
heat at once.

   Put the egg yolks with the salt and
lemon juice in a basin over a pan of
hot but not boiling water and beat
till thick and creamy. Remove from
the heat and gradually stir in the
parsley cream a tablespoon at a
time. Season to taste with salt and
pepper and sprinkle with the
remaining parsley and the chives.
Makes about 450 ml/¾ pint

Egg and herb dip

2 hard-boiled eggs, sieved
1 teaspoon made English mustard
100 ml/4 fl oz vegetable oil
2 tablespoons vinegar or
   3 tablespoons lemon juice
salt and freshly ground black pepper
1 tablespoon finely chopped parsley
1 tablespoon finely chopped chives
2 tablespoons finely chopped fresh
   mixed herbs

Blend the eggs with the mustard to
make a smooth paste. Whisk in the
oil, a drop at a time, to make a
mayonnaise-like cream. Season to
taste with the vinegar or lemon
juice, salt and pepper.

   Stir the herbs into the egg
mayonnaise. Serve at once to enjoy
the full flavour of the herbs.
Makes about 150 ml/¼ pint

Vegetable
Accompaniments

Vegetables

Asparagus

For each person

100–175 g/4–6 oz fresh asparagus,
* stems scraped and trimmed to even*
* lengths*
25 g/1 oz butter
pinch each of salt and sugar
hot water (see method)

When preparing the asparagus, use a sharp knife and take care to remove any hard, woody parts from the stems. Arrange the trimmed stems in small bundles with the tips pointing in the same direction. Tie firmly in place with fine string just below the tips and about 2.5 cm/ 1 in from the base of the stems.

Melt the butter in a large pan or fish kettle, without allowing it to brown. Lay the bundles of asparagus carefully in the melted butter, season with salt and sugar and add enough hot water almost to cover.

Cover the pan, bring the water to the boil, then lower the heat and cook the asparagus for 15–20 minutes, or until tender (the younger the shoots, the less time they will take). Do not allow the asparagus to overcook or it will be unpleasantly soft.

Drain well and arrange on a heated plate for serving. The classic accompaniments are Vinaigrette dressing (p 118) or a butter-based sauce such as Hollandaise (p 110) or Maltese or Béarnaise sauce (below).

Variations

Serve cooked asparagus as a starter with 100 g/4 oz smoked or Parma ham per person, cut into strips, or smoked chicken or smoked salmon or trout. New potatoes tossed in butter and parsley, and a butter sauce (see above) make perfect accompaniments if the asparagus is to be served with a main dish.

Flemish-style asparagus Serve each portion with 1–2 hard-boiled eggs mashed with a little softened butter.

German-style asparagus To each serving add 100 g/4 oz smoked or Parma ham, cut into strips, a portion of Pancake crisps (see below) and a helping of melted butter and a butter sauce.

Pancake crisps

Serves 4

150 g/5 oz flour
pinch of salt
450 ml/¾ pint milk
4 eggs
butter for frying

Sieve the flour and salt into a large mixing bowl. Make a well in the centre.

Whisk together the milk and eggs. Pour into the well in the flour and gradually whisk in the flour to form a smooth, thin batter. Cover and leave to stand for 30 minutes.

Melt a knob of butter in a frying pan, tilting it so the fat coats the sides. Pour off any surplus.

Pour enough of the batter to cover the base of the pan thinly. Swirl it round quickly, then cook for about 1 minute till golden-brown underneath. Flip over with a spatula or toss, take the pan off the heat, and cut or tear the pancake into small, thin strips. Replace the pan and toss the strips, frying them until crisp, adding extra butter, if necessary.

Turn out on to a hot plate, cover with another hot plate and keep warm in the oven. Repeat until all the batter is used up. Serve with cooked asparagus.

Béarnaise sauce

Serves 4

2 shallots, peeled and finely chopped
6 peppercorns
3 tablespoons tarragon vinegar
¼ teaspoon meat extract (optional)
3 egg yolks
1 tablespoon hot water
100 g/4 oz butter
1 teaspoon chopped fresh tarragon
1 tablespoon chopped fresh chervil
* or parsley*
pinch of cayenne
pinch of salt

Put the shallots in a pan with the peppercorns, vinegar and meat extract (if used). Bring the liquid to the boil and continue boiling until it is reduced by half. Strain and allow to cool. In a bowl over a pan of hot, but not boiling, water (or in the top of a double boiler over hot water), whisk the egg yolks with the reduced

vinegar mixture and hot water until thick and creamy.

Melt the butter, skim off any foam that rises to the surface, then add this to the egg yolks a teaspoon at a time, whisking between each addition. Stir in the chopped herbs and season the sauce to taste with cayenne and salt.

Variation

Choron sauce Add 1 tablespoon concentrated tomato purée to the finished Béarnaise sauce.

Maltese sauce

Serves 4

150 g/5 oz butter
2 egg yolks
2 teaspoons hot water
1 tablespoon lemon juice
2 tablespoons fresh orange juice
pinch of salt
pinch of cayenne
1–2 teaspoons thinly grated orange
* rind*

Melt the butter in a pan, without allowing it to brown. Remove the pan from the heat. Skim off any froth that rises to the surface. Whisk the egg yolks with the water and lemon and orange juice in a bowl set over a pan of hot, but not boiling, water or use the top of a double boiler. Remove the pan from the heat and whisk in the clarified butter, a teaspoon at a time. Season to taste with salt and cayenne and sprinkle with the grated orange rind for serving.

Vegetables

Cauliflower — basic recipe

Serves 4

*medium cauliflower, trimmed and
    divided into florets*
salt
25 g/1 oz butter (optional)

Drain the cauliflower well, and set
aside. Bring a large pan of salted
water to the boil, add the
cauliflower florets, lower the heat
and simmer, uncovered, for 10–15
minutes, or until the florets are
tender but not too soft. Drain well
and add a knob of butter before
serving with roast beef, lamb or
veal.

Cauliflower polanaise

Serves 4

50 g/2 oz butter
2 tablespoons fresh breadcrumbs
salt and freshly ground pepper
*1 medium cauliflower, cooked as
    above without butter*
1 hard-boiled egg, sieved
1–2 tablespoons chopped parsley

Melt the butter in a pan, skim off
any foam and discard. Take care not
to allow the butter to colour. Add
the breadcrumbs and fry until
golden brown, then season and pour
over the cauliflower florets.
    Sprinkle the hard-boiled egg over
the cauliflower with the parsley and
serve at once.

Broccoli — basic recipe

Serves 4

*450 g/1 lb broccoli, well washed,
    stems removed and heads cut into
    florets*
salt
pinch of grated nutmeg
25 g/1 oz butter

Cut the stems into 2.5-cm/1-inch
slices. Bring a pan of water to the
boil, season with salt and nutmeg,
then add the broccoli, lower the
heat and allow it to simmer for 5–6
minutes, or until cooked but still
slightly crisp. (If using frozen
broccoli, cook according to the
directions on the packet in salted
water flavoured with nutmeg. Snip

into florets and slice the stalks when
cooked.) Drain thoroughly.
    Melt the butter in a pan over low
heat and toss the cooked broccoli
for a minute or two, until coated
with butter and glossy.
    Serve with Hollandaise sauce
(page 110) or Mornay sauce (page
108).

Variation
Broccoli omelette Soften 1 chopped
onion and 1 crushed clove of garlic
in 25 g/1 oz butter and 2 tablespoons
oil. Add 75 g/3 oz chopped cooked
ham and 225 g/8 oz broccoli, cooked
as above. Season to taste. Beat 4
eggs with 4 tablespoons single
cream, add 2 tablespoons chopped
parsley and season with salt and
paprika. Pour over the broccoli and
cook until the eggs are set.

Broad beans in cream sauce

Serves 4

450 g/1 lb frozen or shelled fresh broad beans
25 g/1 oz butter
1 small onion, peeled and finely chopped
1 clove garlic, crushed with a little salt
150 ml/¼ pint cream
4 tablespoons cooking liquid from the beans
pinch of salt
pinch of grated nutmeg
pinch of sugar
2 tablespoons chopped parsley or chervil to garnish

Cook the beans in salted water to cover. Drain, reserving 4 tablespoons of the cooking liquid. Allow the beans to cool slightly, then remove the grey-green outer skins.

Melt the butter in a pan and cook the onion and garlic over gentle heat until transparent but not browned. Stir in the cream and the reserved bean cooking liquid and cook until the sauce is thoroughly heated and slightly thickened. Season to taste with salt, nutmeg and sugar.

Add the beans and heat them through in the sauce. Serve, sprinkled with the chopped parsley or chervil, with roast beef, grilled lamb or pork and poultry or game dishes.

Glazed carrots

Serves 4

50 g/2 oz butter
450 g/1 lb young carrots, wiped and scraped
1 tablespoon sugar
pinch of salt

Melt two-thirds of the butter in a pan over gentle heat, add the carrots and stir until coated with the butter. Sprinkle in the sugar, and cook until the carrots are lightly glazed. Pour over just enough water to cover, add the salt and bring to the boil.

Lower the heat, and cook the carrots slowly until all the water has evaporated. Add the rest of the butter and toss the carrots so that the butter blends into the glaze.

Serve with roast meat, especially beef; poultry; grilled pork chops or veal escalopes.

Note Young new carrots are best for this dish. If using older carrots, trim and peel them, then quarter and cut them into even lengths.

Variation
Put the prepared carrots into a pan with enough cold water to cover. Add 2 teaspoons sugar and 50 g/2 oz butter. Cook as above until all the liquid has evaporated, then stir in a little double cream or soured cream for serving. Sprinkle with chopped parsley, if liked.

Vegetables

Italian-style beans

Serves 4

1 onion, peeled and halved
1 clove garlic, chopped
2 sprigs savory or parsley
10 peppercorns
salt
450 g/1 lb young French beans,
*   topped and tailed*
25 g/1 oz grated Parmesan cheese
25 g/1 oz butter

Put the onion, garlic, savory or parsley and peppercorns into a pan with 900 ml/1½ pints well-salted water. Bring rapidly to the boil, then add the beans and bring the water back to the boil. Lower the heat and cook gently for 10–15 minutes until the beans are tender but still crisp.

Drain the beans in a colander and rinse them quickly under cold running water. Remove the onion, herbs and peppercorns. Toss the beans in a clean pan over gentle heat for a minute or two until thoroughly dry and reheated. Arrange the beans lengthways in a heated serving dish, sprinkle with Parmesan and keep hot. Heat the butter in a pan over gentle heat until very lightly browned (take care not to allow it to burn) and pour it over the beans and Parmesan just before serving.

Italian-style beans go with most roast meat or poultry dishes and are particularly good with grilled or poached fish.

Variations
Choose very new French beans; top and tail them and cook in fast-boiling salted water until tender but still crisp. Drain well in a colander and rinse briefly under cold running water. Drain again.

Meanwhile cook a chopped, medium-sized onion with a crushed clove of garlic in a little olive oil until transparent, then add the beans with 225 g/8 oz peeled, deseeded and chopped tomatoes. Season to taste with salt, pepper, a pinch of dried savory or thyme or basil, and cook gently until heated through. Sharpen the sauce with a little herb or cider vinegar before serving, if liked.

French beans in bacon rolls

Serves 4

6 peppercorns
salt
450 g/1 lb young French beans,
*   topped and tailed*
40 g/1½ oz butter
2 shallots or 1 small onion, peeled
*   and finely chopped*
1–2 tablespoons chopped parsley
8 rashers of streaky bacon, rind
*   removed*

Put the peppercorns in a pan with water to a depth of 5 cm/2 inches and a little salt. Bring the water rapidly to the boil, add the beans and lower the heat once the water has returned to the boil. Cook the beans over gentle heat for 5–10 minutes, or until they are tender but still crisp. Rinse the beans briefly under cold running water and drain well.

Melt the butter over gentle heat and fry the shallots or onion until soft but not browned. Add the drained beans and parsley and toss until well coated with the butter and shallot or onion mixture. Keep hot.

Meanwhile fry the bacon rashers in a non-stick frying pan, turning once during cooking. Drain on absorbent kitchen paper, if necessary, and lay them on a work surface. Divide the beans between the rashers and roll up each one.

Arrange on a serving dish and serve hot with roast lamb, grilled or fried steak or lamb or pork chops.

Cook's Tip

Frozen French beans are very good and can be used successfully in these recipes provided they are not overcooked. Remember that frozen beans have already been blanched and so require less cooking time than fresh beans.

Green bean purée

Serves 4

675 g/1½ lb green beans, topped and
*   tailed, strings removed and halved*
4 tablespoons soured cream
2 tablespoons double cream
15 g/½ oz butter
salt and freshly ground black pepper
pinch of dried savory
2 teaspoons chopped parsley
1 teaspoon chopped chervil

Bring a pan of salted water to the boil, add the beans and bring the water back to boiling point, then lower the heat. Cook the beans for 15 minutes, or until tender. Drain well and allow them to cool slightly. Purée the beans by pushing them through a sieve, or using a liquidiser, vegetable mill or food processor, then pushing them through a sieve again to obtain a really fine purée.

Beat the soured cream into the bean purée with the double cream and the butter, then heat the mixture, stirring constantly, without allowing it to boil. Season to taste with salt, pepper and savory. Stir in half the chopped herbs and arrange the mixture on a heated serving dish. Sprinkle with the remaining herbs and serve with roast beef, veal, chicken, turkey breast or game birds.

Variations
Use 225 g/8 oz green beans and 225 g/8 oz shelled broad beans. Cook the beans together in a pan with a peeled onion, cut in quarters, added to the cooking water; or add a chopped clove of garlic or a generous squeeze of lemon juice to the cooking water. Remove the onion before puréeing the beans.

For a smoother, more delicate-tasting purée, use double the quantity of broad beans to that given above, and blanch them for a few minutes in boiling water before draining well, then removing the grey-green outer skins. Rinse the skinned beans in cold water before puréeing as above.

Vegetables

Carrot purée

Serves 4–6

675 g/1½ lb carrots, peeled and sliced
40 g/1½ oz long-grain rice, rinsed well
*   to remove excess starch*
pinch of salt
50 g/2 oz butter
4 tablespoons double cream
freshly ground white pepper
pinch of sugar

Put the carrots in a pan with the rice and water to cover, then add the salt and half the butter and bring the water to the boil. Lower the heat and cook for about 15 minutes until the carrots are soft and the rice is cooked. Drain well and purée rice and carrots by pushing through a sieve, or using a liquidiser, vegetable mill or food processor. Return the purée to the rinsed-out pan and heat gently with the cream, stirring constantly. Season with pepper and sugar to taste. When thickened, remove the pan from the heat and beat in the rest of the butter little by little until the purée is light and fluffy. Adjust the seasoning and serve hot.

Fennel purée

Serves 4

50 g/2 oz butter
1 clove garlic, chopped
675 g/1½ lb fennel bulbs, trimmed and
*   coarsely chopped*
200 ml/7 fl oz chicken stock
100 ml/4 fl oz double cream
pinch of salt
freshly ground white pepper
dash of lemon juice

Melt half the butter in a pan over gentle heat and fry the garlic until soft but not browned. Add half the chopped fennel to the pan, pour in the chicken stock, bring to the boil then lower the heat and cook the fennel until tender. Purée the cooked fennel by pushing through a sieve, or using a liquidiser, vegetable mill or food processor. Return to the rinsed out pan.

Purée the raw fennel by grating as finely as possible or using a liquidiser, vegetable mill or food processor. Add to the cooked purée in the pan and stir in the cream over low heat. Continue stirring until the purée is thick and creamy, then

remove the pan from the heat and beat in the rest of the butter, a little at a time.

Season the purée with salt, pepper and a little lemon juice and serve hot.

Brussels sprout purée

Serves 4–6

675 g/1½ lb Brussels sprouts, cleaned
*   and trimmed, with a cross cut in*
*   the base of each stalk*
1 medium potato, peeled and
*   quartered*
salt
150 ml/¼ pint double cream
50 g/2 oz butter
freshly ground black pepper
pinch of grated nutmeg

Put the sprouts and potato in a pan with salted water to cover; bring the water to the boil and cook until tender. Take out the potatoes with a slotted spoon and set aside. Drain the sprouts and rinse briefly under cold running water. Drain thoroughly then add the potatoes and purée both together by pushing through a sieve, or using a blender,

128

vegetable mill or food processor, then pushing through a sieve again for a very smooth purée. Return the purée to the rinsed-out pan and stir in the cream over gentle heat. Continue stirring until the purée thickens. Beat in the butter, a little at a time, and season to taste with salt, pepper and nutmeg. Serve hot.

Cook's Tip

Vegetable purées are a delicious and unusual way of serving vegetables. Some such as root vegetables and peas naturally form quite a thick purée whereas others such as watercress or spinach form a thinner purée and therefore make an excellent basis for sauces. The secret of a smooth purée is making sure that all the vegetables are evenly cooked, so cut them into pieces of equal size before cooking.

Summer vegetables

Serves 4–6

6 small artichokes, washed, trimmed,
   quartered and choke removed
juice of 1 lemon
3 tablespoons olive oil
2 medium-size onions, peeled and
   quartered
2 cloves garlic, crushed with a little
   salt
225 g/8 oz carrots, peeled and cut
   into julienne strips
1 medium kohlrabi, peeled and cut
   into julienne strips
150 ml/¼ pint dry white wine
300 ml/½ pint veal or chicken stock
salt and freshly ground white pepper
4 sprigs fresh thyme or ½ teaspoon
   dried thyme

Sprinkle the prepared artichokes with lemon juice to prevent discoloration. Heat the oil in a pan and add the artichokes, onions, garlic, carrots and kohlrabi. Stir them as they cook to seal the vegetables without allowing them to brown — about 5 minutes. (If a less pronounced garlic flavour is required, add the garlic 2 minutes

before the end of the frying time.) Pour in the wine and stock, bring to the boil, then lower the heat, cover the pan and finish cooking the vegetables over low heat for 10–15 minutes. They should be tender, but still a little crisp. Season to taste with salt and pepper, then flavour with thyme.

Serve with grilled or fried meat, especially veal.

Variation
To make this into a satisfying main dish add a few small new potatoes and some peas to the mixture and increase the quantity of each vegetable, and both wine and stock, by half again. When the vegetables are cooked, add 225 g/8 oz cooked ham, cut in strips. Serve hot.

Vegetables

Baked fennel

Serves 4–6

250 ml/8 fl oz clear beef stock
100 ml/4 fl oz dry white wine
50 g/2 oz butter
salt and freshly ground white pepper
pinch of grated nutmeg
8 small fennel bulbs wiped, trimmed
*   and halved lengthways*
50 g/2 oz grated Parmesan cheese
2 tablespoons fresh white
*   breadcrumbs*
parsley to garnish

Bring the stock to the boil in a pan with the wine and a third of the butter. Season to taste with salt, pepper and nutmeg. Lay the fennel in the pan, cut sides down, then cover and simmer gently for 15–20 minutes, or until the fennel is tender but still a little crisp.

Set the oven at hot (230c, 450f, Gas 8). Remove the fennel with a slotted spoon and lay, alternate sides down, in a heated ovenproof dish. Keep hot.

Briskly boil the cooking liquid in the pan, until it is reduced by half, then pour over the fennel. Mix the Parmesan and breadcrumbs and sprinkle over the fennel. Dot with the rest of the butter and bake in the hot oven for about 10 minutes, until the butter has melted and the top is lightly browned and crisp. Garnish with parsley.

Serve with grilled or fried meat, or as an accompaniment to any white fish dish.

Variations
Mix strips of cooked ham with the cooked fennel before baking, or serve it with a tomato sauce. The dish can also be grilled under high heat to finish off the butter and crumbs instead of cooking in the oven. In this case, put the fennel and other ingredients in a flameproof gratin dish.

Fennel in white sauce Instead of dotting the rest of the butter (two thirds) on top, make a roux by cooking it with 20 g/¾ oz flour until straw-coloured. Take the pan off the heat and stir in the cooking liquid. Replace the pan on the heat and cook, stirring constantly, for 5 minutes. Add 100 ml/4 fl oz cream and any chopped green feathery leaves from the fennel. Add a pinch of garlic salt, if liked, or a few drops of Worcestershire sauce. Pour over the fennel in the heated serving dish. Sprinkle with the grated Parmesan cheese, omitting the breadcrumbs, and bake as above.

Tip If the fennel bulbs still have their feathery, bright green leaves, trim these away, chop them and save them for sprinkling over the fennel before baking or use in a salad.

Kohlrabi in soured cream sauce

Serves 4

4 kohlrabi, each weighing about
*   150 g/5 oz, peeled, trimmed and*
*   finely sliced*
3 slender leeks, washed and thinly
*   sliced*
50 g/2 oz butter
150 ml/¼ pint soured cream
salt
pinch of sugar
pinch of cayenne (optional)
1 tablespoon chopped parsley

Cut away and reserve any small leaves from the kohlrabi when preparing them. Blanch the kohlrabi and leeks together in boiling salted water for 3 minutes, then rinse under cold running water, or plunge into a bowl of iced water to stop further cooking, and drain well. Melt the butter in a pan over gentle heat and, before it is coloured, stir in the soured cream to make a thick, smooth sauce. Season to taste with the salt and sugar, then add the drained vegetables. Cover and cook over gentle heat for 10–12 minutes, or until the vegetables are cooked through but still slightly crisp. Adjust the seasoning, if necessary, and sprinkle with a little cayenne, if liked. Slice any reserved kohlrabi leaves and sprinkle over the vegetables, with the parsley, for serving.

This accompaniment goes well with delicately flavoured meats such as chicken or veal, or with poached or baked fish.

Tip Kohlrabi can either be pale green — when grown in a greenhouse — or purplish, from the garden plot. The former is more delicate in flavour and can be served raw, in salads. Young kohlrabi need only to be scrubbed, not peeled, and thus retain more of the vitamins in the skin. Always use any young, tender leaves and shoots, as these, too, are rich in nutrients.

Variations
Use spring onions instead of leeks. Trim and blanch them first, or soften in the melted butter. Snip any darker green parts from the tops of the shoots into small rings and scatter over the dish before serving. Chopped chives also make a good garnish.

Try mixing the soured cream with 2 tablespoons double cream for a milder-tasting sauce.

Substitute young carrots, thinly sliced, and petits pois, for the leeks. Blanch carrots for 4–5 minutes (depending on how thinly they are sliced) before being added to the sauce. Cook frozen peas, if used, according to the directions on the packet, then drain and rinse under cold running water before draining thoroughly and adding them to the vegetables cooking in the sauce.

Vegetables

Braised red cabbage

Serves 4

50 g/2 oz margarine or lard
1 medium red cabbage, core
  removed and leaves finely
  shredded
1 small onion, peeled and grated
2 cooking apples, peeled, cored and
  chopped
3 tablespoons redcurrant jelly
salt and freshly ground black pepper
2 tablespoons wine vinegar
1 bay leaf

Melt the margarine or lard in a large
saucepan, add the shredded cabbage
and stir briskly until coated with the
fat. Add the grated onion and
apples and stir to mix with the
cabbage. Add the redcurrant jelly,
season with salt and pepper and
sprinkle over the vinegar. Add
about 300 ml/½ pint water and stir
the mixture. Put the bay leaf on top
and braise over low heat in a
covered pan for 30–40 minutes.
Take out the bay leaf and adjust the
seasoning before serving.

Cabbage braised in white wine

Serves 4

25 g/1 oz butter
2 tablespoons oil
2 medium onions, peeled and
  chopped
1 medium white cabbage, core
  removed and leaves shredded
300 ml/½ pint chicken stock
150 ml/¼ pint dry white wine
salt and freshly ground white pepper

Heat the butter and oil in a large
saucepan and cook the onion until
transparent. Add the shredded
cabbage and continue cooking for 5
minutes, stirring continuously. Pour
in the stock and wine and season to
taste. Cover the pan and cook for
5–10 minutes, then remove the lid
and cook gently until the cabbage is
tender and the liquid almost
evaporated. Serve with white meats
and poultry.

Savoy cabbage with bacon

Serves 4

1 medium size Savoy cabbage, core
  removed and coarsely shredded
50 g/2 oz smoked bacon, derinded
  and diced
1 medium onion, peeled and
  chopped
1 clove garlic, peeled and crushed
salt and freshly ground pepper
pinch of grated nutmeg

Blanch the cabbage by bringing it to
the boil in a pan of salted water,
then draining well and rinsing under
cold running water. Meanwhile,
cook the diced bacon in a pan until
the fat runs, then add the onion and
garlic. Cook briskly in the bacon fat
until transparent, but not browned.
Add the drained cabbage, season
with salt, pepper and nutmeg, then
cover the pan and cook over low
heat for 20–30 minutes, or until
tender but still a little crisp.
  Serve with dark or light roast
meat, or with grilled meats.

Old-fashioned Brussels sprouts

Serves 4

*450 g/1 lb Brussels sprouts, trimmed
and stems cross-cut at the base*
salt and freshly ground black pepper
*50 g/2 oz streaky bacon, derinded
and finely diced*
50 g/2 oz butter or margarine
*1 medium onion, peeled and
chopped*
1 slice of white bread, toasted
1 clove of garlic, halved
a little grated nutmeg

Cook the sprouts in boiling salted
water for 10–15 minutes.
Meanwhile, cook the bacon in a
frying pan until the fat runs, then
add half the butter or margarine and
allow it to melt. Add the onion and
cook over medium heat until golden
brown. Meanwhile, rub both sides of
the toast with the cut garlic clove,
then cut the toast into neat, small
dice. Heat the remaining butter or
margarine in a separate pan and fry
the bread dice, or croûtons, until all
the butter or margarine has been
absorbed and the croûtons are
evenly browned. Sprinkle with a
little salt and set aside.

Thoroughly drain the cooked
sprouts and add them to the bacon
and onion mixture, stirring well to
mix them together. Adjust the
seasoning, sprinkle with grated
nutmeg and sprinkle over the
croûtons for serving.

Brussels sprouts with chestnuts

Serves 4

20 g/¾ oz sugar
450 g/¾ pint hot chicken stock
*225 g/8 oz chestnuts, blanched and
peeled (see below)*
*450 g/1 lb Brussels sprouts, trimmed
and stems cross-cut at the base*
salt
50 g/2 oz butter
freshly ground black pepper
2 tablespoons fresh breadcrumbs

Put the sugar in a pan and let it
caramelise gently over low heat,
without allowing it to burn. Remove
the pan from the heat, cover the
hand holding it with a teatowel and
carefully add the stock. Return the
pan to the heat and cook gently
until the caramel has dissolved. Add
the chestnuts and simmer for 25
minutes. Meanwhile, cook the
sprouts in boiling salted water for
10–15 minutes. Drain well.

Lift out the chestnuts from the
pan with a slotted spoon and keep
them hot. Reduce the remaining
stock by two-thirds, then replace the
chestnuts, with 40 g/1½ oz of the
butter and stir over gentle heat until
the chestnuts are coated with a
sticky brown glaze. Turn into a
heated serving dish with the sprouts.
Fry the breadcrumbs in the
remaining butter and spoon over the
sprouts before serving.

Tip To blanch and peel chestnuts,
make a crosswise cut in the base of
each and put them in a pan with
enough boiling water to cover.
Allow them to cook for 5–6
minutes, then drain and peel off
both outer and inner skins.

Vegetables

Baked jacket potatoes

Serves 4

*4 large floury potatoes, scrubbed and
   dried*
1–2 tablespoons oil
salt

Set the oven at moderately hot
(200 c, 400 f, gas 6).

Cut a shallow cross on the surface
of each potato, brush with a little oil
and sprinkle with salt. Wrap each
potato in kitchen foil, making sure
each one is securely sealed. Do not
wrap the potatoes too tightly, as the
potato will swell a little as it cooks.
Bake the potatoes in the heated
oven for about 1 hour, or until one
feels soft right through when tested
with a fork or skewer.

Unwrap the potatoes and lightly
press each one to open out the cut
on top. Fill this with a tablespoonful
of soured cream for each potato and
sprinkle with snipped chives.
Alternatively, serve with a pat of
chilled butter.

Baked potatoes go well with most
grilled or fried meat, especially
steaks; try them with sausages or
grilled fish steaks.

Baked caraway potatoes

Serves 4

1 tablespoon coarse salt
2–3 tablespoons caraway seeds
*8 medium potatoes, scrubbed, dried
   and halved*
50 g/2 oz melted butter

Set the oven at moderately hot
(200 c, 400 f, gas 6). Mix the salt and
caraway seeds together and dip the
cut surfaces of each halved potato in
the mixture. Set the potatoes on a
baking sheet, spoon a little melted
butter over each and bake them in
the preheated oven for 30–35
minutes. Serve piping hot, with
grills, roast pork and a crisp green
salad.

Fan potatoes

Serves 4

675 g/1½ lb medium potatoes, peeled
salt
paprika
75 g/3 oz butter

Set the oven at moderately hot
(200 c, 400 f, gas 6). Cut each potato
across in the thinnest possible slices,
without cutting right through to the
base. Gently separate the slices so
that the potato 'fans' out. Season by
sprinkling lightly with salt and
paprika. Grease an ovenproof
baking dish or tin with a little of the
butter and set the potatoes in it,
uncut side down.

Melt the rest of the butter and
pour it over the potatoes. Bake
them in the moderately hot oven for
45–50 minutes, basting frequently as
they cook, until they are golden-
brown.

Serve with grilled, poached or
fried fish, game and steaks or grills.

Variation
Sprinkle the fan potatoes with a
little grated Parmesan or Cheddar
cheese 10 minutes before the end of
the cooking time. Serve with freshly
ground black pepper.

Ardennes-style potatoes

Serves 4

4 equal-sized potatoes
100 g/4 oz lean cooked ham, diced
2 tablespoons chopped chives
50 g/2 oz butter
salt and freshly ground black pepper
*50 g/2 oz grated Emmental or
   Cheddar cheese*

Bake the potatoes following the
recipe above. Leave the oven set at
moderately hot, (200 c, 400 f, gas 6).

Unwrap each foil-baked potato
and cut a 'lid' from the top of each.
Scoop out the inside, leaving a
1-cm/½-in shell. Mash the cooked

potato until smooth and stir in the
diced ham, chives and butter.
Sprinkle inside the hollowed-out
potato shells with a little salt, then
pile the mixture back into each
potato. Sprinkle with cheese and
bake for 10–15 minutes until the
cheese is melted and golden. Season
with pepper and serve with roast
poultry or game and baked or fried
fish steaks or fillets.

Anna potatoes

Serves 4

*675 g/1½ lb potatoes, peeled and very
   thinly sliced*
75 g/3 oz softened butter
salt
pinch of paprika

Set the oven at moderately hot
(200 c, 400 f, gas 6). Rinse the sliced
potatoes in cold water to rid them of
excess starch, then dry them well.
Generously grease the inside of an
ovenproof baking dish with some of
the butter. Arrange the sliced
potatoes in layered circles, with the
edges overlapping. Dot every second
layer with softened butter and
sprinkle it with salt and a little
paprika. Continue in this way until
the baking dish is filled. Season the
top layer and dot with the remaining
butter. Cover the dish with foil and
bake in the moderately hot oven for
40–45 minutes. Test with a skewer
— the exact cooking time depends
on the type of the potatoes and the
thickness of the slices.

Turn the potatoes out whole on to
a heated dish and serve with calf's
or lamb's liver, veal escalopes or
baked or steamed fish.

Vegetables

Potato purée

Serves 4

675 g/1½ lb potatoes, peeled and
  cooked
about 200 ml/7 fl oz hot milk
salt and freshly ground pepper
40 g/1½ oz butter or margarine
a little grated nutmeg

Drain the potatoes well and, if
necessary, return them to the pan
and toss over gentle heat until all
excess water has evaporated and
they are quite dry. Mash them
throughly or pass through a sieve.
Beat in the hot milk a little at a time
and season to taste with salt and
pepper. Add the butter or margarine
piece by piece, beating between
each addition until a light, fluffy
purée is formed. Season with a little
nutmeg before serving.

Variations
Special potato purée Use half the
given amount of milk, making up
the quantity with an equal amount
of cream. An egg yolk and up to
100 g/4 oz grated cheese may also be
beaten into the potato. For an extra

special finish, spread the potato in a
heated serving dish and finish off
under a preheated hot grill until the
top bubbles and turns a golden-
brown. Onion softened in a little
butter or a handful of mushrooms,
sliced and sautéed, also make tasty
additions.
    A little crushed garlic and/or
chopped fresh herbs in season lend a
distinctive touch. Or try beating in
some soured cream and one or two
chopped hard-boiled eggs for
flavour.

Duchesse potatoes Replace 2–3
tablespoons of the milk with single
cream and add an egg yolk to the
seasoned potato purée, as above.
Spoon the potato into a piping bag
fitted with a vegetable nozzle.
Grease a baking tray and pipe out
large rosettes on to it, keeping them
apart. Bake in a moderately hot
oven (200 c, 400 f, gas 6) for about
15 minutes, or until the tops are
crisp and golden brown.

Potato nests or baskets Make the
purée as for Duchesse potatoes
(above) and spoon it into a piping
bag fitted with a vegetable nozzle.

Pipe circles of potato, about the size
of the palm of your hand, on to a
greased baking tray. Decorate round
the edge of each one with small
rosettes, using up all the potato.
Bake as for Duchesse potatoes.
Serve on a heated serving dish, filled
with diced cooked vegetables, or
lightly scrambled egg.

Potato croquettes Beat 2 egg yolks
into the potato purée, then stiffen it
by beating in 2 tablespoons flour.
Shape the mixture into balls about
3-cm/1-in. in diameter, or into
small, cork-shaped rolls. Dip these
in beaten egg and coat with dried
breadcrumbs. Fry in deep hot fat, a
few at a time, and drain on
absorbent kitchen paper.

Rösti

Serves 4

675 g/1½ lb potatoes, peeled
50 g/2 oz butter
salt and freshly ground black pepper

Boil the potatoes for 15 minutes only then drain and allow them to cool. Shred or grate the potatoes, using a coarse grater. Melt half the butter in a heavy based frying pan, add the grated potato and season with salt and pepper. Spread out the potato into an even layer, pressing it down with a fork or spatula to flatten the 'cake'. Fry over medium heat until golden-brown and crisp on the underside, then slide it out on to a plate, flip over the rösti and fry on the other side, adding a little extra butter, if necessary. Serve hot.

A classic Swiss dish, it makes the perfect accompaniment to veal escalopes, but can also be served with ragoûts, or grilled meat.

Tiny individual rösti are sometimes made and served as canapés.

Variations
Try mixing a little finely diced bacon or blanched onion with the grated potato. Flavour the rösti with a little garlic, a few chopped fresh herbs, or sprinkle with cheese (Swiss for preference) and finish off under the grill.

Fried potatoes with onions

Serves 4

675 g/1½ lb potatoes, peeled and very
* thinly sliced*
6 tablespoons oil
3 medium onions, peeled and sliced
* in thin rings*
2–3 cloves of garlic, crushed with a
* little salt*
salt and freshly ground white pepper
1–2 tablespoons chopped chives

Make sure the potatoes are dry by patting with absorbent kitchen paper. Heat the oil in a pan and, when hot, fry the sliced potatoes, turning them constantly, for a minute or two before adding the onion rings. Continue frying, stirring and turning constantly; the potatoes should take 15–20 minutes depending on thickness. Five minutes before the end of the cooking time, mix in the garlic and season to taste with salt and pepper. Arrange on a heated serving dish and sprinkle with the chives.

These fried potatoes make a savoury accompaniment to fried eggs, bacon, sausages, or fried or baked fish.

Tip For really thinly sliced potatoes, use a mandoline grater.

Salads
for all Seasons

Salads

Dandelion salad

Serves 4

*100 g/4 oz rashers streaky bacon,
  derinded and finely chopped or
  diced*
*1 medium onion, peeled and finely
  chopped*
*2 cloves of garlic, peeled and crushed
  with a little salt*
2 slices white bread, finely diced
*450 g/1 lb dandelion leaves, picked
  over, washed and dried*

Dressing
2 hard-boiled eggs, halved
*4 tablespoons dry sherry vinegar or
  wine vinegar*
1 teaspoon made English mustard
salt and freshly ground black pepper

Dry fry the bacon in a heavy-based
pan over medium heat, stirring
constantly until the fat runs and the
bacon is lightly browned and crisp.
Add the onion and garlic with the
bread dice and continue frying until
both the onion and the bread are
golden brown, adding a little extra
fat if necessary. Set aside to drain
on absorbent kitchen paper.
  Remove the yolks from the eggs
and push through a fine-meshed
sieve, then beat to a creamy
consistency with the dry sherry or
wine vinegar and mustard. Season to
taste with salt and pepper. Finely
chop the egg whites.
  Arrange the dandelion leaves in a
large bowl or serving dish and pour
over the dressing. Gently reheat the
bacon mixture and spoon it over the
salad. Garnish with the chopped egg
whites.

Variations
This recipe also works well with
finely shredded raw spinach instead
of dandelion leaves. And for those
who like a contrast between a cold
salad and a hot dressing, arrange the
salad leaves on the dish, then stir
the egg-yolk dressing into the bacon
and crouton mixture. Pour this hot
dressing over the salad, add the egg
whites and serve at once.

Avocado salad

Serves 4

*225 g/8 oz fresh asparagus spears,
  cooked and drained or
  1 (298-g/10½-oz) can of asparagus
  spears, drained*
*1 (225-g/8-oz) can palm hearts,
  drained and thinly sliced*
2 tablespoons capers, drained
3 ripe avocados
juice of 1 lemon
150 ml/¼ pint natural yogurt
salt and freshly ground white pepper
pinch each of sugar and cayenne
1 small carton cress

Slice the asparagus spears into
5-cm/2-in lengths and put them in a
salad bowl with the palm hearts and
capers. Halve two of the avocados,
remove the stones and peel. Thinly
slice the flesh and sprinkle with
lemon juice to prevent discoloration.
Add them to the salad bowl.
  For the dressing, halve, stone,
peel and purée the third avocado
with the rest of the lemon juice and
the yogurt. Season to taste with salt,
pepper and sugar, then add a
sprinkling of cayenne and stir
thoroughly to mix.
  Rinse the cress in cold water and
strip off the leaves. Reserve about a
third for the garnish and stir the rest
into the dressing. Arrange the salad
in the bowl, pour over the dressing
and sprinkle with the reserved cress.

Note Serve the salad as soon as
possible after making otherwise the
avocados may turn brown.

Variations
For a stronger flavour, add 2 spring
onion stalks. Either cut these into
thin slices, or cut each into 5-cm/
2-in lengths and cut halfway down
the stalk, making cross cuts so that
the cut end of each looks like a
brush. Soak them in iced water so
the ends curl outwards, before
draining and adding to the salad.
  Try adding a few coarsely
chopped shelled walnuts or
hazelnuts to the dressing for a
contrast in texture, and to
complement the slightly nutty
flavour of the avocados.

Green pea salad

Serves 4

350 g/12 oz cooked peas
*1 (142-g/5-oz) can sweet corn
  kernels, drained*
*1 medium green pepper, deseeded
  and finely chopped*
*1 medium yellow or red pepper,
  deseeded and finely chopped*
*2 celery stalks, washed and thinly
  sliced*
1 tablespoon chopped parsley
*1 head of chicory, washed and
  separated into leaves*

Dressing
2 tablespoons herb or cider vinegar
salt and freshy ground pepper
pinch of cayenne
pinch of sugar
*3 tablespoons olive oil or 2
  tablespoons olive oil and 1
  tablespoon walnut oil*

Combine all the vegetables except
the chicory and stir in the parsley.
Season the vinegar with salt and
pepper, and sprinkle in a little
cayenne to taste. Add the pinch of
sugar, then whisk in the oil, drop by
drop, until the mixture thickens.
Pour the dressing over the salad
ingredients and chill for 15–20
minutes.
  Line a salad bowl with the chicory
leaves and pile the salad on top.

Cook's Tip

Nut oils are ideal for giving a
simple salad dressing an unusual
flavour. Walnut, hazelnut and
almond are those most commonly
available and should be used to
replace some or all of the olive or
vegetable oil used in a dressing. The
amount required will depend on the
strength of the oil and individual
taste so experiment until you find
the right combination of flavours.

Salads

Radiccio salad

Serves 4

2–3 heads of radiccio, washed, trimmed and torn into strips
1 red pepper, deseeded, cored and cut into thin rings
2 red-skinned (Welsh) onions, peeled and cut into thin rings
1 small bunch radishes, trimmed, washed, drained and sliced
½ small carton cress to garnish

Dressing
2 tablespoons red wine vinegar
salt and freshly ground black pepper
3–4 tablespoons oil
1 clove of garlic, peeled and crushed with a little salt

Mix together the radiccio, pepper and onion rings in a bowl and arrange the sliced radishes on top.

For the dressing, season the vinegar with salt then add plenty of freshly ground black pepper. Whisk in the oil, drop by drop, until the mixture thickens. Add the garlic and pour the dressing over the salad. Toss lightly. Rinse and snip the leaves from the cress and sprinkle them over the salad.

Serve at once, before the leaves lose their crispness.

Note Radiccio is a red-leaved, white-stemmed salad plant with crisp leaves, similar to lettuce in taste. It is generally imported from Italy and is becoming increasingly available in Great Britain as its attractive leaves are a popular addition to many salads.

Variations
Add 2–3 tomatoes, skinned, deseeded and sliced. For a main course at lunch, add strips of cold cooked beef and 2 sliced hard-boiled eggs.

Red bean salad

Serves 4

1 (425-g/15-oz) can red kidney beans, rinsed and drained
1 red pepper, deseeded and diced
2 ripe tomatoes, skinned, deseeded and diced
1 red-skinned (Welsh) onion, peeled and diced

Dressing
1 tablespoon wine vinegar or cider vinegar
salt and freshly ground black pepper
3 tablespoons olive oil
dash of Tabasco sauce
1 clove of garlic, peeled and crushed with a little salt

Garnish
2 sprigs fresh thyme
2 sprigs fresh basil

Put the beans in a salad bowl with the diced pepper, tomatoes and onion and mix the ingredients well.

For the dressing, season the vinegar with a little salt and plenty of freshly ground black pepper. Whisk in the oil a little at a time. Add the Tabasco and garlic. Pour the dressing over the salad and toss lightly. Cover the salad and chill for 20 minutes.

Before serving, adjust the seasoning and garnish with sprigs of thyme and basil.

Tip If fresh thyme and basil are not obtainable, sprinkle ½ teaspoon each of dried thyme and basil into the dressing with the garlic.

Beetroot salad

Serves 4

350 g/12 oz cooked beetroot, cut in julienne strips
1 small cooking apple, peeled, coarsely grated and sprinkled with the juice of 1 lemon

Dressing
1–2 tablespoons horseradish sauce or creamed horseradish
150 ml/¼ pint natural yogurt
salt and freshly ground black pepper
pinch of sugar

Mix together the beetroot and apple in a salad bowl.

For the dressing, beat the horseradish into the yogurt and season well with salt and pepper, then add a pinch of sugar. Pour over the beetroot and apple mixture and stir well. Cover and chill for 15–20 minutes to allow the flavours to mingle.

Adjust the seasoning before serving.

Variation
Substitute 3–4 tablespoons soured cream for half the yogurt in the dressing, and substitute finely grated fresh celeriac for up to one third of the beetroot.

Cook's Tip

Spread a piece of moistened grease-proof paper over the chopping board before slicing beetroot to prevent the juice staining the board.

Salads

Potato salad

Serves 4

*675 g/1½ lb small potatoes, boiled in
    their skins*
*2 medium onions, peeled and finely
    chopped*
salt and freshly ground pepper
2 tablespoons oil
*100 g/4 oz lean bacon rashers,
    derinded and chopped*
4 tablespoons herb vinegar

Garnish
*2 tablespoons finely chopped dill or
    parsley*
2 tablespoons chopped chives

Drain the potatoes, rinse under cold
running water then, holding each in
turn on a fork, peel while still hot
and slice them. Put them in a bowl
and add half the chopped onion.
Season with salt and pepper.

Heat the oil in a pan and briskly
fry the bacon until cooked, then
remove the bacon from the pan with
a slotted spoon and set aside.

Fry the rest of the onion in the
hot fat and oil until transparent but
not browned.

Return the bacon to the pan and
mix with the cooked onion. Pour
this mixture with the vinegar, into
the potato salad, cover the bowl and
leave to stand for 10 minutes for the
flavours to mingle.

Adjust the seasoning if necessary.
Serve with the chopped herbs
sprinkled over.

Tip It is important to use waxy-
textured potatoes such as Desirée or
Pentland Crown for salads, as floury
varieties such as King Edward or
Maris Piper will disintegrate when
cooked and sliced.

Special potato salad

Serves 4–6

*675 g/1½ lb small potatoes, cooked,
    drained, then peeled and sliced*
*1 medium onion, peeled and finely
    chopped*
*1 dessert apple, peeled, cored and
    thinly sliced, then sprinkled with
    the juice of ½ lemon*
150 g / 5 oz cooked ham, cut in strips
½ small cucumber, thinly sliced
*1 small pickled cucumber, thinly
    sliced or chopped*
2 tablespoons pickled onions, halved
*small bunch of radishes, trimmed,
    washed and sliced*
*2 hard-boiled eggs, chopped to
    garnish*

Dressing
3 tablespoons mayonnaise (page 112)
3 tablespoons natural yogurt
1–2 teaspoons made French mustard
1 tablespoon herb or cider vinegar
*1 teaspoon juice from the pickled
    cucumber jar*
salt and freshly ground black pepper
pinch of paprika

Mix together the potatoes, onion,
apple, ham, fresh and pickled
cucumber, the pickled onions and
radishes and turn into a salad bowl.

For the dressing, beat together the
mayonnaise and yogurt, then beat in
the mustard, vinegar and pickle
juice. Season to taste with salt,
pepper and paprika and stir it into
the salad. Cover the bowl and chill
for 30 minutes. Adjust the seasoning
before serving and garnish with
hard-boiled egg.

Variations
Slices of your favourite continental
sausage can be substituted for the
cooked ham. Vary the other
ingredients according to taste: add 4
or 5 canned artichoke hearts, cut in
quarters, or 4 sticks of celery,
washed and chopped, or 1 small
leek, blanched and sliced, or 50 g/
2 oz stuffed olives, drained and
sliced.

Potato salads are always improved
by a sprinkling of fresh, leafy herbs
or parsley just before serving. Sliced
mushrooms whether raw or lightly
blanched also make a good addition
to a potato salad.

If you substitute fish or shellfish
— pieces of smoked fish or shelled,
cooked prawns — for the meat, add
a tablespoon of creamed horseradish
to the dressing, with plenty of
chopped parsley.

Tip Really small new potatoes can
be left unpeeled. Choose ones of an
even size for the best appearance in
the finished dish.

Cook's Tip

Always cook potatoes for a salad
until just tender but no more so that
they slice well. Remember to mix all
the ingredients together very gently
so that the potato slices do not
break up.

Salads

Chicken salad

Serves 4

*1 Iceberg or Webbs Wonder lettuce,
    washed and torn into strips*
*3 sticks of celery, washed and thinly
    sliced*
*4 cooked chicken joints, skinned and
    flesh cut into chunks*
½ carton cress, washed and snipped
*2 ripe pears, peeled, cored and
    sliced, then sprinkled with juice of
    ½ lemon*
*2 tablespoons coarsely chopped
    salted peanuts to garnish*

Dressing
150 ml/¼ pint natural yogurt
2 tablespoons soured cream
a little extra lemon juice (optional)
salt and freshly ground white pepper
*pinch each of sugar, cayenne and
    paprika*

Put the lettuce in a bowl with the
celery and chicken. Sprinkle over
the snipped cress and add the pears.
   For the dressing, stir the yogurt
into the soured cream and add a

little extra lemon juice, if liked.
Season to taste with salt and pepper,
sugar, cayenne and paprika. Pour
the dressing over the salad, toss
gently once or twice and sprinkle the
peanuts over the salad before
serving.

Variation
Substitute canned or fresh peaches
or pineapple chunks for the ripe
pears.

Summer beef salad

Serves 4

*175 g/6 oz fillet steak, fried in a little
    oil, then seasoned and left to cool*
*175 g/6 oz cooked French beans, cut
    in 5-cm/2-inch lengths*
*100 g/4 oz fresh button mushrooms,
    thinly sliced*
1 shallot, peeled and thinly sliced
*1 large head radiccio or Iceberg
    lettuce, washed and leaves
    separated*
*a little chopped lemon balm
    (optional) to garnish*

Dressing
salt and freshly ground black pepper
2 tablespoons wine vinegar
4 tablespoons oil
*½ level teaspoon made French
    mustard*
1 tablespoon chopped parsley
1 tablespoon chopped tarragon

Cut the steak into thin strips and
mix with the beans, mushrooms and
shallot. Line a salad bowl with
radiccio or lettuce leaves and tear
the rest into strips. Mix the torn
leaves with the rest of the salad
vegetables and turn these into the
salad bowl.
   For the dressing, whisk salt and
pepper into the vinegar to season it
to taste, then whisk in the oil a little
at a time. Stir in the mustard and
chopped herbs and pour the dressing
over the salad, garnishing with
lemon balm, if liked.

Mixed pepper salad

Serves 4–6

175 g/6 oz cooked tongue or smoked
*   beef, cut in thin strips*
1 red pepper, deseeded and sliced
1 green pepper, deseeded and sliced
1 yellow pepper, deseeded and sliced
1 large, mild-flavoured onion
1 small fennel heart, washed,
*   trimmed and thinly sliced*
½ small cos lettuce, washed and torn
*   into thin strips*
2 tomatoes, skinned and chopped
3 hard-boiled eggs, halved
2 tablespoons tarragon vinegar or
*   white wine vinegar*
1 teaspoon made French mustard
4 tablespoons oil
salt and freshly ground black pepper
½ teaspoon paprika pepper
pinch of cayenne
2 teaspoons capers
1 tablespoon snipped chives
1 tablespoon chopped parsley

Put the meat into a salad bowl and
add the prepared vegetables. Toss
them to mix lightly. Remove the
yolks from the hard-boiled eggs and
finely chop the whites. Sieve the
yolks, then beat them into the
vinegar with the mustard. Whisk in
the oil, drop by drop, then season
with salt, pepper, paprika and
cayenne to taste and pour the
dressing over the salad. Add the
capers, chives and parsley and toss
well. Garnish with chopped egg
white.

Courgette and cheese salad

Serves 4–6

100 ml/4 fl oz dry white wine
4 tablespoons olive oil
3 medium courgettes, wiped, trimmed
*   and thinly sliced*
salt and freshly ground black pepper
2 medium onions, peeled and sliced
*   into rings*
1 green pepper, deseeded and cut
*   into thin rings*
100 g/4 oz lean cooked ham, cut into
*   strips*
2 ripe tomatoes, cut into eighths
2 tablespoons white wine vinegar
100 g/4 oz cheese such as White
*   Stilton, Cheshire or Wensleydale,*
*   crumbled or diced*
shredded lettuce to garnish (optional)

Bring the wine to the boil in a pan
with the olive oil and add the sliced
courgettes. Season with salt and
pepper and allow them to cook for 3
to 5 minutes, until cooked but still
slightly crisp. Lift out the courgette
slices, set them aside and leave to
cool, then reduce the cooking liquid
in the pan by about two-thirds by
boiling rapidly. Set the pan aside,
reserving the cooking liquid.

Put the onion rings in a colander
and pour boiling water over them to
soften them slightly. Allow to cool.

Put the pepper, ham and tomatoes
into a bowl and stir to mix them
together. Add the cooled courgettes
and the onion rings and mix the
ingredients again.

Beat the vinegar into the cooled
cooking liquid then pour it over the
salad. Sprinkle over the white
cheese and garnish with shredded
lettuce.

Salads

Endive and grapefruit salad

Serves 4

*1 head endive, wiped, trimmed and
  thinly sliced*
*1 large grapefruit, peeled and cut into
  neat segments*
*1 shallot or small onion, peeled and
  finely chopped*
50 g/2 oz roughly chopped walnuts

Dressing
150 ml/¼ pint natural yogurt
1 teaspoon walnut or olive oil
salt and freshly ground black pepper
*pinch each of sugar and ground
  ginger*
1–2 teaspoons brandy

Put the endive in a bowl with the
grapefruit and onion, toss gently,
then add the nuts. For the dressing
whisk the yogurt with the oil and
season it well with salt, pepper,
sugar and ginger. Stir in enough
brandy to add a little extra
piquancy, then pour the dressing
over the salad. Turn the salad lightly
and serve immediately.

Winter salad with chicken livers

Serves 4

225 g/8 oz chicken livers, trimmed
40 g/1½ oz butter or 3 tablespoons oil
salt and freshly ground black pepper
*small bunch (about 100 g/4 oz) corn
  salad (lamb's lettuce), rinsed and
  dried*
*2 small heads of chicory, wiped,
  trimmed and thinly sliced*
*1 head radiccio, trimmed and leaves
  separated (optional)*
*1 small leek, very thinly sliced, then
  washed and dried*

Dressing
2 tablespoons white wine vinegar
salt and freshly ground black pepper
4 tablespoons olive oil

Pat the chicken livers with absorbent
kitchen paper to remove any excess
moisture. Melt the butter, or heat
the oil, in a pan and fry the livers
briskly on all sides for about 3
minutes, or until cooked. Lift out
with a slotted spoon and leave to
drain on absorbent kitchen paper.
Season with salt and pepper.

Whisk the vinegar with salt and
pepper to taste, then whisk in the
oil, a little at a time.

Pour the dressing into a large
salad bowl, add all the salad
ingredients except the chicken livers
and toss them in the dressing. Thinly
slice the cooked chicken livers and
arrange on top, then spoon a little
of the dressing from the bottom of
the bowl over the livers before
serving.

Tip This winter salad also goes well
with thin slices of rare roast beef,
cut into strips, or poultry, cut into
shreds. Try adding half an onion,
peeled and grated or very finely
chopped, to the dressing, or crush a
clove of garlic with a little salt for a
stronger flavour, and add this to the
dressing.

Salad frisée

Serves 4

½ small head of endive, washed, dried and torn into bite-sized pieces
1 bulb of fennel, wiped, trimmed and sliced
1 red pepper, deseeded and sliced
1 green pepper, deseeded and sliced
2 onions, peeled and cut into thin rings
100 g / 4 oz button mushrooms, wiped and thinly sliced, sprinkled with 1 – 2 tablespoons lemon juice
2 hard-boiled eggs, cut into eighths
2 tablespoons chopped parsley

Dressing
2 tablespoons white wine vinegar
½ teaspoon made English mustard
salt and freshly ground black pepper
pinch of sugar
1 – 2 cloves of garlic, crushed with a little salt
4 tablespoons olive oil

Mix all the salad ingredients in a large bowl, adding the chopped parsley, then make the dressing. Whisk together the vinegar and mustard, then add salt, pepper and sugar, stirring well until the salt and sugar have dissolved. Add the garlic and whisk in the oil a little at a time. Pour the dressing over the salad and toss lightly. Serve immediately.

Salade niçoise

Serves 4 – 6

450 g / 1 lb small potatoes, boiled in their skins, then peeled and sliced
350 g / 12 oz cooked green beans, drained and refreshed in cold water
2 large ripe tomatoes, skinned, deseeded and thinly sliced
8 green olives, stoned and sliced
8 black olives, stones and sliced
1 shallot, peeled and finely diced
1 (50-g / 1¾-oz) can anchovies, rinsed and drained
2 tablespoons capers

Dressing
3 tablespoons red wine vinegar
salt and freshly ground black pepper
pinch of sugar
5 tablespoons olive oil

Mix together all the salad ingredients in a large bowl, then make the dressing. Whisk the vinegar with the salt, pepper and sugar, then whisk in the oil a little at a time. Pour it over the salad, cover and chill for 30 minutes before serving.

Cook's Tip

A (198-g / 7-oz) can of tuna fish, drained and flaked, can be added to the salad to make it into a light luncheon dish. Hard-boiled eggs, peeled and cut into eighths, make a good addition as do courgettes, sliced and lightly cooked.

149

Salads

Rice salad

Serves 4

225 g/8 oz long-grain rice, cooked
  and drained
1 large mild onion, peeled and finely
  chopped
1 red pepper, deseeded and diced
1 green pepper, deseeded and diced
2 pickled cucumbers, drained and
  finely sliced
1 apple, peeled, cored and diced,
  then sprinkled with lemon juice
225 g/8 oz continental sausage (e.g.
  Mortadella or salami), skinned and
  sliced
10 black olives, drained and stoned

Dressing
2 tablespoons wine or cider vinegar
salt and freshly ground pepper
1 teaspoon paprika
1 clove of garlic, peeled and crushed
  with a little salt
2 tablespoons chopped parsley
1 tablespoon chopped chives
2 tablespoons mayonnaise (page 112)
1 teaspoon concentrated tomato
  purée (optional)
150 ml/¼ pint natural yogurt

To serve
few large lettuce leaves
extra chopped chives

Mix together all the salad
ingredients in a large salad bowl and
leave, covered, to chill while making
the dressing. Whisk the vinegar with
a generous seasoning of salt and
pepper until the salt dissolves.
Whisk in the paprika, add the garlic
and stir in two-thirds of the parsley
and chives. Mix in the mayonnaise,
tomato purée (if using) and yogurt.
Stir gently to mix all the dressing
ingredients and adjust the seasoning
— it should be piquant and a little
sharp.
  Mix the dressing into the salad,
cover and chill for about 1 hour.
Line four individual serving plates
with lettuce leaves and top with the
salad. Garnish with the remaining
parsley and chives.

Variations
Try adding a small can of sweet corn
kernels, well drained, to the salad,
or 2 – 3 tablespoons leftover cooked
peas. Sliced fresh button mushrooms
make a good variation, and a few
capers or pickled onions add extra
piquancy.

Oriental rice salad

Serves 4

225 g/8 oz long-grain, saffron-
  flavoured rice (see Note below)
4 dried Chinese mushrooms, soaked
  in tepid water for up to 1 hour and
  sliced
1 (298-g/10½-oz) can bamboo
  shoots, drained and sliced
175 g/6 oz bean sprouts, rinsed and
  drained
small bunch spring onions, washed
  and sliced into thin rings

Dressing
3 tablespoons rice wine or dry sherry
1 tablespoon soy sauce
2 tablespoons wine vinegar
freshly ground white pepper
½ teaspoon hot chilli sauce (optional)
1 clove of garlic, peeled and crushed
  with a little salt
pinch each of ground ginger and
  sugar
5 tablespoons oil
salt (optional)

Pile the rice in a bowl, then drain
and add the mushrooms. Mix in the
bamboo shoots, bean sprouts and
most of the spring onion and set
these ingredients aside while making
the dressing.
  For the dressing, stir the rice wine
or sherry with the soy sauce and
vinegar, then add a generous
sprinkling of pepper. Add the chilli
sauce, if using, then the garlic,
ginger and sugar. Whisk in the oil, a
little at a time. Adjust the
seasoning, adding a little salt, if
necessary, although the soy sauce
and hot seasoning may make the
sauce quite salty enough for most
tastes.
  Stir the dressing into the salad,
cover and leave to stand for about
30 minutes. Adjust the seasoning
again, if necessary, and serve
sprinkled with the reserved spring
onion. This salad goes well with cold
meat, especially pork.

Note Use 3 saffron strands, or a
large pinch ground saffron to flavour
the cooking water for the rice, and
from ½ – 1 tablespoon curry powder,
depending on individual taste.
Turmeric can be substituted for the
more expensive saffron as it will
colour the rice although, of course,
the flavour will be rather different–
spicy rather than aromatic.

Cold meat and rice salad

Serves 4 – 6

225 g/8 oz long-grain rice, cooked,
  drained and cooled
225 g/8 oz lean cooked meat (pork,
  veal or chicken), cut into neat
  cubes
1 small leek, sliced into thin rings,
  then washed and drained
2 canned pineapple rings, drained
  and cut into chunks
1 orange, peeled and segmented with
  all pith and membrane removed
1 tablespoon mango chutney
1 canned pimiento, drained and
  finely diced
a few lettuce leaves
1 small bunch of watercress, washed
  and drained (optional)

Dressing
1 – 2 tablespoons pineapple juice
150 ml/¼ pint double cream, lightly
  whipped
pinch of chilli powder
salt and freshly ground pepper
pinch of cayenne

Pile the rice into a bowl, add the
meat, leek, and pineapple and mix
into the rice. Cut each orange
segment across into three and stir
into the salad. Add the chutney and
pimiento and mix all these
ingredients together well. Cover and
set aside while making the dressing.
  Stir the pineapple juice into the
cream, add the chilli powder and
season to taste with salt, pepper and
cayenne. Pour the dressing over the
uncovered salad.
  Turn the salad carefully in the
dressing, cover the bowl and leave
to stand for about 30 minutes before
adjusting the seasoning and serving.
Serve on indvidual plates, lined with
a few lettuce leaves. Garnish with
watercress, if liked.

Tip Rice salads are good for serving
at buffet parties as they need to
stand for a while for the flavours to
mingle and stay fresher longer. They
are also convenient for taking on
picnics.

Salads

Scandinavian mushroom salad

Serves 4

*1 small lettuce, washed and leaves
 separated*
*225 g/8 oz button mushrooms, wiped
 and thinly sliced, then sprinkled
 with 2 tablespoons lemon juice*

Dressing
*150 ml/¼ pint double or whipping
 cream*
juice of ½ lemon
salt and freshly ground pepper
*pinch each of sugar and mustard
 powder*
½ onion, peeled and grated
*½ small carton cress, snipped, or
 small bunch fresh dill, finely
 chopped*

Divide any large lettuce leaves into
two and use them to line 4
individual plates. Arrange a portion
of mushrooms on top of each.

For the dressing, whisk the cream
with the lemon juice and season
with salt and freshly ground pepper.
Add the sugar and mustard powder
and stir in the onion. Spoon a

portion on each plate and sprinkle
with cress, or dill. Serve
immediately—if left for long the
mushrooms may discolour.

Tip Parsley may be used instead of
dill, though it is the dill which adds
the Scandinavian touch to this
simple salad.

Radish salad

Serves 4

*2 bunches radishes, topped, tailed
 and thinly sliced, then spread out
 and sprinkled with salt*
*2 tart dessert apples, peeled, cored
 and thinly sliced, then sprinkled
 with lemon juice*
*1 small cucumber, wiped and very
 thinly sliced*

Dressing
*50 g/2 oz blue or white Stilton,
 mashed or crumbled*
100 ml/4 fl oz soured cream
3 tablespoons natural yogurt
salt and freshly ground pepper
dash of wine vinegar
pinch of sugar

Thoroughly drain the radishes and
pat dry with absorbent kitchen
paper. Mix with the apple and
cucumber and arrange in a salad
bowl or dish.

For the dressing, mash the cheese
with the soured cream and yogurt,
then season well with salt and
pepper and continue beating until
the mixture is smooth. Whisk in the
vinegar and add a pinch of sugar.
Adjust the seasoning, if necessary
and pour the dressing over the
salad. Serve immediately, tossing the
salad at the table.

Fish and vegetable salad

Serves 4

½ head of crisp lettuce, washed and
    torn into strips
450 g/1 lb white fish fillets, poached
100 g/4 oz cooked peas
100 g/4 oz button mushrooms, wiped
    and thinly sliced, then sprinkled
    with a little lemon juice
2 hard-boiled eggs, cut lengthways
    into eighths
1 (298-g/10½-oz) can asparagus
    spears, drained

Dressing

100 ml/4 fl oz soured cream
150 ml/¼ pint natural yogurt
salt and freshly ground white pepper
pinch of cayenne
dash of Worcestershire sauce
1-2 tablespoons chopped dill or
    parsley

Line a salad bowl with the lettuce.
Pat the cooked fish dry with
absorbent kitchen paper and break it
into large flakes. Place these in the
salad bowl, add the peas,
mushrooms, eggs and asparagus
spears. Cover and set aside while
making the dressing.

Whisk together the ingredients for
the dressing and pour over the salad
before serving.

Curried fish salad with fruit

Serves 4

450 g/1 lb white fish fillets, poached,
    cooled and drained
1 medium onion, peeled and
    chopped
1 apple, peeled, cored and diced,
    then sprinkled with a little lemon
    juice
1 orange, peeled and segmented
1 banana, cut in slices and sprinkled
    with a little lemon juice
2 canned pineapple rings, drained
    and cut into chunks
salt and freshly ground pepper
a few leaves of lettuce, washed and
    drained (optional)
25 g/1 oz roasted salted peanuts

Dressing

5 tablespoons single cream
150 ml/¼ pint natural yogurt
1 tablespoon mango chutney
salt and freshly ground pepper
1 teaspoon curry paste
pinch each of sugar, cinnamon,
    paprika and cayenne

Pat the fish dry with absorbent
kitchen paper and break into large
flakes. Place these in a salad bowl
with the onion and apple. Cut each
orange segment into two and add to
the salad. Put in the banana and
pineapple and stir very gently to mix
the ingredients. Sprinkle with a little
salt and pepper.

For the dressing, stir the cream
into the yogurt, add the mango
chutney, season to taste with salt
and pepper, then add the curry
paste, sugar, cinnamon, paprika and
cayenne.

Mix together all the ingredients
for the dressing and stir this gently
into the salad. Serve on individual
plates lined with lettuce leaves and
sprinkle each portion with salted
peanuts.

Salads

Oriental chicken salad

Serves 4

4 dried Chinese mushrooms, soaked
  in tepid water for up to 1 hour
1 small (1-kg/2½-lb) chicken,
  cooked, skinned and jointed or
  4 cooked chicken pieces, skinned
1 small leek, trimmed and sliced into
  thin rings, then washed and
  drained
225 g/8 oz bean sprouts, rinsed and
  drained
1 (298-g/10½-oz) can bamboo
  shoots, drained and cut into thin
  strips
8–10 leaves of crisp lettuce or
  Chinese leaves
1 tablespoon chopped chives

Dressing
2 tablespoons soy sauce
4 tablespoons rice wine or dry sherry
salt and freshly ground pepper
pinch each of ground ginger and
  sugar
2 tablespoons oil

Drain the mushrooms, pat dry with
absorbent kitchen paper and slice.
Cut the chicken flesh into neat bite-
sized pieces, discarding the bones
(use these for stock). Put the
chicken pieces into a bowl with the
mushrooms and leek, then add the
bean sprouts and bamboo shoots.
Stir to mix the ingredients lightly,
then set aside while making the
dressing.
  For the dressing, stir the soy sauce
into the rice wine or sherry, then
season lightly with salt (the soy
sauce may already be salty enough)
and generously with pepper, ginger
and sugar. Whisk in the oil, a little
at a time. Pour the dressing over the
salad ingredients, toss gently, then
cover the bowl and leave to
marinate for 15–20 minutes.
  Meanwhile, line a salad bowl with
the lettuce leaves. Adjust the
seasoning of the salad, arrange it on
the lettuce and garnish with chopped
chives before serving.

Variation
If a packet of Chinese egg noodles is
obtainable, cook about 100 g/4 oz in
boiling salted water, drain them,
allow to cool and cut into 2.5-cm/
1-in lengths. Add them to the salad
and leave to stand for a few minutes
to absorb the flavour from the
dressing.

Chicken and sweet corn salad

Serves 4

1 (1-kg/2½-lb) chicken, cooked,
  skinned and jointed or 4 cooked
  chicken pieces, skinned
1 (326-g/11½-oz) can sweet corn
  kernels, drained
1 red pepper, deseeded and finely
  chopped
1 green pepper, deseeded and finely
  chopped
2 ripe tomatoes, skinned, deseeded
  and finely chopped
1 large mild onion, peeled and finely
  chopped
salt and freshly ground white pepper
1 small carton cress, washed and
  snipped

Dressing
2 tablespoons mayonnaise (page 112)
150 ml/¼ pint natural yogurt
juice of ½ lemon
salt and freshly ground white pepper
pinch each of paprika, cayenne and
  sugar

Cut the chicken flesh into bite-sized
pieces, discarding the bones (use
these for stock). Place in a bowl or
dish with the sweet corn, peppers,
tomato and onion, and stir to mix.
Season with salt and pepper and mix
again.
  For the dressing, whisk the
mayonnaise with the yogurt and
lemon juice, then season to taste
with salt and pepper and the spices.
Add a pinch of sugar to lighten the
taste.
  Pour the dressing over the salad
and toss all the ingredients well,
then cover and chill for 20–30
minutes. Adjust the seasoning just
before serving and sprinkle with
snipped cress.

Tip A little chopped garlic, or a
good pinch of garlic salt in the
dressing complements the flavour of
the salad. For a really spicy
dressing, add a dash of Tabasco
sauce, or 1–2 teaspoons
concentrated tomato purée and extra
salt and paprika.

Chicken and cucumber salad

Serves 4

1 (1-kg/2½-lb) chicken, cooked,
  skinned and jointed or 4 cooked
  chicken pieces, skinned
1 small cucumber, wiped and thinly
  sliced
225 g/8 oz button mushrooms, thinly
  sliced and sprinkled with 2
  tablespoons lemon juice
1 small bunch dill or parsley, washed
  and finely chopped with a few
  sprigs reserved for garnish

Dressing
150 ml/¼ pint natural yogurt
4 tablespoons soured cream
4 tablespoons single cream
2 cloves of garlic, peeled and crushed
  with a little salt
salt and freshly ground black pepper
1–2 teaspoons white wine vinegar

Cut the chicken flesh into bite-sized
pieces, discarding the bones (use
these for stock). Put the chicken
into a bowl with the cucumber
slices, reserving a few for garnish.
Add the mushrooms and chopped
dill or parsley. Set aside.
  For the dressing, stir the yogurt
with the soured cream and single
cream, add the crushed garlic, then
season to taste with salt, pepper and
vinegar.
  Pour the dressing over the salad
and toss until all the ingredients are
well coated, then cover the bowl and
let the salad chill for 20–25 minutes.
Adjust the seasoning and garnish
with the reserved cucumber slices
and dill or parsley sprigs for serving.
  This salad is best served while still
chilled.

Variation
A few halved or sliced stoned black
olives add a delicious flavour to this
salad.

Salads

Courgette salad

Serves 4–6

100 ml/4 fl oz olive oil
juice of ½ lemon
150 ml/¼ pint dry white wine
150 ml/¼ pint water
salt and freshly ground black pepper
675 g/1½ lb small courgettes, wiped,
    trimmed and thinly sliced
1 onion, peeled and thinly sliced
2 cloves of garlic, peeled and crushed
    with a little salt
pinch each of dry mustard and sugar
2 ripe tomatoes, skinned and roughly
    chopped
50 g/2 oz roughly chopped walnuts
2 slices dry white bread, crusts
    removed, and cut into dice
1–2 tablespoons chopped parsley

Heat 1 tablespoon of the oil in a
thick-based pan, add the lemon
juice, wine and water and season
with salt and pepper. Once the
liquid has come to the boil, add the
courgettes, and when the liquid
returns to the boil, lower the heat
and cook the sliced courgettes for 2–
3 minutes, until tender but still a
little crisp. Lift out the courgettes
with a slotted spoon, drain well on
absorbent kitchen paper and leave in
a salad bowl to cool. Reduce the
cooking liquid in the pan by boiling
rapidly until about half remains.
Take the pan off the heat, measure
out about 3 tablespoons of the
cooking liquid into a bowl and
discard the rest.
    Beat 2 tablespoons of the oil into
the cooking liquid, then add the
onion, garlic, dry mustard and
sugar. Season with salt and pepper,
and pour over the sliced courgettes
in the salad bowl. Add the tomatoes
and walnuts and turn all the
ingredients lightly to coat with the
liquid.
    Heat the rest of the olive oil in a
heavy-based pan and fry the bread
cubes on all sides until an even,
golden brown, adding an extra clove
of garlic, peeled and crushed with a
little salt, if liked.
    Pour the croûtons and oil over the
salad in the bowl, sprinkle with
parsley and serve immediately.

Note Add a few stuffed green olives,
sliced into rings, for a variation in
flavour.

Mixed vegetable salad

Serves 4–6

1 small cauliflower, trimmed, washed
    and separated into florets
4 sprigs broccoli, trimmed, washed
    and separated into florets, stems
    chopped into 2.5-cm/1-in slices
1 small kohlrabi, peeled and cut into
    julienne strips
2 carrots, peeled and cut into julienne
    strips
100 g/4 oz cooked French beans
175 g/6 oz cooked asparagus spears,
    trimmed if fresh and stems cut into
    2.5-cm/1-in lengths
100 g/4 oz cooked peas
100 g/4 oz button mushrooms, wiped
    and thinly sliced, then sprinkled
    with 1–2 tablespoons lemon juice
1–2 tablespoons chopped chervil or
    parsley

Dressing
juice of 1 lemon
salt and freshly ground white pepper
150 ml/¼ pint soured cream
1 teaspoon French mustard
1–2 cloves of garlic, peeled and
    crushed with a little salt
1 small onion, peeled and grated
2 tablespoons chopped mixed herbs
    (parsley, basil, thyme, chives)

Blanch all the uncooked vegetables
except the mushrooms for a few
minutes in boiling salted water, then
drain and rinse under cold running
water to set the colours and prevent
further cooking. Allow to cool. Trim
the beans into equal lengths and
make the dressing.
    Stir the lemon juice with salt and
pepper until the salt dissolves. Mix
into the soured cream, then add the
mustard, garlic and onion and mix
well. Stir in the mixed herbs.
    Combine all the vegetables in a
bowl with the dressing, then cover
the bowl and leave to stand for
15–20 minutes. Adjust the seasoning
and sprinkle with the chopped mixed
herbs before serving.
    This salad makes a good first
course, or goes particularly well with
boiled ham as a main course.

Prawn and artichoke salad

Serves 4–6

225 g/8 oz corn salad (lamb's
    lettuce), washed and dried
6 canned artichoke hearts, drained
    and quartered
3 hard-boiled eggs, sliced into eighths
75 g/3 oz button mushrooms, wiped
    and thinly sliced, then sprinkled
    with 1–2 tablespoons lemon juice
100 g/4 oz peeled prawns
salt and freshly ground pepper

Garnish
1 tablespoon chopped dill or parsley
1 tablespoon chopped chives

Dressing
2 tablespoons herb or cider vinegar
salt and freshly ground black pepper
pinch of celery salt
dash of Worcestershire sauce
4 tablespoons oil

Put the corn salad in a bowl with the
artichoke hearts, eggs, mushrooms
and prawns. Season lightly with salt
and pepper and set aside while
making the dressing.
    Combine the vinegar with salt and
pepper and a pinch of celery salt,
whisking until the salts dissolve.
Add the Worcestershire sauce, then
beat in the oil a little at a time.
    Pour the dressing over the salad,
turning once so the ingredients are
evenly coated, then sprinkle with dill
or parsley and chives and serve at
once.
    This salad makes an excellent
starter, light lunch dish or side dish.

Variation
This salad is also excellent made
with fresh spinach. The leaves
should be thoroughly washed and
dried then torn into strips.

Salads

Mediterranean cheese salad

Serves 4

½ cucumber, wiped and thinly sliced
1 red pepper, deseeded and cut in
  thin rings
1 green pepper, deseeded and cut in
  thin rings
1 medium onion, peeled and cut in
  thin rings
2 ripe tomatoes, skinned, deseeded
  and quartered
50 g/2 oz stuffed green olives,
  drained and halved crossways
50 g/2 oz black olives, stoned and
  halved
175 g/6 oz Gorgonzola or Roquefort
  cheese, crumbled
freshly ground black pepper
1 tablespoon chopped basil or
  parsley

Dressing

1 tablespoon wine vinegar
salt and freshly ground black pepper
1–2 cloves of garlic, peeled and
  crushed with a little salt
4–5 tablespoons olive oil

Combine all the vegetables in a bowl
and sprinkle over the cheese. Stir to
mix well and season with pepper,
then add the herbs and mix lightly.
  For the dressing, season the
vinegar with a little salt and freshly
ground black pepper, then add the
garlic and whisk in the oil a little at
a time. Pour this over the salad and
toss and serve it at once.

Dutch cheese salad

Serves 4

225 g/8 oz small potatoes, cooked,
  drained and cooled, then peeled
225 g/8 oz Gouda cheese
2 red onions, peeled and sliced
150 g/5 oz cooked tongue, cut in thin
  strips
2 pickled cucumbers, drained and cut
  in thin strips
1 dessert apple, peeled, cored and
  sliced then sprinkled with a little
  lemon juice
salt and freshly ground pepper

Dressing

150 ml/¼ pint soured cream
salt and freshly ground pepper
dash of Worcestershire sauce
1–2 teaspoons French mustard
1 anchovy fillet, rinsed well and
  finely chopped
1 tablespoon tarragon vinegar or
  cider vinegar
1 tablespoon chopped chives

Cut the potatoes and cheese into
small pieces and place in a bowl
with the onion, tongue strips,
cucumber and apple and season with
salt and pepper.
  Beat the soured cream with a little
salt and pepper, the Worcestershire
sauce, mustard, anchovy and
vinegar, then stir in the chives. Pour
the dressing over the salad and turn
the salad ingredients lightly in the
dressing, taking care not to break
the potatoes, cheese or tongue
strips. Cover and chill for about 1
hour, then adjust the seasoning and
serve.

Spiced summer fruit salad

Serves 4

juice of 1 lemon
2 tablespoons whisky
1 tablespoon orange liqueur
225 g/8 oz ripe strawberries, hulled and halved
2 peaches or nectarines, peeled, halved, stones removed and flesh thinly sliced
1 tablespoon bottled green peppercorns, drained (optional)
small sprig of fresh tarragon (optional)
1 crisp lettuce heart (Iceberg or Webbs Wonder), divided into 4
150 ml/¼ pint whipping or double cream
pinch of cayenne

First, combine the lemon juice, whisky and orange liqueur, then add the strawberries, peaches or nectarines and peppercorns, if using. Turn the fruit so it is coated with the liquid, add the tarragon, if using, then chill for 30 minutes.

Meanwhile, line 4 individual dishes with small lettuce leaves and stiffly whip the cream with the cayenne. Arrange a portion of fruit in each dish and top with a spoonful of cream before serving.

Note Instead of lining the dishes with lettuce leaves, the little sprigs from the heart of the lettuce can be left whole and added as a garnish.

Fresh fruit salad

Serves 4

450 g/1 lb mixed soft fruit in season (apples, pears, peaches, strawberries, melon, grapes)
75–100 g/3–4 oz caster sugar
juice of 1 lemon
4 tablespoons rum, brandy or a fruit brandy (cherry or apricot)

Pick over, clean and prepare the fruit as appropriate (e.g. cut melon into cubes, deseed grapes, hull and halve strawberries). Sprinkle with sugar to taste and lemon juice, then pour over the rum, brandy or liqueur. Cover the dish and chill for 20–30 minutes before serving.

Tropical fruit salad

Serves 4

1 small fresh pineapple, peeled, cored and cubed
1 mango, peeled, quartered, stoned and sliced
2 kiwi fruits, peeled and cut across in very thin slices
1 banana, peeled, sliced and sprinkled with a little lemon juice
6 fresh or preserved kumquats, wiped (if fresh) or drained (if preserved), then halved lengthways
2 teaspoons caster sugar
100 ml/4 fl oz Marsala
pinch of ground ginger

Combine the pineapple chunks, mango, kiwi fruit, banana and kumquats in a bowl. Add the sugar to the Marsala and stir well before adding the ginger. Pour the dressing over the fruit and chill for 15–20 minutes before serving.

Rice
and
Pasta

Rice and Pasta

Rice

To cook rice, say the Orientals, is as difficult for Europeans as it is for them to make good tea, because for both one needs a little peace and quiet. And they aren't far wrong, for whoever cooks rice too fast (that is to say over too great a heat) cannot be surprised when all the grains stick together and the rice ends up mushy. So here are two simple, foolproof ways of cooking rice so you'll never again break into a panic because the rice just won't work. You'll get the best results if you use long-grain rice for savoury dishes, short round grain rice for milk puddings and most other desserts.

Rice Indian-style

Serves 4

175 g/6 oz long-grain rice
3 litres/5 pints water
15 g/½ oz salt
75 g/3 oz butter

Set the oven at moderate (180 C, 350 F, gas 4).

Wash and drain the rice as for Rice Chinese-style. Put it in a large deep pan with the water and salt. Bring to the boil and cook rapidly for 6 minutes over high heat, then strain off the water.

Transfer the rice to a warmed casserole. Mix in the butter, put on the lid and continue cooking for 25 minutes in the oven. Serve at once.

Variations
Increase the butter to 100 g/4 oz. Fry 1 chopped onion and 100 g/4 oz chopped mushrooms in it, then mix these into the cooked rice. Or blend a pinch of saffron with the melted butter. Curry powder, ground ginger, chopped blanched almonds, pistachio nuts and raisins all make tasty additions.

Rice Chinese-style

Serves 4

225 g/8 oz long-grain rice
water
1 teaspoon salt

Wash the rice in a sieve under running cold water until the water runs clear, stirring the rice round all the time with your fingers or a spoon. Shake in the sieve to drain thoroughly, then put into a large, ideally non-stick, pan. Cover with water to barely twice the amount of rice in the pan, salt it and cook over high heat till the grains have absorbed all the water.

Cover the pan with a tight-fitting lid and continue cooking over gentle heat for 20 minutes more. Do not stir the rice during this time. Serve as soon as it is ready.

Cheese risotto

Serves 4

50 g/2 oz butter
2 small onions, peeled and chopped
225 g/8 oz long-grain rice, washed
  and drained
100 ml/4 fl oz dry white wine
600 ml/1 pint chicken stock
small pinch of saffron
50 g/2 oz grated Parmesan cheese
50 g/2 oz grated Emmental cheese
salt

Heat half the butter in a deep frying pan. Add the onions and cook till soft and transparent. Add the rice and cook till transparent also, stirring all the time.

Slowly pour in the wine and when it has been completely absorbed, pour in all but 6 tablespoons of the stock
Cover the pan and cook the rice for 10 minutes over a very gentle heat. Stir in the saffron, blended with the remaining stock, cover the pan again and cook 10 minutes longer. Just before serving, stir in the cheeses and the rest of the butter. Season to taste with salt.

This risotto can be served with salads or to accompany veal escalopes, grilled steaks of chops.

Variation
To make the risotto into a main dish, fry diced lamb or pork in the fat (or olive oil if you like) before frying the onions and rice; add chopped deseeded peppers and peeled, deseeded, diced tomatoes.

Pilaff
Pilaff, or more correctly pilau, is the Turkish version of risotto. It is made with 25 g/1 oz butter or dripping and 3 tablespoons olive oil to 225 g/8 oz long-grain rice. Garlic is added with the onions and the cheese is omitted.

Californian pilaff
After the onions and garlic have been softened in the fat, cook 100 g/ 4 oz sliced mushrooms in it until the liquid has evaporated. Add the rice and cook it in chicken stock as above, then add 100 g/4 oz sultanas and 70 g/2½ oz tomato purée. Season to taste with cayenne or chilli powder.

Lamb pilaff
Trim off all the fat from 450 g/1 lb boneless lamb, and cut into small dice. Heat the fat as above, adding a little olive oil if necessary, and seal the meat in it. Put in the onions and cook with a little garlic, and rice as above, mixing in diced deseeded peppers, chopped tomatoes, and cheese to taste.

Chicken liver pilaff
Cook the rice as for Cheese risotto above but substitute extra stock for the wine. Dice 225 g/8 oz chicken livers and fry them in the butter with 2 diced apples for about 4 minutes. Stir into the rice at the end of the cooking time.

Rice and Pasta

Spaghetti with various sauces

Serves 4

450 g/1 lb spaghetti
1–2 tablespoons salt
good dash of olive oil

Bring to the boil a generous quantity of water in a large saucepan. Add the salt and slide the spaghetti gradually into the water. Cook for about 12 minutes till 'al dente' or retaining some bite. About 2 minutes before the end of the cooking time, add the oil.

When cooked, drain the spaghetti in a large colander, return it to the pan and steam-dry for a moment. It can then be refreshed quickly with cold water to prevent it sticking together but this shouldn't be necessary.

Tomato and basil sauce

Serves 4

1 (794-g/1¾-lb) can peeled tomatoes, strained and juice reserved
1 onion, peeled and finely chopped
2 cloves of garlic, peeled and finely chopped
4 tablespoons olive oil
pinch of dried oregano
1 tablespoon chopped basil or 1 teaspoon dried basil
salt and freshly ground black pepper

Chop the tomatoes finely or crush with a potato masher. Gently cook the onion and garlic in the oil until soft and transparent. Pour over the reserved tomato liquid. Add the tomato pulp, the oregano and half the basil. Season to taste with salt and pepper and cook rapidly, uncovered, to a thick creamy consistency. Adjust the seasoning and sprinkle with the remaining basil. Serve with grated Parmesan cheese separately.

Note To make this sauce more piquant, flavour it with a mashed anchovy fillet, or a little anchovy paste, and/or season it with a pinch of grated nutmeg. It will be especially delicious if made with fresh tomatoes, although not so red in colour, in which case add a little tomato purée, cooked for a few minutes with the onions and garlic.

Blue cheese cream sauce

Serves 2–4

1 tablespoon butter
175 g/6 oz blue cheese, mashed with a fork
300 ml/½ pint double cream
freshly ground black pepper
pinch of grated nutmeg
salt

Melt the butter, without browning, in a wide saucepan or a frying pan. Add the cheese and cream and simmer until thick, stirring all the time. Season to taste with plenty of pepper, nutmeg and only a very little salt as the cheese is salty.

Serve the sauce with the cooked pasta and plenty of freshly ground black pepper. Or toss the pasta quickly in the sauce, spoon on to a serving plate and then season with pepper.

Bolognese sauce

Serves 4

25 g/1 oz butter
50 g/2 oz rindless smoked streaky bacon, diced
1 onion, peeled and finely chopped
1 medium-sized carrot, peeled and finely chopped
1 celery stalk, finely chopped
1 tablespoon olive oil
350 g/12 oz minced beef, lamb or veal
1–2 tablespoons tomato purée
100 ml/4 fl oz stock
100 ml/4 fl oz red wine
100 ml/4 fl oz milk or cream
salt and pepper
good pinch of dried oregano

Heat the butter in a large frying pan. Add the bacon and vegetables and cook for about 10 minutes until lightly browned, stirring from time to time. Transfer them to a large saucepan.

Heat the olive oil in the frying pan, add the minced meat and cook rapidly, stirring constantly, until it is browned and crumbly; add to the saucepan and heat through thoroughly.

Stir in the tomato purée, stock and wine. Bring to the boil, lower the heat, cover and simmer for a least 45 minutes. If possible, continue to cook very gently for another ½–1 hour, stirring from time to time to prevent it from catching and burning.

Stir in the milk or cream and cook, uncovered, for a few minutes. Season to taste with salt, pepper and oregano and serve very hot with the cooked pasta.

Note There are many variations of this sauce, which the Italians call *ragu alla bolognese*. It can be made with chopped mushrooms, chicken livers sautéed in butter, or chopped parsley may be added. Peeled canned tomatoes may be used instead of or as well as the tomato purée, and extra flavour added with garlic, chilli or cayenne. But for a really exclusive and expensive bolognese, add a small chopped truffle.

Variation
Try this simple but quite delicious way of flavouring spaghetti. Fry several sliced cloves of garlic till golden in a little olive oil. Add a couple of fresh chilli peppers, seeded and cut into fine rings. Toss the cooked drained spaghetti in the flavoured oil and grind plenty of black pepper over. A sprinkling of fresh basil leaves can be added as the spaghetti is brought to table.

Cook's Tip

For a change try these recipes using wholewheat spaghetti—it has a delicious flavour and an interesting nutty texture. Other types of wholewheat pasta such as rings or macaroni are also suitable.

Rice and Pasta

Gnocchi alla romana

Serves 3–4 as an accompaniment

300 ml/½ pint of milk
150 ml/¼ pint water
½ teaspoon salt
100 g/4 oz semolina
2 egg yolks
75 g/3 oz butter
*150 g/5 oz grated Parmesan or
   Emmental cheese*

In a large pan, bring the milk and
water to the boil. Add the salt. Pour
the semolina in a thin stream into
the boiling liquid stirring all the
time, and continue stirring over
gentle heat for 10 minutes while it
cooks and thickens.

Blend in the egg yolks. Remove
from the heat and leave until cool
enough to handle. Using the back of
a tablespoon, press the mixture out
to a thickness of about 1 cm/½ in on
a plate or tray that has been rinsed
with cold water. Let it rest for 1
hour. Then cut out small circles or
crescents with a small plain pastry
cutter, or cut into squares. Set the
oven at hot (230c, 450f, gas 8).

Grease a large shallow ovenproof
dish with a little of the butter. Put
the unshaped paste trimmings in
first, then cover with the shaped
pieces, overlapping them to form a
neat pattern. Sprinkle each layer
with a little grated cheese and finish
the top layer with the rest of the
cheese. Dot the remaining butter all
over the top and cook in the heated
oven for 12–15 minutes. Serve hot
with stews, goulash, or roast game
birds.

Potato dumplings
Piedmontese-style

Serves 3–4 as an accompaniment

1 kg/2 lb potatoes, well scrubbed
50 g/2 oz butter
salt
100 g/4 oz flour
2 eggs, lightly beaten
1 litre/1¾ pints salted water
450 ml/about ¾ pint milk
50 g/2 oz grated Parmesan cheese

Boil the potatoes in their skins.
Quickly refresh them with cold
water then peel. Mash them
thoroughly, then beat in 15 g/½ oz of
the butter and season with salt to
taste. Stir them over a low heat to
dry them out a little, then leave
until cool enough to handle. Turn
them into a bowl and knead in the
flour and eggs.

Using 2 teaspoons, form the
potato mixture into little dumplings.
Heat the salted water and milk
together in a large pan until barely
simmering. Put in the dumplings and
cook gently in the simmering liquid
for 6–8 minutes; do them in several
batches if necessary. Lift out with a
slotted spoon and drain on
absorbent kitchen paper. Put in a
warm serving dish. Melt the rest of
the butter and pour it over the
dumplings. Sprinkle with Parmesan.

Serve with fried liver or liver
ragoût, roast lamb, or beef olives.

Variation
Reduce the amount of potatoes to
450 g/1 lb. Use 2 egg yolks instead
of whole eggs, and add 225 g/8 oz of
mashed quark or other cream cheese
to the potato mixture. Shape as
above. These dumplings need 5–6
minutes cooking only. Finish by
topping with the flaked butter and
grated cheese and brown under a
hot grill.

Pasta with ham and egg

Serves 3–4 or 6 as a starter

*350 g/12 oz bow-shaped pasta (use a
  mixture of green and white shapes)
2 litres/3½ pints boiling salted water
3 tablespoons olive oil
100 g/4 oz mildly cured gammon,
  finely diced
4 eggs
4 tablespoons double cream
50 g/2 oz grated Parmesan cheese
freshly ground black pepper*

Cook the pasta in the boiling salted
water in a large uncovered pan for 8
minutes; then add 2 tablespoons of
the oil to prevent the pasta sticking
together, and cook about 4 minutes
more or until the pasta is 'al dente'.
  Meanwhile, gently fry the
gammon in the remaining oil till
browned. Beat the eggs with the
cream and cheese, adding black
pepper to taste.
  Drain the cooked pasta well and
turn at once into a warmed dish.
Quickly stir in the egg mixture,
spoon over the gammon and serve
with more grated Parmesan cheese if
you wish.

Serve on its own as a starter, or
with broccoli, green beans, or fennel
sautéed in butter, as an inexpensive
main course.

Green noodles with peas

Serves 3–4 or 6 as a starter

*350 g/12 oz green ribbon noodles
2 litres/3½ pints of boiling salted
  water
2 tablespoons olive oil
150 ml/¼ pint double cream
1 (454-g/1-lb) packet of frozen peas,
  cooked and drained
salt
freshly ground black pepper*

Cook the noodles in the boiling
salted water in a large pan,
uncovered, for 10 minutes, then add
the oil to stop the noodles sticking
together, and cook for about 5
minutes more till 'al dente'.
  In another pan, heat the cream
and boil it rapidly, uncovered, until
reduced to about two-thirds. Add
the peas and drained noodles and
bring to the boil again. Season to
taste with salt and pepper. Serve at
once, as the cream is quickly

absorbed by the noodles.
  This is an ideal accompaniment to
roast meats, fried escalopes of veal
or pork chops.

Note The cream can be flavoured
with a little garlic or chopped basil
or chervil if liked.

Variation
The addition of 100 g/4 oz cooked
chopped ham makes this an
excellent first course. Serve
sprinkled with chopped parsley.

Rice and Pasta

Lasagne

Serves 6

20 sheets (about 225 g/8 oz) lasagne
4 tablespoons oil
1 large onion, peeled and finely
    chopped
100 g/4 oz mushrooms, wiped and
    chopped
2 carrots, peeled and finely chopped
2 cloves of garlic, peeled and crushed
225 g/8 oz minced beef
1 (396-g/14-oz) can tomatoes
salt and freshly ground black pepper
pinch of cayenne
½ teaspoon dried basil
½ teaspoon dried oregano
100 g/4 oz frozen peas

For the sauce
65 g/2½ oz butter
100 g/4 oz cooked ham, chopped
50 g/2 oz flour
600 ml/1 pint milk
pinch of grated nutmeg
4 tablespoons chopped parsley

To finish
225 g/8 oz mozzarella cheese, cubed
50 g/2 oz Parmesan cheese, grated
6–8 black olives, stoned and halved

Set the oven at moderate (180c,
350f, gas 4). Cook the lasagne for
8–10 minutes in boiling salted water
to which a tablespoon of the oil has
been added. Drain, refresh under
cold water and lay out to dry on
sheets of absorbent kitchen paper or
a clean tea towel.

Heat the remaining oil in a
saucepan and add the onion,
mushrooms and carrots. Cook
gently, stirring from time to time,
until the onion is transparent but not
brown. Add the garlic and the meat
and continue cooking until the meat
is brown and crumbly. Pour in the
tomatoes with their liquid and
season to taste with salt, pepper,
cayenne and the herbs. Simmer
gently for 30–45 minutes, stirring
occasionally to prevent sticking.

Meanwhile cook the peas for a
few minutes in a little boiling salted
water. Drain, then refresh with cold
water. Melt all but 15 g/½ oz of the
butter in a saucepan and fry the ham

for a few minutes. Sprinkle in the
flour and continue cooking for 1–2
minutes. Blend in the milk a little at
a time, stirring continuously, to
make a thick sauce. Season to taste
with salt, pepper and nutmeg.
Remove from the heat and stir in
the parsley.

Grease an oblong oven proof dish
(about 15 × 25 cm/6 × 10 in) and
cover the bottom with a layer of
lasagne. Spread over some meat
mixture and pour over a little of the
white sauce. Scatter over equal
amounts of peas, mozzarella and
Parmesan. Continue to build layers
in this way, adding the olives to the
top layer with the peas and cheese.
Dot with the remaining butter and
bake in the heated oven for 25–30
minutes until golden brown and
bubbling.

Serve with a fresh green salad,
tossed in an Italian dressing of oil,
vinegar and mustard. A light Italian
red wine goes very well with
lasagne.

Note This dish is even more
attractive if you use green lasagne
(lasagne verdi) and is also tastier as
fresh spinach juice is used in the
manufacture of green lasagne. If you
cannot obtain green lasagne you can
use 225 g/8 oz fresh spinach with the
white lasagne. Wash it well, blanch
for a few minutes in boiling water
and refresh with cold water. Drain
well, squeezing out excess moisture
and place in layers over the white
lasagne before spreading over the
meat mixture.

Variation
Try adding some sweet corn,
quartered artichoke hearts or strips
of tomato or pepper to the dish.
Replace the black olives with stuffed
green ones for a milder flavour.

Cook's Tip

Lasagne makes an ideal dish for a
large informal buffet party. It can be
assembled in advance, then frozen.
Either use a dish which is both
oven- and freezer-proof or line the
dish with foil. When the lasagne is
frozen lift the foil out of the dish
and fold it tightly to make a sealed
parcel.

Defrost the lasagne overnight at
room temperature. If you have
removed it from the dish, unwrap
the foil parcel while still frozen and
replace it in the original dish for
defrosting and reheating. Before
serving, place in a moderately hot
oven (180 C, 350 F, gas 4) for 30–40
minutes or until heated through and
golden and bubbling on top.

Egg Dishes

Egg Dishes

Poached eggs

Serves 2–4

2 litres/3½ pints water
2 teaspoons salt
1 tablespoon vinegar
4 fresh eggs

Bring the water to the boil with the salt and vinegar then reduce the temperature so that it simmers steadily. Break the eggs one at a time into a ladle and slide them quickly into the water. Cook for about 3–5 minutes until the whites are set and the eggs are cooked to taste. Carefully lift them out using a slotted spoon, transfer to a warmed serving dish and trim the edges to neaten the eggs. Serve immediately.

Tip Eggs used for poaching must be as fresh as possible as slightly stale ones will be more apt to fall apart during cooking.

Note Poached eggs are delicious served with a variety of sauces. Try them with Mustard or Horseradish sauce (see page 111) or Mushroom or Mock béchamel (see page 108). For an unusual variation serve the Tomato and basil sauce on page 164, made thinner by stirring in a little red wine or soured cream just before serving.

Poached eggs with vegetable purée

Serves 4

450 g/1 lb prepared cabbage, broccoli
   or carrots
150 ml/¼ pint boiling chicken stock
50 g/2 oz cream cheese
15 g/½ oz butter
2 tablespoons soured cream
salt and pepper
pinch of nutmeg
1 tablespoon chopped parsley
1 tablespoon chopped dill or chives
4 eggs

Prepare the vegetables and cook them in the stock in a covered pan until they are tender — about 5–15 minutes depending on their type. Strain them, reserving any stock for use in soups or casseroles, then purée in a liquidiser or food processor. Beat in the cream cheese, butter and soured cream and season to taste with salt, pepper and a little

nutmeg. Stir in the chopped herbs and divide the vegetable purée between four individual, warmed serving dishes. Keep hot while you poach the eggs, following the instructions above. Make a hollow in the mixture and place a poached egg on each. Serve immediately.

Poached eggs Olivet

Serves 4

½ quantity Béchamel sauce (page 108)
25 g/1 oz butter
4 shallots, peeled and finely chopped
1 clove of garlic, peeled and crushed
450 g/1 lb fresh sorrel or spinach,
   washed, trimmed and dried
salt and pepper
4 tablespoons double cream
4 eggs

Make the Béchamel sauce according to the recipe instructions and keep it hot. Melt the butter in a saucepan, add the shallots and garlic and cook until soft but not browned. Add the sorrel or spinach, cover the pan and cook it over low heat for about 10 minutes. Chop the cooked vegetables or purée in a liquidiser or food processor. Season the purée generously. Whip the cream until stiff and fold it into the sorrel or spinach, then divide the mixture between four individual serving dishes and keep warm while you poach the eggs according to the instructions above. Pour the sauce around the vegetable mixture and top with a poached egg. Serve immediately.

Poached eggs Beaugency

Serves 4

½ quantity Béarnaise sauce (page 122)
4 canned artichoke bottoms
15 g/½ oz butter
4 canned scallops or button
   mushroom caps
4 eggs
1 tablespoon chopped parsley

Make the sauce according to the recipe instructions. Heat the artichoke bottoms in their liquid but do not let them boil. Melt the butter, add the drained scallops or mushroom caps and heat through gently for 2–3 minutes. Drain the artichokes and place them on individual, warmed serving dishes or

one large dish. Poach the eggs according to the instructions above. Pour the sauce over the artichoke bottoms and top each with a poached egg. Garnish with the scallops or mushrooms and sprinkle the chopped parsley over. Serve immediately.

Cook's Tip

Special egg poaching pans can be obtained or you can use greased plain pastry cutters set in a frying pan filled with boiling water to help poached eggs keep their shape. It is sometimes necessary to trim the edge of the egg a little to obtain a neat shape.

Egg Dishes

Scrambled eggs

Serves 4

8 eggs
4 tablespoons single cream
salt and freshly ground white pepper
50 g/2 oz butter
1 tablespoon chopped chives
*   (optional)*

Whisk the eggs with the cream and
seasoning to taste until the
ingredients are thoroughly combined
and frothy. Melt three-quarters of
the butter in a non-stick or heavy-
based saucepan over gentle heat,
swirling it round the sides of the
pan. Do not allow it to overheat.
Pour the eggs into the pan and cook
them, stirring continuously, over
gentle heat until they are just set
and very creamy. Remove the pan
from the heat immediately and
quickly stir in the remaining butter.
    Serve the eggs at once — the heat
of the pan continues to cook the
eggs so they should not be left in it
for too long. Sprinkle the scrambled
eggs with chopped chives, if using.

Tip For a lower calorie content
substitute milk for the cream.

Variations
Scrambled eggs with bacon Chop
100 g/4 oz rindless streaky bacon
and dry fry it gently in the pan until
the fat runs. Add 25 g/1 oz butter
before pouring in the egg mixture,
then cook as above.

Scrambled eggs with herbs Any
finely chopped, fresh herbs are
suitable for this dish, for example,
parsley, thyme, sage, lemon balm,
tarragon, rosemary or chives. Add
small quantities of the herbs to the
beaten eggs before cooking.

Scrambled egg Antoine Cook the
bacon as above and add 2
tablespoons chopped mixed fresh
herbs and 1 tablespoon chopped
capers to the beaten eggs as they are
poured into the pan. Pour Noisette
butter sauce (see page 110) over the
cooked eggs before serving.

Scrambled eggs with shrimps Finely
chop 50 g/2 oz lean rindless bacon

and sauté this with 50 g/2 oz canned
shrimps in 15 g/½ oz of the butter.
Remove this mixture from the pan
and keep it hot. Cook the eggs as
above, then stir in the shrimp
mixture and 2 tablespoons chopped
parsley. Serve immediately.

Scrambled eggs jardinière

Serves 4

175 g/6 oz carrots, peeled and thinly
*   sliced*
175 g/6 oz French beans, trimmed
salt
100 g/4 oz frozen peas
75 g/3 oz butter
175 g/6 oz shallots or pickling
*   onions, peeled*
1 quantity Scrambled eggs (see
*   above)*
100 g/4 oz mature Cheddar cheese,
*   finely grated*

Cook the carrots and French beans
separately in boiling salted water for
about 10 minutes or until cooked to
taste then drain well. Cook the peas

according to the instructions on the packet and drain. Keep the vegetables warm. Melt two-thirds of the butter in a frying pan and fry the shallots or pickling onions, seasoning them lightly first, until golden brown. Meanwhile make the scrambled eggs according to the instructions above, then stir in the grated cheese until it melts.

Spoon the scrambled eggs into a serving dish and arrange the cooked vegetables, including the onions, around them. Dot the remaining butter over the peas, beans and carrots and serve with warm French bread as an accompaniment.

Plain omelette

Serves 1

2 large or 3 small eggs
salt and pepper
2 teaspoons water
25 g/1 oz butter

Beat the eggs with the seasoning and water until the yolks and whites are just amalgamated. Melt the butter in an omelette pan over high heat then pour in the egg mixture. Lift the edge of the omelette as it sets and tilt the pan to allow the uncooked egg to run on to the pan and set. The underside of the omelette should be golden brown and the top just set. Carefully fold the omelette in half or roll it up and slide it on to a warmed serving plate.

Tip When making a filled omelette it is essential that the filling is prepared and hot before the eggs are cooked. Spoon the filling over half the omelette and fold the other half over to cover. Serve as above. Fricassée of chicken or veal, lightly cooked vegetable or cooked fish or prawns are all ideas for fillings.

Omelette fines herbes

Serves 1

2 large or 3 small eggs
pinch of salt
2 teaspoons single cream or milk
1 teaspoon chopped parsley
1 teaspoon chopped chives
1 teaspoon chopped chervil
25 g/1 oz butter

Mix the eggs with the salt, cream or milk and the herbs. Melt the butter in an omelette pan, pour in the egg mixture and cook as for the Plain omelette. Fold the omelette in half and serve immediately.

Variations
Pour the egg mixture over lightly cooked mushrooms, chopped onion or crispy fried chopped bacon or ham and cook as above. The omelette may be filled with a little grated Emmental or Gruyère cheese.

Egg Dishes

Savoury soufflé pancakes

Makes 6

150 g/5 oz plain flour
pinch of salt
3 eggs, separated
250 ml/8 fl oz water
a little grated lemon rind (optional)
butter for frying

Sift the flour and salt into a bowl and make a well in the centre. Add the egg yolks and gradually beat in the water, incorporating the flour to make a fairly thick batter. Stir in the lemon rind, if used, and allow the mixture to stand for 15 minutes. Whisk the egg whites until stiff and fold them into the batter.

Melt a little butter in a medium-sized frying pan, pour in enough of the batter to make a thin layer over the base and cook until golden brown on the underside and lightly set on top. Carefully flip it over using a fish slice or spatula and cook until golden on the other side. Keep the pancakes warm until they are all cooked then fill and serve.

Note This basic recipe for soufflé pancakes can be enriched by the addition of milk or cream and up to 40 g/1½ oz melted butter can be folded into the batter.

Steak and kidney filling

Enough for 6 pancakes

225 g/8 oz lamb's kidneys, halved, cored and sliced
350 g/12 oz frying steak, trimmed and cut in thin strips
juice of ½ small lemon
75 g/3 oz button mushrooms, thinly sliced
25 g/1 oz butter
2 tablespoons oil
1 onion, peeled and finely chopped
1 clove of garlic, peeled and crushed
150 ml/¼ pint single cream
salt and freshly ground black pepper
dash of Worcestershire sauce
2 tablespoons chopped parsley

Soak the kidneys in cold water for 30 minutes. Drain well and dry the pieces carefully, then mix with the steak. Sprinkle the lemon juice over the mushrooms and allow to stand for 10 minutes.

Melt the butter with the oil in a frying pan. Add the onion and garlic and cook until soft but not browned. Stir in the steak and kidney mixture and cook until browned, stirring occasionally to prevent burning. When the meat is cooked, add the mushrooms and cook for 2–3 minutes. Add the cream, seasoning and a little Worcestershire sauce and heat it through without allowing the mixture to boil. Finally stir in the parsley. Divide the mixture between the pancakes, fold them over and serve immediately.

Variations
Melt 25 g/1 oz butter in a saucepan and sauté 1 finely chopped onion until soft but not browned. Add the juice of 1 lemon and about 6 tablespoons dry white wine. Stir in 175 g/6 oz smoked haddock or smoked eel, cooked and flaked or 175 g/6 oz cooked chicken meat, finely diced. Heat through gently for 5 minutes then mix in 2 tablespoons double cream. Remove from the heat at once and season to taste before serving.

Vegetable filling

Enough for 6 pancakes

1 medium aubergine, thinly sliced
salt
2 tablespoons olive oil
15 g/½ oz butter
1 large onion, peeled and sliced
1 courgette, cut into thin strips
2 ripe tomatoes, peeled, deseeded and roughly chopped
1 clove of garlic, peeled and crushed
5 tablespoons red wine
freshly ground black pepper
1 teaspoon chopped mixed herbs
1 teaspoon green peppercorns
a few basil leaves to garnish (optional)

Place the aubergine in a dish, sprinkle with salt and leave to stand for 15 minutes then rinse and dry throughly. Heat the oil and butter together in a frying pan, add the prepared vegetables and garlic and cook until soft but not browned. Pour over the wine and season with a little pepper, then stir in the herbs and peppercorns and cook for 5 minutes. Divide the filling between the soufflé pancakes and fold them in half. Garnish with the basil leaves, if using. Serve immediately.

Variation
Sweet soufflé pancakes These pancakes are also delicious with a sweet filling. Try a sweetened fruit purée such as apricot flavoured with a little orange rind or apple purée flavoured with cinnamon. Alternatively spread the pancakes with a little jam before folding over and serve dusted with icing sugar.

Egg Dishes

Stuffed eggs

Stuffed eggs can be served as a first course or as a snack and they are ideal for serving as part of a cold buffet.

Columbus eggs

1 boneless chicken breast, cooked, skinned and finely chopped
2 anchovy fillets, chopped
2 tablespoons capers, finely chopped
1 small onion, peeled and grated
8 hard-boiled eggs
1 tablespoon chopped parsley
150 ml/¼ pint mayonnaise
1 teaspoon made mustard
sprigs of dill or parsley to garnish

Mix the chicken, anchovy fillets, capers and onion together. Halve the eggs lengthways, remove the yolks and sieve them into the chicken mixture. Stir in the chopped parsley and spoon this mixture into the whites. Beat the mayonnaise and mustard together and place it in a piping bag fitted with a small star nozzle. Garnish the eggs with rosettes of the mayonnaise mixture and sprigs of dill or parsley.

Russian eggs

8 hard-boiled eggs
50 g/2 oz butter
juice of ½ lemon
50 g/2 oz caviar or lumpfish roe

Halve the eggs lengthways, remove the yolks and sieve them. Cream the butter with the lemon juice and sieved yolks until soft then spoon it back into the whites. Garnish each with a little caviar or lumpfish roe.

Pâté-stuffed eggs

8 hard-boiled eggs
100 g/4 oz foie gras or liver pâté
salt and freshly ground white pepper
3 tablespoons grated Parmesan cheese
50 g/2 oz butter

Halve the eggs lengthways and scoop out the yolks. Beat the pâté with the yolks and seasoning and use this mixture to fill the egg whites. Sprinkle the Parmesan cheese over the top and dot each with a little of the butter. Place the stuffed eggs under a hot grill until lightly browned. Serve immediately.

Prawn-stuffed eggs

8 hard-boiled eggs
175 g/6 oz peeled prawns
50 g/2 oz butter
salt and freshly ground white pepper
150 ml/¼ pint double cream
parsley sprigs to garnish

Halve the eggs lengthways and remove the yolks. Reserve 16 prawns for garnish and chop the remainder very finely. Cream the butter with the yolks, seasoning and chopped prawns until soft. Fill the egg whites with this mixture. Whip the double cream until stiff and place in a piping bag fitted with a small plain nozzle. Pipe a cream border round the stuffed eggs, then top with the reserved prawns and parsley sprigs.

Eggs in salt pickle

1.15 litres/2 pints water
40 g/1½ oz salt
2 small onions
8 hard-boiled eggs in their shells

Boil the water with the salt and the onions, with their skins, for 10 minutes. Allow the liquid to cool then strain and reserve it. Crack the eggs but do not remove their shells, then place them in an earthenware crock or preserving jar. Pour the cooled brine over the eggs to cover them completely. Cover the crock or jar and leave for about 3 days. Do not allow the eggs to stand for more than 5 days.

Serve the eggs from the crock or jar with fresh wholemeal bread or pumpernickel. The eggs should be shelled, halved and seasoned with mustard, Worcestershire sauce or Tabasco sauce.

Tip To make a spicier brine a little fresh root ginger may be added. Use about 2.5 cm/1 inch of ginger and add 1 teaspoon peppercorns, ½ teaspoon mustard seeds and 2–3 bay leaves.

Coddled eggs

An egg-coddler is a small decorative china or glass vessel with a lid which is traditionally used for lightly cooking eggs. Most coddlers are big enough for 2 eggs or 1 egg plus additional flavourings.

Place a small knob of butter inside the coddler and place in a pan of simmering water until the butter has melted. Swirl the butter round the sides and drop in the egg. Put the lid on the coddler and simmer the water for 8–10 minutes until the egg is just set.

Variations
Spinach egg Lightly season 2 tablespoons drained, cooked, chopped spinach with salt, pepper and nutmeg. Stir in a little double cream. Put half this mixture in the greased coddler. Drop in the egg and cover with the remaining spinach. Cook as above. A little chopped, cooked ham may also be stirred into the spinach, if liked.

Cheese egg Beat 1 tablespoon finely grated Cheddar cheese with 2 tablespoons double cream and use in place of the spinach mixture above. Season with a pinch of paprika.

Tuna egg Use 2 tablespoons drained, flaked tuna fish instead of the spinach mixture and omit the nutmeg.

Bacon egg Chop 2 rashers of lean bacon and fry lightly. Place half in the bottom of the egg coddler then put in the egg and sprinkle the rest of the bacon over the top before cooking as above. Chopped cooked ham or tongue can be used in this way without frying first.

Soufflés and Bakes

Soufflés and Bakes

Gratin dauphinois

Serves 4

800 g/1¾ lb potatoes, peeled, washed
 and thinly sliced
2 cloves garlic, halved
salt and freshly ground white pepper
freshly grated nutmeg
300 ml/½ pint milk
300 ml/½ pint single cream
1 egg, beaten
100 g/4 oz Gruyère or Emmental
 cheese, grated
50 g/2 oz butter

Set the oven at moderately hot
(200 C, 400 F, gas 6).
   Rinse the sliced potatoes under
running water and pat them dry on
absorbent kitchen paper. Rub the
inside of a gratin or ovenproof dish
with the cut cloves of garlic. Grease
the dish and layer the potatoes in it,
seasoning each layer with salt,
pepper and nutmeg. The potatoes
should come to about 1 cm/½ in
below the rim of the dish.
   Heat the milk and cream together
until just lukewarm. Stir in the egg
and two-thirds of the grated cheese
then slowly pour this mixture over
the potatoes, allowing it to run
between the layers. Sprinkle the
remaining cheese over the top, dot
with the butter and bake for 50–60
minutes or until the potatoes are
cooked and the top is crisp and
golden brown.

Note Instead of half milk and cream,
this dish may be enriched by using
all cream.

Leek and potato gratin

Serves 4

575 g/1¼ lb potatoes, peeled, washed
 and thinly sliced
1 large leek, thinly sliced and washed
25 g/1 oz butter
1–2 cloves garlic, crushed
2 egg yolks
250 ml/8 fl oz single cream
salt and freshly ground white pepper
pinch of cayenne pepper
75 g/3 oz grated cheese

Set the oven at moderately hot
(200 C, 400 F, gas 6).
   The potatoes should be sliced very
thinly — a mandoline or slicing
attachment to a food processor or
mixer will make this easier. Rinse
the slices and dry them on absorbent
kitchen paper. Separate the leek
slices into rings and dry them
thoroughly. Grease an ovenproof
dish thickly with the butter and layer
half the potatoes in it. Arrange the
leek and garlic evenly over them and
then top with the remaining
potatoes. Whisk the egg yolks and
cream together and season
thoroughly with salt, pepper and a
little cayenne. Pour this mixture
over the potatoes and sprinkle the
cheese evenly over the top.
   Bake for 45–50 minutes until
golden brown. Serve immediately —
this dish is particularly good with
roast lamb or game.

Note For extra flavour layer a thinly
sliced green pepper with the
potatoes and leeks and sprinkle
Parmesan cheese over the top
instead of the grated cheese. The
gratin would then be ideal for a
supper or light luncheon dish.

Quick potato gratin

Serves 4

50 g/2 oz butter
2 onions, peeled and sliced into rings
1 clove garlic, crushed
100 g/4 oz cooked ham, chopped
2 tablespoons chopped parsley
salt and freshly ground white pepper
pinch of freshly grated nutmeg
generous pinch of caraway seeds
450 g/1 lb boiled potatoes, cooled
 and sliced
150 ml/¼ pint soured cream
1 egg, beaten
50 g/2 oz mature Cheddar cheese,
 grated

Set the oven at moderately hot
(200 C, 400 F, gas 6).
   Melt the butter in a frying pan,
add the onion slices, separated into
rings, and cook them, turning
frequently, until they are golden
brown. Add the garlic and toss well
then mix in the ham and parsley.
Season to taste with salt, pepper,
nutmeg and caraway seeds. Remove
the pan from the heat and carefully
mix in the potatoes. Spoon this
mixture into an ovenproof dish.
   Whisk the soured cream into the
egg and stir in half the cheese. Pour
the egg mixture over the potatoes,
sprinkle the remaining cheese evenly
over the top and bake for about 20
minutes until golden brown. Serve
immediately. Quick potato gratin
goes particularly well with grilled
steak.

Soufflés and Bakes

Oven-baked kohlrabi

Serves 6

450 g/1 lb kohlrabi
50 g/2 oz butter
2–3 onions, peeled and sliced
225 g/8 oz lean bacon, cut in strips
2 tablespoons chopped chives
2 tablespoons chopped parsley
salt and freshly ground black pepper
450 g/1 lb potatoes, peeled and thinly
  sliced
450 g/1 lb tomatoes, peeled and sliced
300 ml/½ pint milk
100 ml/4 fl oz soured cream
175 g/6 oz Emmental cheese, grated
2 eggs, beaten
freshly grated nutmeg

Heat the oven to moderately hot
(200 C, 400 F, gas 6).
   Trim any leaves and stalks from
the kohlrabi, then peel and slice
thinly. Melt half the butter in a
frying-pan, add the onion and cook
the slices until soft but not browned.
Add the bacon, herbs and seasoning
and stir the ingredients together.
Remove the pan from the heat.
   Layer the potatoes, kohlrabi and
tomatoes in a well-greased
ovenproof dish together with the
onion mixture, ending with a layer
of potatoes. Heat the milk and
soured cream together to just
lukewarm then gradually stir in the
cheese, standing the saucepan over
low heat until the cheese melts. Do
not allow the mixture to boil.
Remove the saucepan from the heat
and stir in the beaten eggs. Season
with nutmeg and a little salt and
pepper, then pour the mixture over
the layered vegetables and dot with
the remaining butter.
   Bake for 45–50 minutes until the
vegetables are cooked and the top
layer of potatoes is crisp and golden.
Serve immediately with French
bread or as an accompaniment to
grilled chops or steaks.

Variation
Broccoli may be substituted for the
tomatoes. Divide the broccoli into
florets and blanch it in boiling water
for a few minutes. Layer it with the
other ingredients, pour over the
sauce and bake as above. Smoked
chicken or turkey may be substituted
for the bacon.

Cook's Tip

Turnips can be used in this recipe if
kohlrabi cannot be obtained as they
have a similar flavour. Choose small
young turnips and prepare as in
recipe above. Turnip tops can be
cooked separately as a green
vegetable.

Moussaka

Serves 4

4 medium aubergines, trimmed and
    sliced
salt
about 50 g/2 oz plain flour
olive oil for frying
2 large onions, peeled and finely
    chopped
675 g/1½ lb minced lamb
2 cloves garlic
450 g/1 lb tomatoes, peeled and
    chopped
4 tablespoons red wine
2 tablespoons concentrated tomato
    purée
4 tablespoons chopped parsley
freshly ground black pepper
generous pinch of cinnamon
250 ml/8 fl oz single cream
2 eggs, beaten
100 g/4 oz finely grated cheese
freshly grated nutmeg

Place the aubergines in a colander,
sprinkle generously with salt and
leave them to stand for 15–20
minutes.
    Set the oven at moderate (180 c,
350 f, gas 4). Rinse them then pat

dry on absorbent kitchen paper and
dust them lightly with the flour.
Heat the oil in a frying pan and fry
the aubergine slices, a few at a time,
for about 1 minute on each side then
drain them on absorbent kitchen
paper. Add more oil to the pan if
necessary, and heat it between
batches so that the aubergine slices
brown quickly.
    Add the chopped onion to the
remaining oil in the pan and cook it
with the minced lamb, stirring
frequently, until lightly browned.
Stir in the garlic and tomatoes, red
wine and tomato purée and cook the
mixture for 5 minutes. Add the
parsley and season the meat mixture
with salt, pepper and a little
cinnamon.
    Layer the aubergine and meat
together in an ovenproof dish,
ending with aubergine on top.
Lightly whisk the cream with the
eggs and stir in the cheese. Season
with a little nutmeg and pour the
egg mixture over the moussaka.
Bake in the moderate oven for
about 1 hour until the egg mixture is
set and golden brown on top. Serve
immediately with a crisp green
salad.

Variation
Sliced, cooked potatoes or sliced
courgettes can be layered in the
moussaka together with the
aubergines and mince. Béchamel
sauce (page 108) may be poured
over the moussaka instead of the
custard mixture. Minced beef or
pork may be substituted for the
lamb.

Cook's Tip

If preparing onions makes you
weep, try putting them in cold water
for half an hour before peeling
them. Alternatively peel onions
under running water and remember
not to lean over the board whilst
chopping them.

Soufflés and Bakes

Baked Chinese cabbage

Serves 4

300 ml/½ pint Béchamel sauce (page 108)
100 g/4 oz grated Emmental cheese
salt and freshly ground white pepper
freshly grated nutmeg
2 eggs, separated
1 large Chinese cabbage, shredded and washed
100 g/4 oz lean bacon, cut in strips

Heat the oven to moderately hot (200c, 400f, gas 6). Make the Béchamel sauce according to the recipe instructions. Stir two-thirds of the cheese into the sauce and season it with salt, pepper and nutmeg. Beat in the egg yolks. Stiffly whisk the egg whites and fold them into the sauce.

Layer the shredded Chinese cabbage with the bacon and sauce in a buttered ovenproof dish, ending with a layer of sauce on top. Sprinkle the remaining cheese over and bake for 30–40 minutes. If the top of the dish becomes too brown during cooking cover it loosely with a piece of cooking foil.

Layered cottage pie

Serves 4

175 g/6 oz salami, finely diced
2 onions, peeled and chopped
450 g/1 lb minced beef
3 tablespoons tomato purée
1 teaspoon dried oregano
salt and freshly ground black pepper
675 g/1½ lb potatoes, peeled
150 ml/¼ pint hot milk
100 g/4 oz Cheddar cheese, grated

Dry fry the salami in a thick-based saucepan, over a moderate heat, until the fat runs. Remove the salami with a slotted spoon. Add the onion to the fat in the pan and fry until golden. Remove a little of the onion and reserve. Add the minced beef and fry until brown and crumbly. Return the salami to the pan and cook for a further 5 minutes over a moderate heat. Drain all excess fat from the pan and stir in the tomato purée and oregano. Season well to taste then cover the pan and cook over a low heat for 20 minutes.

Meanwhile cook the potatoes in boiling salted water until tender.

Drain then mash well and push through a sieve to make a smooth purée. Whilst still hot, beat in the milk and some extra seasoning. Stir in 75 g/3 oz of the grated cheese. Heat the oven to moderately hot (200c, 400f, gas 6).

Grease a 1-litre/2-pint ovenproof dish and layer the meat and potato mixtures in it, ending with a layer of potato. Sprinkle with the remaining cheese. Bake for 20 minutes in the moderately hot oven or until golden.

Variations

The salami can be replaced with 175 g/8 oz chopped streaky bacon and minced cooked beef can be used to replace the fresh beef mince. Try adding 1 green pepper, deseeded and chopped or 100 g/4 oz mushrooms, wiped and sliced to the mince mixture.

Jack's cherry pudding

Serves 6

75 g/3 oz butter
100 g/4 oz sugar
4 eggs, separated
1 teaspoon cinnamon
grated rind of ½ lemon
few drops vanilla essence
4 tablespoons Kirsch or sherry
40 g/1½ oz blanched almonds,
  chopped
4 tablespoons fresh white
  breadcrumbs
8 slices white bread
450 g/1 lb black cherries, stoned
icing sugar to dust

Set the oven at moderately hot
(180 c, 350 f, gas 4).

Cream the butter with the sugar
and egg yolks. Add the cinnamon,
lemon rind, vanilla essence, Kirsch
or sherry and stir in the chopped
almonds. Whisk the egg whites until
stiff and fold them into the creamed
mixture.

Grease a 1.75-litre/3-pint soufflé
dish and sprinkle the breadcrumbs
into it, tilting it to ensure that they
coat the sides. Layer the bread,

cherries and creamed mixture in the
dish, ending with the creamed
mixture on top. Bake for 50–60
minutes. Dust with icing sugar
before serving.

Cream cheese soufflé

Serves 4–6

100 g/4 oz soaked prunes, stoned and
  roughly chopped
75 ml/3 fl oz dry white wine
¼ cinnamon stick
2 cloves
75 g/3 oz butter
100 g/4 oz sugar
3 eggs, separated
3 tablespoons double cream
20 g/¾ oz semolina
375 g/13 oz cream cheese
25 g/1 oz ground hazelnuts

Sauce
5 egg yolks
75 g/3 oz sugar
2 tablespoons lemon juice
250 ml/8 fl oz dry white wine

Mix the prunes with the wine,
cinnamon and cloves and leave to

soak for a few hours.

Set the oven at moderately hot
(190 c, 375 f, gas 5). Reserve about
15 g/½ oz of the butter and beat the
remainder with the sugar, egg yolks
and cream. Gradually beat in the
semolina and cream cheese. Whisk
the egg whites until stiff and fold
them into the cheese mixture
together with the drained prunes.
Grease a 1.75-litre/3-pint,
ovenproof soufflé dish and coat it
with half the hazelnuts. Pour in the
soufflé mixture and sprinkle with the
remaining hazelnuts. Dot with the
reserved butter and bake for
20 minutes, then reduce the
temperature to moderate (180 c,
350 f, gas 4) and cook for a further
30 minutes.

Make the sauce about 10 minutes
before the soufflé is ready. Beat the
egg yolks with the sugar and lemon
juice, gradually adding the wine.
Stand the bowl over a saucepan of
hot water and whisk the mixture,
preferably using an electric whisk,
until it thickens. Serve the hot sauce
with the soufflé immediately it is
removed from the oven.

Soufflés and Bakes

Rhubarb pudding

Serves 4–6

*450 g/1 lb rhubarb, trimmed and cut
    into 2.5-cm/1-in lengths
4 tablespoons raspberry syrup or
    strawberry syrup
350 g/¾ lb frozen strawberries
150 g/5 oz caster sugar
2 eggs, separated
1 teaspoon vanilla essence
75 g/3 oz plain flour
50 g/2 oz cornflour
grated rind ½ lemon
1 egg white
pinch of salt
icing sugar to dust*

Put the rhubarb in a saucepan with
the raspberry or strawberry syrup.
Heat gently until the juice runs,
bring to the boil and simmer for 5
minutes then allow to cool. Sprinkle
the strawberries with 50 g/2 oz of
the caster sugar and leave to thaw.
   Heat the oven to moderate (180 C,
350 F, gas 4). Beat the egg yolks with
the remaining sugar and vanilla
essence until thick and creamy. Sift
together the flour and cornflour and
fold into the egg yolk mixture.
Drain the strawberries and rhubarb
and gradually fold the juice into the
mixture together with the lemon
rind. Whisk all the egg whites with
the salt until stiff and fold into the
egg yolk mixture.
   Grease a 1.75-litre/3-pint soufflé
dish with butter. Put the rhubarb
and strawberries in the bottom of
the dish and cover with the sponge
mixture. Bake the pudding in the
preheated oven for 1 hour. If the
pudding browns too quickly cover
with foil towards the end of the
cooking time. Dust whilst still hot
with icing sugar and serve
immediately.

Variations
Flavour the rhubarb with 2
tablespoons redcurrant jelly instead
of the raspberry or strawberry syrup.
The strawberries can be omitted and
the quantity of rhubarb increased to
675 g/1½ lb; replace the syrup with
the grated rind and juice of 1
orange, adding a little extra sugar, if
necessary.

Sauce sabayon I

*3 egg yolks
pinch of salt
40 g/1½ oz vanilla sugar
250 ml/8 fl oz medium dry white
    wine
1 teaspoon Kirsch*

Beat the egg yolks with the salt and
sugar in a bowl over a saucepan of
hot water until foamy. Gradually
whisk in the wine and continue to
whisk until the sauce thickens
slightly. Lastly, whisk in the Kirsch
and continue whisking the mixture,
off the heat, until the sauce has
cooled. Serve the sauce
immediately.

Sauce sabayon II

*6 egg yolks
pinch of salt
1 teaspoon lemon juice
25 g/1 oz vanilla sugar
100 ml/4 fl oz medium-dry sherry or
    Marsala*

Whisk the egg yolks with the salt
and lemon juice in a bowl over a
saucepan of hot water. Gradually
whisk in the sugar. Continue
whisking, slowly pouring in the
sherry or Marsala, until the sauce is
slightly thickened. Serve
immediately.

Cook's Tip

.To make your own vanilla sugar
break a vanilla pod in half and mix
it thoroughly into 100 g/4 oz caster
sugar. Spoon the sugar and the
vanilla pod into a jar and cover it
with a tight-fitting lid. Keep the
sugar for 1–2 weeks before using.
Shake the jar occasionally during
this storage time to allow the vanilla
flavour to mingle with the sugar.

Soufflés and Bakes

Cheese soufflé

Serves 4

40 g/1½ oz butter
200 g/7 oz Emmental or Gruyère
cheese, finely grated
40 g/1½ oz plain flour
250 ml/8 fl oz milk
salt and freshly ground white pepper
pinch of freshly grated nutmeg
4 eggs, separated
½ teaspoon lemon juice

Set the oven at moderately hot (180c, 350f, gas 4).

Grease a 900-ml/1½ pint soufflé dish with a little of the butter and sprinkle a little of the cheese around the inside of it. Melt the remaining butter, add the flour and cook it over low heat, stirring continuously, for 3 minutes. Gradually stir in the milk and bring the sauce to the boil, then reduce the heat and cook it, stirring continuously, until it is thick and smooth. Season the sauce with salt, pepper and nutmeg and remove the saucepan from the heat. Stir in the egg yolks and most of the remaining cheese, reserving about 2 tablespoons for garnish. Allow to cool until just warm.

Whisk the egg whites and lemon juice until they are very stiff and quite dry. Fold a little of the whites into the sauce, then fold in all the remaining whites and turn the mixture into the prepared dish. Sprinkle the reserved cheese on top and bake the soufflé for 40–45 minutes until well risen and golden brown. Serve immediately.

Raspberry soufflé

Serves 6

225 g/8 oz raspberries
100 g/4 oz sugar
4 egg yolks
15 g/½ oz vanilla sugar (page 188) or
few drops of vanilla essence
40 g/1½ oz cornflour, sifted
5 egg whites
pinch of salt
1 teaspoon lemon juice
icing sugar to dust

Set the oven to moderately hot (190c, 375f, gas 5).

Purée the raspberries with 25 g/1 oz of the sugar in a liquidiser then press the purée through a sieve to remove the seeds. Whisk the remaining sugar with the egg yolks and vanilla sugar or vanilla essence until pale and creamy then fold in the cornflour. Whisk the egg whites with the salt and lemon juice until they are stiff and dry then carefully fold them into the yolk mixture. Lastly, fold in the raspberry purée and turn the mixture into a greased 1.75-litre 3-pint soufflé dish. Bake the soufflé for 15 minutes then increase the oven temperature to (200c, 400f, gas 6) for a further 10–15 minutes. Dust the hot soufflé with icing sugar, wrap a napkin around the dish for a professional look, and serve it immediately.

Alaska surprise

Serves 6

225 g/8 oz strawberries
150 g/5 oz caster sugar
16 boudoir biscuits
2 tablespoons Framboise or Kirsch
4 egg whites
1 teaspoon lemon juice
40 g/1½ oz ground almonds
1 (485-ml/17.6-fl oz) carton vanilla
ice cream

Trim, wash and hull the strawberries then halve and sprinkle 2 tablespoons of the sugar over them. Arrange the biscuits over the base of a 20-cm/8-in flan dish, cutting some to fill in the gaps and form an even base. Arrange the strawberries on top and sprinkle the liqueur over them. Whisk the egg whites with the lemon juice until they are very stiff and dry. Whisk the remaining sugar in and continue to whisk until stiff and glossy. Divide the whites into two equal portions and fold the ground almonds into one half. Cut the ice cream into slices and lay it on top of the strawberries, then cover it with the almond meringue. Place the remaining meringue in a piping bag fitted with a star nozzle and, working quickly, cover the top of the dessert with piped meringue. Cover the top completely, right up to the edge of the dish. Brown the meringue in a very hot oven (230c, 450f, gas 8) for about 2 minutes until meringue peaks are lightly browned. Serve immediately.

Perfect Desserts

Desserts

Bavaroise

Serves 4

1 vanilla pod
300 ml/½ pint milk
pinch of salt
15 g/½ oz gelatine
2 tablespoons hot water
4 egg yolks
100 g/4 oz icing sugar, sifted
300 ml/½ pint double cream

Break the vanilla pod, place it in a saucepan with the milk and a pinch of salt and bring slowly to the boil. Dissolve the gelatine in 2 tablespoons hot water in a basin over a saucepan of hot water. Beat the egg yolks with the icing sugar until frothy then gradually strain the milk over them, whisking continuously. Place the bowl over a saucepan of hot water and continue whisking until the custard thickens slightly. Do not overcook or the mixture will curdle.

Stir the dissolved gelatine into the custard and allow to cool until it begins to set. Whip the cream until stiff and fold it into the bavaroise then spoon it into a 900-ml/1½-pint mould and chill until set. Just before serving, turn out and decorate with whipped cream.

Bavaroise with gooseberries

Serves 4

225 g/8 oz gooseberries, washed, topped and tailed
100 g/4 oz sugar
1 cinnamon stick
4 cloves
100 ml/4 fl oz white wine
1½ teaspoons gelatine
2 tablespoons hot water
1 quantity bavaroise (see left)
150 ml/¼ pint double cream, whipped
a few fresh gooseberries for decoration (optional)

Cook the gooseberries with the sugar, cinnamon, cloves and white wine for about 20–25 minutes in a covered saucepan over medium heat. Remove the cinnamon and cloves and purée the fruit in a liquidiser then press it through a sieve to remove the seeds. Dissolve the gelatine in the hot water in a basin over a saucepan of hot water then stir it into the gooseberry purée.

Prepare the bavaroise according to the recipe instructions and pour half of it into a 1-litre/2-pint mould or glass serving dish. Chill it quickly until just set then carefully spoon the gooseberry purée over the layer of bavaroise. Chill the gooseberry purée until just set then spoon the remaining bavaroise over the top. Chill until the layers are quite set then turn the bavaroise out, if it is in a mould, and decorate it with whipped cream and a few fresh gooseberries.

Note A little gin may be added to the gooseberry purée or 1 teaspoon juniper berries can be substituted for the cinnamon stick and cloves.

Cook's Tip

Always make sure that gelatine is completely dissolved before adding to another mixture. Do not let the gelatine boil or become overheated as it will become stringy.

Bavaroise with red and blackcurrants

Serves 4

225 g/8 oz redcurrants
225 g/8 oz blackcurrants
100 g/4 oz sugar
3–4 tablespoons crème de cassis (blackcurrant liqueur)
½ (600-ml/1-pint) tablet raspberry jelly
1 quantity bavaroise (see left)

Wash, trim and dry the currants, reserving a few redcurrants for decoration. Sprinkle them with sugar, then leave them to stand for 30–40 minutes until most of the sugar has dissolved. Pour over the liqueur and stir the currants to dissolve the remaining sugar and mix well. Dissolve the jelly tablet in 150 ml/¼ pint hot water then stir it into the fruit and leave it until half set.

Meanwhile, make the bavaroise according to the recipe instructions and spoon half of it into a 1½-litre/2-pint mould or glass serving dish. Chill it until just set. Spoon the currant mixture on top and chill again until just set. Finally top with the remaining bavaroise and chill until quite set. Turn out on to a serving dish (if the bavaroise is set in a mould) and decorate with the reserved redcurrants.

Variation
Substitute your favourite jam or preserve for the jellied currant mixture. Spoon a thin layer of it over the bavaroise base, top with the second half of the bavaroise and chill thoroughly. Turn it out just before serving and decorate with fresh fruit in season. A mixture of crumbled macaroons and raisins or sultanas steeped in rum or brandy is delicious layered with the bavaroise instead of the currants.

Alternatively, layer drained canned or bottled fruit with the bavaroise and sprinkle a little coarsely grated chocolate over the finished dessert.

Desserts

Figs with raspberry purée

Serves 4

8 ripe figs, peeled and halved
4 tablespoons Kirsch
350 g/12 oz raspberries
1 tablespoon lemon juice
50 g/2 oz caster sugar
150 ml/¼ pint whipping cream
1 tablespoon vanilla sugar (page 188)
2 tablespoons icing sugar

Arrange the figs in individual serving dishes and sprinkle the Kirsch over them. Leave them in the refrigerator for about 1 hour. Meanwhile purée the raspberries with the lemon juice and caster sugar in a liquidiser then sieve to remove the seeds. Whip the cream with the vanilla and icing sugars then spoon it over the chilled figs and top each serving with raspberry purée. Serve with wafer biscuits.

Variation
Vanilla or chocolate ice cream can be served with the figs, either with the whipped cream or instead of it. Alternatively the Kirsch-flavoured figs can be served in meringue nests then topped with the cream and raspberry purée.

Apricots flambé

Serves 4

100 ml/4 fl oz white wine
2.5-cm/1-in piece cinnamon stick
¼ vanilla pod
40 g/1½ oz sugar
12 large, ripe apricots
25 g/1 oz butter
50 g/2 oz slivered almonds
4 tablespoons Kirsch

Heat the wine with the cinnamon, vanilla and sugar. Then cover the pan and allow it to simmer for 10 minutes. Blanch the apricots in boiling water for a minute, then drain, peel, halve and stone them. Remove the cinnamon and vanilla pod from the wine. Add the apricots and poach them gently for about 5 mintues. Removed them from the wine and pat them on absorbent kitchen paper. Melt the butter, add the apricot halves and almonds and cook for a few minutes until the almonds are lightly browned. Pour over the warmed Kirsch, set it alight and serve immediately with a little of the cooking wine.

Tip Serve these apricots with vanilla or chocolate ice cream. They are also good with pancakes.

Variation
Peaches flambé Use four large ripe peaches instead of the apricots and replace the vanilla pod with a strip of thinly pared lemon rind.

Semolina fritters

Serves 4

450 ml/¾ pint milk
pinch of salt
40 g/1½ oz sugar
25 g/1 oz butter
100 g/4 oz semolina
40 g/1½ oz ground almonds
2 eggs
grated rind of 1 orange
50 g/2 oz dry white breadcrumbs
75 g/3 oz butter for frying

Bring the milk to the boil with the salt, sugar and butter. Sprinkle in the semolina and ground almonds and stir for 10 minutes over low heat until thickened. Remove the pan from the heat and blend a little of the semolina in a small bowl with one of the eggs and the orange rind. Return this mixture to the pan, stir well and allow it to stand for 10 minutes.

Rinse a 23 × 33-cm/9 × 13-in Swiss roll tin with cold water and spread the semolina evenly over it. Leave it in the refrigerator until quite firm then use a wet knife to cut it into squares.

Beat the second egg and dip the semolina squares first in the egg then in the breadcrumbs to coat.

Fry these fritters in the butter until they are crisp and golden brown, turning once to ensure even browning. Drain them carefully on absorbent kitchen paper and serve them immediately with canned or bottled fruit or seasonal fresh fruit. Alternatively sweeten and purée the fruit or serve warmed jam with the fritters.

Rice pudding

Serves 4

600 ml/1 pint milk
pinch of salt
50 g/2 oz butter
1 vanilla pod, split
thinly pared rind of ½ lemon
50 g/2 oz sugar
40 g/1½ oz pudding rice
a little freshly grated nutmeg

Heat the milk slowly in a heavy-based saucepan with the salt, half the butter, vanilla pod, lemon rind and sugar. As soon as the milk reaches boiling point, remove it

from the heat and leave to infuse for 10 minutes. Strain the milk, return it to the pan, add the rice and bring it to the boil stirring occasionally. Reduce the heat to the lowest setting, cover the pan and cook the rice for about 50–60 minutes. Stir the pudding occasionally to ensure that it does not stick.

Turn the rice into a warmed serving dish. Melt the remaining butter in a saucepan and pour it over the pudding together with a generous sprinkling of nutmeg. The butter should be stirred into the pudding just before it is eaten to enrich the rice.

Desserts

Mocha charlotte

Serves 6

15 g/½ oz gelatine
4 tablespoons water
5 eggs, separated
75 g/3 oz caster sugar
1 tablespoon instant coffee, dissolved
   in 2 tablespoons hot water
grated rind and juice of 1 orange
4 tablespoons orange liqueur
100 g/4 oz plain chocolate
100 g/4 oz milk chocolate
2 tablespoons water
75 g/3 oz butter
300 ml/½ pint double cream, whipped
28 boudoir biscuits

Decoration
a little chocolate vermicelli
coarsely grated orange rind

Dissolve the gelatine in the water in a basin over a saucepan of hot water. Whisk the egg yolks with the sugar until pale and creamy. Whisk the coffee into the yolks together with the orange rind and juice and 1 tablespoon of the orange liqueur. Stir in the dissolved gelatine. Melt the plain and milk chocolate with the cold water and butter in a bowl over a saucepan of hot water. Stir it lightly to ensure that the ingredients are well blended then carefully fold it into the yolk mixture. Whisk the egg whites until stiff then fold them in followed by half the cream.

Moisten the biscuits with the remaining liqueur and use them to line a 1.75-litre/3-pint charlotte mould or straight-sided deep dish. Fill it with the mocha cream and top with any remaining biscuits. Chill until set then turn out and decorate with the remaining cream, piped in swirls, a little chocolate vermicelli and a little coarsely grated orange rind.

Yogurt charlotte

Serves 8

Sponge
3 eggs
75 g/3 oz caster sugar
75 g/3 oz plain flour
a little icing sugar
100 g/4 oz raspberry jam, warmed

Cream
3 eggs, separated
150 g/5 oz caster sugar
20 g/¾ oz gelatine
3 tablespoons water
grated rind and juice of 1 lemon
100 ml/4 fl oz dry white wine
250 ml/8 fl oz natural yogurt

Decoration
150 ml/¼ pint double cream, whipped
20 g/¾ oz pistachio nuts, chopped

Set the oven at hot (220c, 425f, gas 7).
   Line and grease a 23 × 33-cm/ 9 × 13-inch Swiss roll tin. Beat the eggs with the sugar until pale, thick and creamy. Sift the flour over the egg mixture and carefully fold it in.

Pour the mixture into the prepared tin and smooth it out evenly. Bake for 5–7 minutes until well risen and golden brown.

Lay a sheet of greaseproof paper on a clean teatowel and sprinkle it with the icing sugar. Turn the cake out on to the paper. Working quickly, remove the greaseproof paper and trim the edges of the cake then spread the warmed jam over it. Roll up the cake using the greaseproof paper and teatowel to help form a neat roll. Leave it to stand, wrapped in the towel for a minute. Remove the roll to a wire rack and allow to cool then slice it thinly.

To make the yogurt cream, beat the egg yolks with the caster sugar until pale and creamy. Meanwhile dissolve the gelatine in the water in a basin over a saucepan of hot water. Stir the lemon rind and juice, wine and yogurt into the egg yolks and whisk thoroughly. Stir in the dissolved gelatine and leave the mixture until it begins to set. Whisk the egg whites until they are stiff, but not too dry, then fold them into the cream. Line a 1.75-litre/3-pint pudding basin with the Swiss roll slices and pour the cream into the middle. Chill until set then turn out and decorate with piped whipped cream and the pistachio nuts.

Tip The yogurt cream can be set in a mould without the Swiss roll slices or a purchased Swiss roll may be used to save time.

Desserts

Raspberries Romanoff

Serves 4

450 g/1 lb raspberries
50 g/2 oz icing sugar
3 tablespoons orange liqueur
300 ml/½ pint double cream
1 tablespoon vanilla sugar (page 188)

Wash and dry the raspberries and remove any stalks. Sprinkle two-thirds of the sugar over and leave them to stand for 15–20 minutes. Reserve 12 of the best raspberries for decoration then pour the orange liqueur over the remainder and leave them to stand for 1–2 hours.

Whip the cream with the remaining sugar and vanilla sugar. Layer the raspberries and cream in sundae glasses (piping the cream if liked) ending with a layer of cream. Decorate with the reserved raspberries.

Tip Port can be used to flavour the raspberries instead of the liqueur and strawberries or blackberries may be used instead of raspberries.

Peaches with fresh fig cream

Serves 4

4 firm ripe peaches
4 tablespoons Kirsch
4 ripe figs
40 g/1½ oz caster sugar
1 teaspoon lemon juice
300 ml/½ pint double cream

Decoration
100 g/4 oz wild or Alpine strawberries
20 g/1 oz slivered almonds

Stand the peaches in boiling water for 1–2 minutes then peel and halve them, removing the stone. Arrange them in a large serving dish or individual dishes, sprinkle over the Kirsch and leave to stand for 1–2 hours. Peel, quarter and purée the figs in a liquidiser or food processor with the sugar and lemon juice. Whip the cream until stiff then stir it into the fig purée.

Pipe the fig cream in large swirls into the halved peaches. Hull, wash and dry the strawberries and use to decorate the peaches together with the almonds. Serve with almond macaroons or other sweet biscuits.

Variation
Pineapple with fresh fig cream Halve a small fresh pineapple lengthways and scoop out the flesh, leaving the skin intact. Discard the hard parts of the core and chop the flesh. Return the flesh to the hollowed-out shell and sprinkle with Kirsch or rum. Decorate the pineapple with Alpine strawberries or raspberries and the piped fig cream.

Cherry jelly

Serves 4–6

25 g/1 oz gelatine
1 (425-g/15-oz) can red or black
  cherries, stoned
2–3 tablespoons caster sugar
pared rind of ½ small lemon
300 ml/½ pint rosé wine
juice of 1 lemon
3 tablespoons Kirsch
150 ml/¼ pint double cream
2 tablespoons vanilla sugar (page
  188)
2 tablespoons pistachio nuts

Dissolve the gelatine in 2
tablespoons water in a basin over a
saucepan of hot water. Drain the
cherries, reserve the syrup and heat
150 ml/¼ pint of it with the sugar
and lemon rind. Stir it thoroughly
then remove from the heat and
leave it to stand for 5 minutes
before removing the lemon rind.

   Stir the dissolved gelatine, wine
and lemon juice into the syrup
together with the Kirsch. Allow it to
set very lightly then stir in the
cherries and pour it into a wetted
600-ml/1-pint mould. Chill the
cherry jelly until set then turn it out
on to a serving dish. Whip the
cream with the vanilla sugar until
stiff and decorate the jelly with
swirls of whipped cream and
pistachio nuts.

Variation
The jelly can be set in individual
moulds. Try serving the jelly with
scoops of your favourite ice cream.
Sauce Sabayon (page 188) or
Zabaglione (page 204) can also be
served as accompaniments. Other
canned fruits, for example
raspberries or strawberries, can be
used instead of the cherries.

Cook's Tip

To unmould a jelly, dip the mould
briefly into hot water then place a
plate over the top and invert the
mould sharply. Give a couple of
vigorous shakes and the jelly should
drop on to the plate.

Desserts

Blackberry and apple soup

Serves 4

5 tablespoons dry white wine
175 g/6 oz granulated sugar
2 dessert apples, peeled, cored and
  sliced
1 litre/1¾ pints water
thinly pared rind of 1 lemon
2 cloves
2.5-cm/1-in piece cinnamon stick
1 kg/2 lb blackberries
1 egg white
pinch of salt
25 g/1 oz cornflour

Heat the wine and sugar together, stirring continuously until the sugar has dissolved. Add the apples and cook them gently for 5 minutes. Remove and reserve the apple slices. Add the water, lemon rind and spices to the pan together with the blackberries and simmer them, covered, for about 20 minutes. Sieve the mixture and return the liquid to the pan.

Whisk the egg white with the salt until stiff. Blend the cornflour with a little of the liquid, add it to the pan and cook it, stirring continuously, over low heat until it boils. Cook for 2–3 minutes return the apples to the soup then remove it from the heat. Drop teaspoonfuls of the egg white onto the hot soup, cover the pan and allow the egg white to set in the steam from the soup for about 15 minutes.

Remove the 'snowballs' carefully from the soup with a slotted spoon, pour the soup into a serving bowl and carefully float the snowballs back on top. Allow to cool and chill thoroughly before serving.

Fruity milk whip

Serves 6

225 g/8 oz mixed soft fruits (plums,
  gooseberries, cherries, peaches,
  strawberries, raspberries,
  redcurrants or blackberries)
100 g/4 oz caster sugar
2 teaspoons gelatine
450 ml/¾ pint milk
150 ml/¼ pint natural yogurt
½ teaspoon vanilla essence
pinch of salt
150 ml/¼ pint whipping cream

Wash or wipe the fruit and prepare it as appropriate, slicing any large fruits. Mix them together in a bowl and sprinkle half the sugar over them. Leave them to stand for about 30 minutes. Meanwhile dissolve the gelatine in 2 tablespoons water in a basin over a saucepan of hot water.

Dissolve the remaining sugar in the milk and stir in the yogurt, vanilla essence and salt. Whisk the gelatine into the milk mixture then chill it until it begins to set. Whisk the half-set jelly thoroughly to incorporate as much air as possible. Whip the cream and fold it into the milk whip then transfer the mixture to a serving bowl and chill it thoroughly. Top the whip with the prepared fruit and serve it immediately.

Note The amount of sugar may vary with the ripeness and quality of the fruit.

Chocolate flakes, small macaroons or cinnamon sugar may be used to top the whip instead of the fruit and a little brandy, rum or other liqueur may be added to the milk mixture.

Cook's Tip

Fruit soups make an unusual and refreshing end to a rich meal. The fruit used can be varied according to season. Black cherries, redcurrants and raspberries would all be suitable in this recipe instead of the blackberries and apples.

Fruit soups should be served with plain sweet biscuits or sponge cakes.

Desserts

Zabaglione

Serves 4

5 egg yolks
75 g/3 oz caster sugar
15 g/½ oz vanilla sugar (page 188)
grated rind and juice of ½ lemon
100 ml/4 fl oz Marsala
a few black grapes for decoration

Whisk the egg yolks with the caster sugar and vanilla until very pale and creamy. Stand the bowl over a saucepan of hot water, add the lemon rind and juice and Marsala and whisk the mixture until thickened. Pour into individual dishes or glasses and decorate with a few grapes. Serve immediately.

Variations

Zabaglione is nearly always served hot as soon as it is made. Other fresh fruits besides grapes may be served with it. For an unusual contrast put a scoop of ice cream or sorbet in the bottom of the glass before pouring in the hot cream. Serve at once before the ice cream has melted.

Note Marsala is a full-bodied dessert wine from Sicily which is gradually regaining popularity in Great Britain. It is available in varying grades of sweetness; the best one to choose for Zabaglione is Marsala all'uovo (Marsala with egg) which is creamy and sweet.

Orange cream

Serves 4

2 teaspoons gelatine
300 ml/½ pint freshly squeezed orange juice
2 egg yolks
75 g/3 oz caster sugar
300 ml/½ pint double cream
3 tablespoons orange liqueur
1 orange

Dissolve the gelatine in 2 tablespoons hot water in a basin over a saucepan of hot water. Warm the orange juice, stir in the gelatine and leave it to cool. Whisk the egg yolks with the caster sugar until thick and creamy then stir it into the orange juice just as it begins to set. Whip the cream with the orange liqueur until it is stiff and fold it into the jellied mixture. Turn the orange cream into individual serving dishes or glasses.

Grate the rind from the orange and peel it, removing all the pith. Cut it into thin slices and use them to decorate the creams then sprinkle the grated orange rind over the top.

Tip To make a light and airy orange cream, fold in 2 stiffly whipped egg whites after the cream.

Variations

Freshly squeezed grapefruit or lemon juice may be substituted for the orange juice in which case the quantity of sugar should be adjusted to taste. Blood oranges taste particularly good in this dessert.

Honey ice cream with kiwi fruit purée

Serves 4

2 eggs
3 egg yolks
2 tablespoons vanilla sugar (page 188)
300 ml/½ pint single cream
100 ml/4 fl oz milk
150 g/5 oz clear honey, warmed
5 kiwi fruit
4 tablespoons Kirsch

Whisk the eggs, extra egg yolks and vanilla sugar until pale and thick. Heat the cream and milk together and pour gradually into the eggs, whisking continuously. Gradually whisk in the honey then leave the mixture to cool. Turn it into a large freezer container and place it in the freezer until it is half frozen. Remove the ice cream from the freezer and whisk it thoroughly to remove any ice crystals. Return it to the freezer and repeat the whisking process once more then allow the ice cream to freeze until firm.

Peel the kiwi fruit and reserve one for decoration. Purée the remaining fruit in a liquidiser with the Kirsch. Serve scoops of ice cream in individual dishes decorated with slices of the reserved kiwi fruit. Pour a little fruit purée over each serving.

Tip Honey ice cream can also be served with blackberry purée. About 450 g/1 lb ripe blackberries should be puréed with sugar to taste then pressed through a sieve. The purée may be flavoured with a little Kirsch and a few whole blackberries used for decoration.

Desserts

Champagne orange sorbet

Serves 4

150 g/5 oz caster sugar
300 ml/½ pint freshly squeezed orange
*   juice*
juice of 1 lemon
300 ml/½ pint well-chilled champagne
*   or sparkling white wine*
1 egg white, stiffly whisked
150 g/5 oz strawberries, hulled and
*   halved*

Dissolve the sugar in the orange juice over low heat. Add the lemon juice and allow the syrup to cool. Pour it into a large freezer container and chill it in the freezer for 30 minutes. Gradually whisk in the champagne or sparkling wine and return the sorbet to the freezer until it is half frozen. Whisk it thoroughly and fold in the stiffly whisked egg white then return the sorbet to the freezer and leave it until frozen, whisking once or twice to prevent ice crystals from forming. Spoon the sorbet into individual dishes and decorate with the strawberries.

Note This sorbet may be served in small quantities to refresh the palate between the courses of a main meal. It may also be served in small quantities in champagne glasses, topped up with champagne.

Coffee parfait

Serves 6

150 g/5 oz caster sugar
100 ml/4 fl oz water
4 tablespoons instant coffee
1 tablespoon drinking chocolate
4 tablespoons boiling water
150 ml/¼ pint double cream
4 egg yolks
1 tablespoon coffee or chocolate
*   liqueur*
candy coffee beans to decorate

Dissolve the sugar in the water over low heat then bring it to the boil and remove it from the heat. Dissolve the coffee and drinking chocolate in the boiling water. Whip the cream with the coffee and chocolate mixture until stiff. Whisk

the egg yolks in a basin over a saucepan of hot water then gradually whisk in the sugar syrup in a slow stream until the mixture is very pale and creamy. Continue whisking until it is quite cold, adding the liqueur drop by drop. Fold in the whipped cream, pour the parfait into individual freezer-proof moulds and freeze for several hours. Turn out and decorate with the candy coffee beans.

Blackberries Astoria

Serves 4

4 large cooking apples, peeled, cored and sprinkled with lemon juice
100 ml/4 fl oz white wine
4 tablespoons sugar
½ teaspoon cinnamon
350 g/12 oz blackberries, washed and dried
150 g/5 oz apricot jam, warmed and sieved
3 tablespoons Kirsch
25 g/1 oz flaked almonds
15 g/½ oz butter
150 ml/¼ pint double cream
20 g/¾ oz icing sugar
2 tablespoons vanilla sugar (page 188)

Stand the apples in a saucepan, pour over the wine and sprinkle the sugar and cinnamon over them. Cover the pan and cook the apples gently for about 10 minutes. Remove them from the pan, arranging them on individual plates or dishes, and leave them to cool.

Mix the blackberries with the jam and Kirsch and divide this between the apples then chill them thoroughly for about 30 minutes. Lightly fry the flaked almonds in the butter until golden. Drain them on absorbent kitchen paper. Whip the cream with the icing sugar and vanilla sugar until stiff and spoon it over the apples. Decorate with the flaked almonds.

Bilberry ice cream

Serves 4

450 g/1 lb fresh bilberries or blackberries
100 g/4 oz caster sugar
2 eggs, separated
1 tablespoon lemon juice
2 tablespoons blackcurrant liqueur
150 ml/¼ pint double cream
100 g/4 oz bilberries or blackberries, trimmed, washed and dried to decorate

Wash, trim and dry the bilberries or blackberries and mix them into the sugar then leave to stand for 30 minutes. Whisk the egg yolks with the lemon juice in a bowl over a saucepan of hot water and whisk in all the juice from the fruit. Continue whisking until the mixture is thick and creamy, then remove it from the heat, add the liqueur and continue whisking till cool. Chill it thoroughly then whisk both the egg whites, and cream separately until they are stiff and fold them into the blackberry cream. Freeze the ice cream in a large freezer container, whisking occasionally to prevent ice crystals forming, until it is firm. Serve the ice cream, scooped into tall glasses, decorated with the whole fruit.

Desserts

Guelph pudding

Serves 4

40 g/1½ oz cornflour
pinch of salt
300 ml/½ pint milk
1 vanilla pod
100 g/4 oz sugar
4 eggs, separated
2 tablespoons lemon juice
300 ml/½ pint dry white wine

Mix the cornflour with the salt and a little of the milk until smooth and creamy. Heat the remaining milk to boiling point with the vanilla pod, remove it from the heat and allow it to cool for a few minutes. Strain the milk into the cornflour mixture, stirring continuously. Return it to the pan, stir in half the sugar and bring the mixture slowly to the boil, stirring continuously. Remove it from the heat and allow to cool to lukewarm, stirring frequently. Whisk the egg whites until stiff and fold them into the sauce then divide it between four individual dishes or glasses.

Whisk the egg yolks with the remaining sugar in a bowl over a saucepan of hot water, gradually adding the lemon juice and wine until the mixture is cooked and thickened; do not allow it to overcook or it will curdle. Remove from the heat and continue whisking until it is quite cold. Divide the custard between the dishes, forming an even layer over each of the cornflour bases. Chill lightly before serving.

Note The cornflour base may be made up to a day in advance and chilled ready for use. The base can also be made using flavoured blancmange powder.

Steamed bread pudding

Serves 6

100 g/4 oz stale white, crustless
  bread, cubed
75 g/3 oz macaroons, crumbled
75 g/3 oz crumbled pumpernickel
  (optional)
150 ml/¼ pint hot milk
150 g/5 oz butter
100 g/4 oz sugar
4 eggs, separated
2 tablespoons vanilla sugar (page
  188)
grated rind and juice of 1 orange
3 tablespoons orange liqueur
50 g/2 oz finely chopped or ground
  almonds
pinch of salt

Mix the bread, macaroons and pumpernickel together and pour over the hot milk then leave the mixture to soak for 10 minutes.

Meanwhile, cream the butter with the sugar then beat in the egg yolks and vanilla sugar, and orange rind and juice. Add the liqueur, chopped or ground almonds and stir in the soaked ingredients.

Whisk the egg whites with the salt until they are stiff then fold them into the pudding. Turn the mixture into a well greased 1-litre/2-pint pudding basin or kugelhopf mould and cover it first with a piece of pleated, greased greaseproof paper and then loosely with foil, sealing it well around the rim of the basin or mould. Boil or steam the pudding for 1½ hours then carefully remove it from the pan or steamer, uncover and turn it out on to a warmed plate. Remember to check the level of the water in the saucepan during cooking and top it up with more boiling water when necessary. Sauce Sabayon (page 188) goes very well with this pudding. Alternatively, serve cream whipped with a little vanilla sugar and orange liqueur as an accompaniment to the pudding.

Tip Pistachio nuts, hazelnuts or walnuts may be used instead of the almonds and a few raisins may be added to the pudding. These may be first soaked in a little brandy or rum for extra flavour. Small scoops of vanilla ice cream make a refreshing contrast to this warming winter pudding.

Entertaining

Menus for Celebration Meals

Entertaining

Dinner party menu

Serves 6

Baked oysters
Stuffed fillet steak
Neapolitan potato balls
Asparagus (page 122)
Filled pineapple

Baked oysters

3 dozen fresh oysters with tightly shut
*   shells (others are inedible)*
50 g/2 oz butter
50 g/2 oz breadcrumbs
2 tablespoons chopped parsley
2 tablespoons Pernod
freshly ground white pepper

Open the oysters. Hold one oyster firmly and insert a strong rigid knife, preferably an oyster knife, between the two shells just beside the hinge. Twist the knife sharply to open the shell. Run the knife under the oyster to remove it from the shell. Reserve any liquid that runs out and discard the shell. Prepare all the oysters in this way.

Set the oven at hot (230 C, 450 F, gas 8). Grease an ovenproof dish with some of the butter and line it with a few of the breadcrumbs.

Mix the rest of the breadcrumbs with the parsley. Sprinkle half the oysters with half the Pernod and some of the reserved oyster liquid then season with pepper and cover with half the breadcrumb mixture and dot with flakes of butter. Repeat with the remaining ingredients. Bake for 10 minutes in the heated oven then serve at once with French bread and a dry white wine.

Note If you prefer you can serve the oysters in their shells. After opening them and removing the oyster lay them back on their shell and place on a baking sheet covered with salt. Sprinkle with lemon juice and a few breadcrumbs and dot with butter. Brown under a grill, preheated to its hottest setting.

Stuffed fillet steak

675-g/1½-lb piece fillet steak
4 tablespoons oil
1 medium onion, peeled and
*   chopped*
100 g/4 oz minced lean beef
salt and freshly ground black pepper
pinch paprika
pinch dried thyme
100 g/4 oz lean cooked ham, finely
*   chopped*
100 g/4 oz button mushrooms, wiped
*   and finely chopped*
1 tablespoon chopped parsley
1 tablespoon chopped chervil
*   (optional)*
1 egg, beaten
25 g/1 oz butter

Trim the steak and cut a pocket down one side with a sharp knife. Melt 2 tablespoons of the oil in a saucepan and fry the onion until soft but not browned. Add the mince and fry until brown and crumbly. Season to taste with salt, pepper, paprika and dried thyme. Stir in the ham and mushrooms and continue to cook until the liquid from the mushrooms has evaporated. Add the parsley and chervil, if using, and remove from the heat. Allow the mixture to cool then mix with beaten egg to bind.

Stuff the pocket in the steak with the meat mixture and sew up the opening with fine string or secure with wooden cocktail sticks. Heat the oil in a large frying pan and cook the steak to seal on all sides. Remove from the pan and rub the steak with salt and pepper. Melt the butter in the oil and return the steak to the pan. Cook the steak for 20 to 25 minutes then allow to rest for a few minutes before carving. Remember to remove the string or cocktail sticks before serving with Neapolitan potato balls and asparagus. A full-bodied red wine goes well with this dish.

Neapolitan potato balls

175 g/6 oz small pasta rings
450 g/1 lb potatoes, peeled
40 g/1½ oz butter
50 g/2 oz flour
150 ml/¼ pint single cream
100 g/4 oz cooked ham, chopped
2 level tablespoons chopped parsley
salt
little grated nutmeg
oil for deep frying

Cook the pasta rings in plenty of boiling salted water until just tender. Drain and refresh with cold water. Cook the potatoes in boiling salted water until tender then drain, mash well and push through a sieve to make a smooth purée. Blend the butter and flour together and add, a little at a time, to the hot potato. Mix well and stir in the cream. Add the ham and parsley and season to taste with salt and nutmeg.

Form the potato mixture into balls about 4-cm/1½-inch across and roll them firmly in the pasta rings. Heat the fat to 185 C/360 F and fry the potato balls for 3–4 minutes or until golden brown.

Filled pineapple

1 ripe pineapple, halved lengthways
*   and core removed*
2 tablespoons Kirsch
2 tablespoons maraschino (optional)
225 g/8 oz raspberries
1–2 tablespoons caster or vanilla
*   sugar*
100 g/4 oz black grapes, halved and
*   pips removed*
1 (485-ml/17.6-fl oz) carton vanilla
*   ice cream*

Remove the flesh from the pineapple with a melon baller or teaspoon and place with any juice that collects in a bowl. Reserve the shells. Sprinkle the pineapple flesh with the Kirsch and maraschino, if using, and leave in a cool place or refrigerator for about 2 hours.

Meanwhile purée the raspberries by pushing through a sieve and sweeten to taste with sugar or vanilla sugar.

Drain the liquid from the pineapple and mix with the raspberry purée. Arrange the pineapple with the grapes in the reserved pineapple shells and chill. Just before serving top with slices of ice cream and pour over the raspberry sauce.

Tip To test whether a pineapple is ripe pull one of the inner leaves from the top of the pineapple. If it comes away easily the pineapple is ripe.

Entertaining

Dinner party menu

Serves 6

Stuffed artichokes
Beef Wellington
Courgette salad (page 156)
Mocha mousse

Stuffed artichokes

6 small artichokes, trimmed and
  chokes removed
3 shallots, peeled and chopped
25 g/1 oz butter
3 level tablespoons chopped parsley
100 g/4 oz lean cooked ham,
  chopped
3 hard-boiled eggs, chopped
1 carton cress, snipped
salt and freshly ground black pepper
12 rashers streaky bacon
2 tablespoons oil
300 ml/½ pint dry white wine
1 tablespoon tomato purée
300 ml/½ pint soured cream

Wash the artichokes and leave upside down to drain. Fry the shallots in the butter until soft but not browned then stir in the parsley, ham, eggs and cress. Season to taste with salt and pepper. Use this mixture to stuff the artichokes.

Wrap 2 rashers of bacon round each artichoke and secure with wooden cocktail sticks. Heat the oil in a frying pan and seal the artichokes all over. Transfer to a large saucepan or flameproof casserole. Pour over the white wine, tomato purée and half the soured cream. Cover tightly and simmer for 35–40 minutes. Arrange the artichokes on a serving dish. Beat the rest of the soured cream into the cooking liquid and pour this sauce over the artichokes. Serve with fresh white bread.

Beef Wellington

800-g/1¾-lb piece fillet of beef
25 g/1 oz lard or vegetable fat
salt and freshly ground black pepper
50 g/2 oz butter
2 onions, peeled and finely chopped
175 g/6 oz mushrooms, wiped and
  thinly sliced
225 g/8 oz lambs liver, trimmed and
  diced
1 teaspoon dried marjoram
1 teaspoon dried thyme
2 tablespoons chopped parsley
2 tablespoons fresh white
  breadcrumbs
2 tablespoons Madeira
1 egg yolk, beaten, to glaze
1 (368-g/13-oz) packet frozen puff
  pastry, thawed

Trim the fillet and wipe with absorbent kitchen paper. Melt the fat in a large frying pan, then sear the meat all over for 10 minutes. Remove from the pan, allow to cool and rub all over with salt and pepper. Melt half the butter in a small pan and cook the onions until soft, but not coloured. Add the mushrooms and cook gently, stirring from time to time, until all the liquid from the mushrooms has evaporated. Meanwhile sauté the diced liver in the rest of the butter until browned on all sides. Combine the liver, onion and mushroom with the herbs, breadcrumbs and Madeira and season to taste.

Heat the oven to moderately hot (200c, 400f, gas 6). Roll out the pastry on a floured surface to a rectangle large enough to wrap the meat in and spread with two-thirds of the mushroom mixture. Place the fillet on top of this and top with the rest of the filling. Fold the pastry over to enclose the meat completely, dampening the edges with a little water to make a good seal. Place the 'parcel' on a dampened baking sheet so that the joins are tucked underneath and brush with egg yolk. Bake in the heated oven for 50 minutes.

Serve with Cranberry sauce (page 115) and a mixed salad.

Mocha mousse

175 g/6 oz plain chocolate
50 g/2 oz milk chocolate
4 eggs, separated
2 teaspoons instant coffee
½ teaspoon vanilla essence
1 teaspoon lemon juice
300 ml/½ pint whipping or double
  cream
1 tablespoon Tia Maria or brandy
2 drops almond essence
candy coffee beans to garnish
  (optional)

Break up the chocolate and place in a bowl over a pan of hot, but not boiling, water. Leave until melted then remove from the pan. Beat the egg yolks with the coffee powder and vanilla essence until creamy. Add to the melted chocolate and mix well.

Whisk the egg whites with the lemon juice until stiff. Whip the cream and reserve about one-third for garnish. Fold the remaining cream into the chocolate mixture and flavour with Tia Maria or brandy and almond essence. Finally fold in the egg whites. Pour into a serving dish and allow to set in the refrigerator. Just before serving, decorate with the reserved cream and candy coffee beans.

Cook's Tip

A fresh young artichoke should have tightly packed leaves of a good fresh green colour. Avoid any whose leaves are beginning to spread out and show the purplish centre.

Entertaining

Cold buffet party

Serves 12

A cold buffet party is one of the easiest and most pleasant ways of entertaining a large number of people. All the work can be done in advance, leaving the hostess free to enjoy the meal with her guests.

The recipes given below are sufficient for a full scale buffet meal, but you may also like to add or substitute some of your favourite recipes from the preceding chapters.

Cold tomato soup

40 g/1½ oz butter
225 g/8 oz onions, peeled and
    chopped
3–4 cloves garlic, peeled and crushed
20 g/¾ oz flour
2 teaspoons paprika
6 (397-g/14-oz) cans tomatoes,
    drained and juice reserved
1 chicken stock cube, crumbled
pinch of sugar
freshly ground black pepper
300 ml/½ pint whipping cream
40 g/1½ oz flaked almonds
4 tablespoons chopped chives

Melt the butter in a large saucepan and use to fry the onion and garlic until soft but not browned. Sprinkle over the flour and paprika and stir until absorbed. Add the tomato liquid, stirring all the time and bring to the boil. Simmer for 5 minutes. Meanwhile chop the tomatoes roughly then add them to the pan. Season with the stock cube, sugar and pepper to taste, bring back to the boil and simmer for 10 minutes. Purée the mixture in a blender or food processor, in batches if necessary, then allow the soup to cool completely.

Lightly whip the cream and stir it into the soup. Just before serving, garnish with the flaked almonds and chives.

Variation

Add a dash of Worcestershire or Tabasco sauce to the soup for a really spicy flavour. Alternatively a few tablespoons of vodka or gin may be added for an unusual flavour.

Palmito cocktail

1 (425-g/15-oz) can palm hearts
    (palmitos), drained and cut into
    strips
150 ml/¼ pint soured cream
150 ml/¼ pint natural yogurt
1 tablespoon concentrated tomato
    purée
2 tablespoons orange juice
1 tablespoon brandy
salt
cayenne
pinch of sugar
225 g/8 oz very thinly sliced smoked
    ham
crushed black peppercorns to garnish

Arrange the palm hearts in a deep dish. Beat together the soured cream, yogurt, tomato purée, orange juice and brandy to make a dressing. Season to taste with salt, cayenne and sugar. Roll up the slices of ham and arrange on the dish with the palm hearts. Pour the dressing over the palm hearts and ham rolls and garnish with a few crushed black peppercorns before serving.

Scampi Chantilly

450 g/1 lb peeled scampi
3 tablespoons lemon juice
150 ml/¼ pint double or whipping
    cream
150 ml/¼ pint mayonnaise (see page
    112)
2–3 tablespoons dry sherry
pinch each of salt, cayenne, paprika
    and sugar
dash of Worcestershire sauce
dash of white wine vinegar
2 tablespoons green peppercorns,
    drained, to garnish

Rinse the scampi quickly and sprinkle with the lemon juice. Divide between individual serving dishes. Whisk the cream until stiff and fold into the mayonnaise. Stir in the sherry and season to taste with salt, cayenne, paprika, sugar, Worcestershire sauce and vinegar. Spoon the dressing over the scampi and garnish with green peppercorns.

Lettuce and ham salad

3 small Iceberg lettuces, washed
225 g/8 oz button mushrooms, wiped
    and thinly sliced
6 stalks celery, washed and sliced
2 red peppers, deseeded, washed and
    chopped
225 g/8 oz lean cooked ham, cut in
    strips
1 bunch radishes, washed, trimmed
    and sliced
300 ml/½ pint mayonnaise (see page
    112)
150 ml/¼ pint natural yogurt
1 shallot, peeled and finely chopped
salt and white pepper
pinch each of cayenne and sugar

Garnish
6 anchovy fillets, soaked in water,
    drained and halved
2 tablespoons capers, drained
2 tablespoons chopped parsley

Cut the hearts from the lettuces from the top and remove and discard any hard core. Separate the inner leaves and ease apart the leaves of the lettuce shells to form rosette shapes.

Shred the reserved inner leaves and mix with the mushrooms, celery, peppers, ham and radishes. Beat the mayonnaise and yogurt well together and add the finely chopped shallot. Season to taste with salt, pepper, cayenne and sugar.

Pile the ham and salad mixture into lettuce cases and pour over the dressing. Garnish with the anchovies, capers and chopped parsley.

Trout in aspic

1 litre/2 pints fish stock (made from scraps of fish)
100 ml/4 fl oz dry white wine
2 large carrots, roughly chopped
2 sticks celery, roughly chopped
1 onion, peeled and quartered
10 peppercorns
salt
6 trout, cleaned
1 egg white
1 egg shell, crushed (optional)
15 g/½ oz powdered gelatine

Garnish
1 cooked carrot, very thinly sliced
sprigs of parsley

Put the fish stock, wine, carrots, celery, onion and peppercorns in a large pan and bring to the boil. Simmer for 10 minutes then season with salt. Put in the trout and let them simmer very gently for 15 minutes. Lift the fish out of the pan, taking care not to break up the flesh. Rub off the skin but leave the head and tail intact. Leave the trout to cool.

Meanwhile strain the stock and reduce to half its original quantity by boiling rapidly. Whisk the egg white and stir into the broth with the crushed egg shell, if using. Bring the stock to the boil and as soon as the froth rises to the top remove the pan from the heat. Reduce the heat and simmer very gently for 10 minutes. Line a fine sieve with scalded muslin or a clean teatowel and pour the broth through.

Dissolve the gelatine in 3 tablespoons of water over a pan of hot water, add to the strained stock and leave to cool.

As soon as the aspic becomes syrupy spoon a thin layer over the base of a large serving platter and lay the fish on it. Coat them with the rest of the aspic and allow to cool. Garnish with the carrot and parsley.

The main roast

The choice of main meat dish is naturally a matter of personal taste, but as it is to be eaten cold it is best to choose a lean cut. Cold stuffed breast of veal (page 220) makes an excellent party dish as does Austrian boiled beef (page 78) or roast chicken or turkey. For a large party choose two different roasts.

The cheese board

It is a good idea to include at least one of each of each type of cheese: a hard cheese (for example mature Cheddar, Cheshire, Wensleydale), a blue cheese (Stilton, Danish blue), a soft cheese (Brie, Camembert, Roquefort) and a cream cheese such as one with herbs added.

As with all party food the presentation is most important. Decorate the cheese board according to the time of year with fruit (grapes, apples, pears, fresh or diced figs), celery leaves or stalks, radish roses, tomato or parsley.

To go with the cheese have a basket of different types of bread along with water biscuits, crackers and bread sticks.

The dessert

The dessert can be chosen from the recipes in the chapter beginning on page 192.

A light mousse made in individual glasses is a good choice or simply serve a selection of delicious fresh fruit to eat by itself or to dip into cream or Caramel sauce, the recipe for which is given below. This goes particularly well with strawberries, kiwi fruit, peaches, apricots and orange or mandarin segments.

Caramel sauce

350 g/12 oz sugar
300 ml/½ pint milk
150 ml/¼ pint single cream
½ teaspoon cinnamon
pinch grated nutmeg
2 tablespoons brandy or Cointreau

Place the sugar in a heavy-based saucepan and allow to caramelise over a low heat. Remove from the heat as soon as it is all golden, cover the hand holding the pan with a teatowel and add the milk in a thin stream. Dissolve the caramel in the milk over a low heat. Remove the pan from the heat and stir in the cream. Flavour to taste with cinnamon, nutmeg and brandy or Cointreau.

Cook's Tip

When planning a meal for a large number of people remember that, as a general rule, the more people that are present the less food is needed per head. This applies particularly to accompaniments such as rice, bread and green salad. For example if you are feeding 20 people allow 50 g/2 oz rice per person but if you are feeding 40 allow only 40 g/1½ oz.

Dinner party menu

Serves 6

Snail Salad
Stuffed breast of veal
Glazed carrots (see page 125)
New potatoes
Champagne peach

Snail salad

25 g/1 oz butter
24 canned snails, drained
2 shallots, peeled and chopped
1 (396-g/14-oz) can artichoke
hearts, drained and quartered
1 (312-g/11-oz) can artichoke
bottoms, drained and quartered
100 ml/4 fl oz white wine
2 tablespoons vinegar
3 tablespoons oil
salt and freshly ground white pepper
2 level tablespoons chopped parsley
lettuce leaves

Melt the butter in a saucepan and
fry the snails with the shallots until
the shallots are soft but not
browned. Add the artichoke hearts

and bottoms with the wine, vinegar
and oil. Season with salt and pepper
to taste, cover the pan and cook
gently for 5 minutes. Allow the
mixture to cool then chill.

Sprinkle with parsley and garnish
with lettuce leaves before serving.

Stuffed breast of veal

1-kg/2½-lb piece boned breast of veal
3 hard-boiled eggs, chopped
3 tablespoons chopped fresh mixed
herbs
75 g/3 oz cooked ham, chopped
50 g/2 oz fresh white breadcrumbs
salt and freshly ground white pepper
600 ml/1 pint veal or chicken stock
450 ml/¾ pint white wine
2 large carrots, scraped and chopped
2 stalks celery, washed and chopped
1 onion, peeled
4 cloves
1 bay leaf
6 peppercorns

Trim the meat and wipe with
absorbent kitchen paper. Mix
together the egg, herbs, ham and
breadcrumbs and season to taste

with salt and pepper to make the
filling. Lay the meat on a flat surface
and spread with the stuffing. Roll up
the meat and tie with fine string.

Heat the stock and wine together
in a large saucepan. Put in the
carrots and celery, the onion, stuck
with the cloves, the bay leaf and the
peppercorns. Lower in the veal and
bring to the boil. Skim, cover and
simmer for 1½ hours. Drain the meat
and leave to rest for 5 minutes
before carving. Strain the stock and
skim off any fat. Boil rapidly until
well reduced and pour a little over
the sliced meat before serving. Hand
the rest separately. Serve with the
glazed carrots and boiled new
potatoes, sprinkled with parsley.

Champagne peaches

6 small peaches
1 bottle champagne or sparkling
white wine

Wash the peaches and prick the
skins all over with a fork. Place each
peach in a rounded glass and top up
with champagne or sparkling wine.

Index

Index

Index